The Meaning of Faith

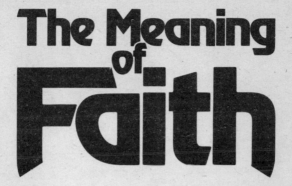

D0721790

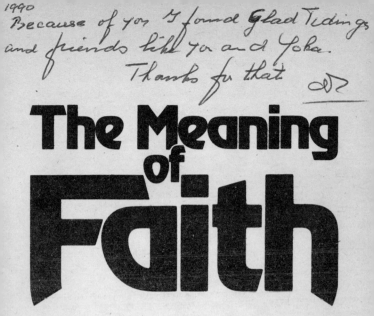

The Meaning of Faith

Harry Emerson Fosdick

festival books

Abingdon/Nashville

THE MEANING OF FAITH

A Festival Book

Festival edition published by Abingdon, October 1982,
by arrangement with New Century Publishers.

ISBN 0-687-23959-1

PRINTED IN THE UNITED STATES OF AMERICA.

To
MY MOTHER
IN MEMORIAM

"'Tis human fortune's happiest height to be
A spirit melodious, lucid, poised, and whole;
Second in order of felicity
To walk with such a soul."

Preface

This book was written during the first world war—"the most terrific war," I called it, "men ever raged, when faith is sorely tried and deeply needed." I little thought that that "war to end war" would so utterly fail of its purpose, and that a second world war would issue in the futility and frustration of the most perilous and threatening generation in human history.

In this last half-century we have gone a long way from the optimism with which the century began. Then the doctrine of inevitable and automatic progress was affirmed, not so much by preachers as by supposedly hard-headed, realistic men of the world. Herbert Spencer foresaw inevitable progress toward perfection; Mark Twain wrote Walt Whitman that thirty years more would see mankind coming at last to full stature; and Swinburne grew lyrical:

> "Glory to man in the highest,
> For man is the master of things."

Such sentimental optimism has blown up in our faces now, and even if pessimism has not universally taken its place, many find faith difficult and scepticism and discouragement easy. Perhaps a new edition of this book, which is now being called for, may still meet a contemporary need, despite the fact that it was written thirty years ago.

There is no sectarianism in the book. I am not pleading for any denominational creed. I had in mind, when I wrote it, what has become more critically evident now, that this world is a battlefield of contending faiths. If one does not believe in democracy, one gives help by his defection to those who believe in totalitarianism. It is the believers who count, the men who verily have convictions to live by and die for. Seldom has the world seen such believers in doctrine as are the Communists. The central question of mankind has become, What do you believe? and for us one by one no question goes deeper. Said Thomas Carlyle: "The thing a man does practically lay to heart and know for certain concerning his vital relations to the mysterious Universe, and his duty and destiny there, *that* is in all cases the primary thing for him and creatively determines all the rest. *That* is his religion." This book was written as one man's testimony about *that*.

My indebtedness is widespread, as the text makes evident but to one person in particular, my friend, Goerge Albert Coe, Ph.D., who still lives to receive my thanks for his careful reading of the manuscript a generation ago, my special gratitude belongs.

HARRY EMERSON FOSDICK

January 9, 1950.

Acknowledgments

Special acknowledgment is gladly made to the following: to E. P. Dutton & Company for permission to use prayers from "A Chain of Prayer Across the Ages" and from "The Temple," by W. E. Orchard, D.D.; to the Rev. Samuel McComb and the publishers for permission to quote from "A Book of Prayers," copyright, 1912, Dodd, Mead & Company; to the American Unitarian Association for permission to draw upon "Prayers," by Theodore Parker; to the Pilgrim Press and the author for permission to use selections from "Prayers of the Social Awakening," by Dr. Rauschenbusch; to the Missionary Education Movement for permission to make quotations from "Thy Kingdom Come," by Ralph E. Diffendorfer; to Fleming H. Revell Co., for permission to make use of "A Book of Public Prayer," by Henry Ward Beecher; and to the publishers of James Martineau's "Prayers in the Congregation and in College," Longmans, Green & Co.

CONTENTS

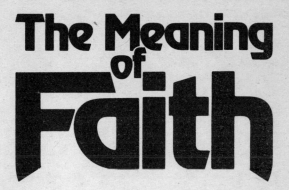

The Meaning of Faith

CHAPTER I

Faith and Life's Adventure

DAILY READINGS

Discussion about faith generally starts with faith's *reasonableness;* let us begin with faith's *inevitableness.* If it were possible somehow to live without faith, the whole subject might be treated merely as an affair of curious interest. But if faith is an unescapable necessity in every human life, then we must come to terms with it, understand it, and use it as intelligently as we can. *There are certain basic elements in man which make it impossible to live without faith.* Let us consider these, as they are suggested in the Epistle to the Hebrews, which, better than any other book in the Bible, presents faith as an unavoidable human attitude.

First Week, First Day

Now faith is assurance of things hoped for, a conviction of things not seen.—Heb. 11:1.

As Moffatt translates: "Now faith means we are confident of what we hope for, convinced of what we do not see." When faith is described in such general terms, its necessity in human life is evident. Man cannot live without faith, because he deals not only with a past which he may know and with a present which he can see, but with a *future in whose possibilities he must believe.* A man can no more avoid looking ahead when he lives his life than he can when he sails his boat, and in one case as in the other, his direction is determined by his thought about what lies before him, his "assurance of things hoped for." Now, this future into which continually we press our way can never be a matter of demonstrable knowledge. We know only when we arrive, but meanwhile we believe; and our knowledge of what is and has been is not more necessary to our quest than our faith concerning what is yet to come. As Tennyson sings of faith in "The Ancient Sage":

"She sees the Best that glimmers thro' the Worst,
  She feels the sun is hid but for a night,
  She spies the summer thro' the winter bud,
  She tastes the fruit before the blossom falls,
  She hears the lark within the songless egg,
  She finds the fountain where they wail'd 'Mirage'!"

However much a man may plan, therefore, to live without faith, he cannot do it. When one strips himself of all convictions about the future he stops living altogether, an active, eager, vigorous manhood is always proportionate to the scope and power of reasonable faith. The great spirits of the race have had the aspiring, progressive quality which the Scripture celebrates:

These all died in faith, not having received the promises, but having seen them and greeted them from afar, and having confessed that they were strangers and pilgrims on the earth. For they that say such things make it manifest that they are seeking after a country of their own. And if indeed they had been mindful of that country from which they went out, they would have had opportunity to return. But now they desire a better country, that is, a heavenly: wherefore God is not ashamed of them, to be called their God; for he hath prepared for them a city.—Heb. 11:13-16.

Almighty God, let Thy Spirit breathe upon us to quicken in us all humility, all holy desire, all living faith in Thee. When we meditate on the Eternal, we dare not think any manner of similitude; yet Thou art most real to us in the worship of the heart. When in the strife against sin we receive grace to help us in our time of need, then are Thou the Eternal Rock of our salvation. When amid our perplexities and searchings, the way of duty is made clear, then art Thou our Everlasting Light. When amid the storms of life we find peace and rest through submission, then art Thou the assured Refuge of our souls. So do Thou manifest Thyself unto us, O God!

Our Heavenly Father, we give Thee humble and hearty thanks for all the sacred traditions which have come down to us from the past—for the glorious memories of ancient days, concerning that Divine light in which men have been conscious of Thy presence and assured of Thy grace. But we would not content ourselves with memories. O Thou who art not the God of the dead, but the God of the living, manifest Thyself unto us in a present communion. Reveal Thyself unto us in the tokens of this passing time. Give us for ourselves to feel the authority of Thy law: give us for ourselves to realize the exceeding sinfulness of sin: give us for ourselves to understand the way of salvation through sacrifice. Teach us, by the Spirit of Christ, the sacredness of common duties, the holiness of the ties that bind us to our kind, the divinity of the still small voice within that doth ever urge us in the way of righteousness. So shall our hearts be renewed by faith; so shall we ever live in God. Amen.—John Hunter.

First Week, Second Day

By faith Abraham, when he was called, obeyed to go out unto a place which he was to receive for an inheritance; and he went out, not knowing whither he went. By faith he became a sojourner in the land of promise, as in a land not his own, dwelling in tents, with Isaac and Jacob, the heirs with him of the same promise: for he looked for the city which hath the foundations, whose builder and maker is God.—Heb. 11:8-10.

By faith Moses, when he was grown up, refused to be called the son of Pharaoh's daughter; choosing rather to share ill treatment with the people of God, than to enjoy the pleasures of sin for a season; accounting the reproach of Christ greater riches than the treasures of Egypt: for he looked unto the recompense of reward. By faith he forsook

Egypt, not fearing the wrath of the king: for he endured, as seeing him who is invisible.—Heb. 11:24-27.

Man cannot live without faith because his relationship with the future is an affair not alone of thought but also of action; *life is a continuous adventure into the unknown.* Abraham and Moses pushing out into experiences whose issue they could not foresee are typical of all great lives that had adventured for God. "By faith" is the first word necessary in every life like Luther's and Wesley's and Carey's. By faith John Bright, when his reforms were hard bestead, said: "If we can't win as fast as we wish, we know that our opponents can't in the long run win at all." By faith Gladstone, when the Liberal cause was defeated, rose undaunted in Parliament, and said, "I appeal to time!" and by faith every one of us must undertake each plain day's work, if we are to do it well. Robert Louis Stevenson said that life is "an affair of cavalry, a thing to be dashingly used and cheerfully hazarded." But so to deal with life demands faith. The more one sees what venturesome risks he takes every day, what labor and sacrifice he invests in hope of a worthy outcome, with what great causes he falls in love until at his best he is willing for their sakes to hazard fortune and happiness and life itself, the more he sees that the soul of robust and seviceable character is faith.

O God, who hast encompassed us with so much that is dark and perplexing, and yet has set within us light enough to walk by; enable us to trust what Thou has given us as sufficient for us, and steadfastly refuse to follow aught else; lest the light that is in us become as darkness and we wander from the way. May we be loyal to all the truth we know, and seek to discharge those duties which lay their commission on our conscience; so that we may come at length to perfect light in Thee, and find our wills in harmony with Thine.

Since Thou hast planted our feet in a world so full of chance and change that we know not what a day may bring forth, and hast curtained every day with night and rounded our little lives with sleep; grant that we may use with diligence our appointed span of time, working while it is called today, since the night cometh when no man can work; having our loins girt and our lamps alight, lest the cry at midnight find us sleeping and the door fast shut.

Since we are so feeble, faint, and foolish, leave us not to our own devices, not even when we pray Thee to; nor suffer us for any care to Thee or for any pain to us to walk our own unheeding way. Plant thorns about our feet, touch our hearts with fear, give us no rest apart from Thee, lest we lose our way and miss the happy gate. Amen.—W. E. Orchard.

First Week, Third Day

Man cannot live without faith because the prime requisite in life's adventures is *courage,* and the sustenance of courage is faith.

And what shall I more say? for the time will fail me if I tell of Gideon, Barak, Samson, Jephthah; of David and Samuel and the prophets: who through faith subdued kingdoms, wrought righteousness, obtained promises, stopped the mouths of lions, quenched the power of fire, escaped the edge of the sword, from weakness were made strong, waxed mighty in war, turned to flight armies of aliens. Women received their dead by a resurrection: and others were tortured, not accepting their deliverance; that they might obtain a better resurrection: and others had trial of mockings and scourgings, yea, moreover of bonds and imprisonment: they were stoned, they were sawn asunder, they were tempted, they were slain with the sword: they went about in sheep-skins, in goat-skins; being destitute, afflicted, ill-treated (of whom the world was not worthy), wandering in deserts and mountains and caves, and the holes of the earth. And these all, having had witness borne to them through their faith, received not the promise, God having provided some better thing concerning us, that apart from us they should not be made perfect.—Heb. 11:32-40.

When in comparison with men and women of such admirable spirit, one thinks of weak personalities, that ravel out at the first strain, he sees that the difference lies in courage. *When a man loses heart he loses everything.* Now to keep one's heart in the midst of life's stress and to maintain an undiscourageable front in the face of its difficulties is not an achievement which springs from anything that a laboratory can demonstrate or that logic can confirm. It is an achievement of faith.

> "The virtue to exist by faith
> As soldiers live by courage."

Consider this account of Havelock, the great English general: "As he sat at dinner with his son on the evening of the 17th, his mind appeared for the first and last time to be affected with gloomy forebodings, as it dwelt on the probable annihilation of his brave men in a fruitless attempt to accomplish what was beyond their strength. After musing long in deep thought, his strong sense of duty and his confidence in the justice of his cause restored the buoyancy of his spirit; and he exclaimed, 'If the worst comes to the worst, we can but die with our swords in our hands!'" No man altogether escapes the need for such a spirit, and, as with Havelock and the Hebrew heroes, confidence in someone, faith in something, is that spirit's source.

O God, who hast sent us to school in this strange life of ours and hast set us tasks which test all our courage, trust, and fidelity, may we not spend our days complaining at circumstances or fretting at discipline, but give ourselves to learn of life and to profit by every experience. Make us strong to endure.

We pray that when trials come upon us we may not shirk the issue or lose our faith in Thy goodness, but committing our souls unto Thee who knowest the way that we take, come forth as gold tried in the fire.

Grant by Thy grace that we may not be found wanting in the hour of crisis. When the battle is set, may we know on which side we ought to be, and when the day goes hard, cowards steal from the field, and heroes fall around the standard, may our place be found where the fight is fiercest. If we faint, may we not be faithless; if we fall, may it be while facing the foe. Amen.—W. E. Orchard.

First Week, Fourth Day

Man cannot live without faith, because the adventure of life demands not only courage to achieve but *patience to endure and wait,* and all untroubled patience is founded on faith. When the writer to the Hebrews speaks of those who "through faith and patience inherit the promises" (Heb. 6:12), he joins two things that in exerience no man successfully can separate. By as much as we need patience, we need faith.

But call to remembrance the former days, in which, after ye were enlightened, ye endured a great conflict of sufferings; partly, being made a gazingstock both by reproaches and afflictions; and partly, becoming partakers with them that were so used. For ye both had compassion on them that were in bonds, and took joyfully the spoiling of your possessions, knowing that ye have for yourselves a better possession and an abiding one. Cast not away therefore your boldness, which hath great recompense of reward. For ye have need of patience, that, having done the will of God, ye may receive the promise.—Heb. 10:32-36.

The most difficult business in the world is *waiting.* There are times in every life when action, however laborious and sacrificial, would be an unspeakable relief; but to sit still because necessity constrains us, endeavoring to live out the admonition of the psalmist, "Rest in the Lord, and wait patiently for him," is prodigiously difficult. *No one can do it without some kind of faith.* "In your patience," said Jesus, "ye shall win your souls" (Luke 21:19), but such an achievement is no affair of logic or scientific demonstration; it is a venture of triumphant faith. The great believers have been the unwearied waiters: faith meant to them not controversial opinion, but sustaining power. As another has phrased it, "Our faculties of belief were not primarily given to us to make orthodoxies and heresis withal; they were given us to *live* by."

We beseech of Thee, O Lord our God, that Thou wilt grant to every one of us in Thy presence, this morning, the special mercies which he needs—strength where weakness prevails, and patience where courage has failed. Grant, we pray Thee, that those who need long-suffering may find themselves strangely upborne and sustained. Grant that those who wander in doubt and darkness may feel distilling upon their soul the sweet influence of faith. Grant that those who are heart-weary, and sick from hope deferred, may find the God of all salvation. Confirm goodness in those that are seeking it. Restore, we pray Thee, those who have wandered from the path of rectitude. Give every one honesty. May all transgressors of Thy law return to the Shepherd and Bishop of their souls with confession of sin, and earnest and sincere repentance. Amen.—Henry Ward Beecher.

First Week, Fifth Day

Man cannot live without faith because he exists in a universe, the complete explanation of which is forever beyond his grasp, so that *whatever he thinks about the total meaning of creation is fundamentally faith.*

By faith we understand that the worlds have been framed by the word of God, so that what is seen hath not been made out of things which appear.—Heb. 11:3.

Not only is this true, but if we think that there is *no* God, that also is faith; and if we hold that the basic reality is physical atoms, that is faith; and whatever anybody believes about the origin and destiny of life is faith. When Haeckel says that the creator is "Cosmic Ether," and when John says that "God is love," they both are making a leap of faith. This does not mean that faith can dispense with reason. In these studies we shall set ourselves to marshal the ample arguments that support man's faith in God. But when the utmost that argument can do has been achieved, the finite mind, dealing with the infinite reality, is forced to a sally of faith, a venture of confidence in goodness at the heart of the world, not opposed to reason but surpassing reason. *Faith always sees more with her eye than logic can reach with her hand.* And especially when men come to the highest thought of life's meaning and believe in the Christian God, they face the fact which the writer to the Hebrews presents:

And without faith it is impossible to be well-pleasing unto him; for he that cometh to God must believe that he is, and that he is a rewarder of them that seek after him.—Heb. 11:6.

Indeed, in all stout conviction about the meaning of life there is a certain defiant note, refusing to surrender to small objections. Cried Stevenson, "I believe in an ultimate decency of things; ay, and if I woke in hell, should still believe it!"

O Thou Infinite Spirit, who needest no words for man to hold his converse with Thee, we would enter into Thy presence, we would reverence Thy power, we would worship Thy wisdom, we would adore Thy justice, we would be gladdened by Thy love, and blessed by our communion with Thee. We know that Thou needest no sacrifice at our hands, nor any offering at our lips; yet we live in Thy world, we taste Thy bounty, we breathe Thine air, and Thy power sustains us, Thy justice guides, Thy goodness preserves, and Thy love blesses us forever and ever. O Lord, we cannot fail to praise Thee, though we cannot praise Thee as we would. We bow our faces down before Thee with humble hearts, and in Thy presence would warm our spirits for a while, that the better we may be prepared for the duties of life, to endure its trials, to bear its crosses, and to triumph in its lasting joys. . . .

In times of darkness, when men fail before Thee, in days when men of high degree are a lie, and those of low degree are a vanity, teach us, O Lord, to be true before Thee, not a vanity, but soberness and manliness; and may we keep still our faith shining in the midst of darkness, the beacon-light to guide us over stormy seas to a home and haven at last. Father, give us strength for our daily duty, patience for our constant or unaccustomed cross, and in every time of trial give us the hope that sustains, the faith that wins the victory and obtains satisfaction and fulness of joy. Amen.—Theodore Parker.

First Week, Sixth Day

Man cannot live, lacking faith, because *without it life's richest experiences go unappropriated.* Opportunities for friendship lie all about us, but only by trustful self-giving can they be enjoyed; chances to serve good causes continually beckon us, but one must have faith to try; superior minds offer us their treasures, but to avail oneself of instruction from another involves teachable humility. A man without capacity to let himself go out to other men in friendly trust or to welcome new illumination on his thought with grateful faith would be shut out from the priceless treasures of humanity. A certain trustful openheartedness, a willingness to venture in personal relationship and in attempts at service is essential to a rich and fruitful life. And what is true of man's relationship with man is true of man's relationship with God. So Prof. William James, of Harvard, states the case: "Just as a man who in a company of gentlemen made no advances, asked a warrant for every concession, and believed no one's word without proof, would cut himself off by such churlishness from all the social rewards that a more trusting spirit would earn—so here, one should shut himself up in snarling logicality and try to make the gods extort his recognition willy-nilly, or not get it at all, might cut himself off forever from his only opportunity of making the gods' acquaintance." *Wherever in life great spiritual values await man's appropriation, only faith can appropriate them.*

Let us fear therefore, lest haply, a promise being left of entering into his rest, any one of you should seem to have come short of it. For indeed we have had good tidings preached unto us, even as also they: but the word of hearing did not profit them, because it was not united by faith with them that heard!—Heb. 4:1-2.

O Infinite Source of life and health and joy! the very thought of Thee is so wonderful that in this thought we would rest and be still. Thou art Beauty and Grace and Truth and Power. Thou art the light of every heart that sees Thee, the life of every soul that loves Thee, the strength of every mind that seeks Thee. From our narrow and bounded world we would pass into Thy greater world. From our petty and miserable selves we would escape to Thee, to find in Thee the power and the freedom of a larger life. . . . We recognize Thee in all the deeper experiences of the soul. When the conscience utters its warning voice, when the heart is tender and we forgive those who have wronged us in word or deed, when we feel ourselves upborne above time and place, and know ourselves citizens of Thy everlasting Kingdom, we realize, O Lord, that these things, while they are in us, are not of us. They are Thine, the work of Thy Spirit brooding upon our souls.

Spirit of Holiness and Peace! Search all our motives; try the secret places of our souls; set in the light any evil that may lurk within, and lead us in the way everlasting. Amen.
—Samuel McComb.

First Week, Seventh Day

Man cannot live without faith, because in life's adventure the central problem is *building character.* Now, character is not a product of logic, but of faith in ideals and of sacrificial devotion to them. What *is* becomes only the starting point of a campaign for what *ought to be,* and in the prosecution of that campaign what ought to be must be believed in with passionate intensity. Faith of some sort, therefore, is necessarily the dynamic of character; only limp and ragged living is possible without faith; and the greatest characters are girded by the most ample faith in God and goodness. The writer to the Hebrews saw this intimate relationship between quality of faith and quality of life, and challenged his readers to judge the Christian faith by its consequence in character.

Remember them that had the rule over you, men that spake unto you the word of God; and considering the issue of their life, imitate their faith.—Heb. 13:7.

Such are the basic elements in human experience that make faith necessary: we deal with a future, about which we must think, with reference to which we must act, and adventuring into which we need courage and patience; this venture of life takes place in a world the meaning of which can be grasped only be a leap of faith; and in this venture the best treasures of the spirit are obtainable only through openheartedness, and character is possible only to men of resolute conviction. Plainly the subject to whose study we are setting ourselves is no affair of theoretical interest alone; it affects the deepest issues of life. No words could better summarize this vital idea of faith which the Epistle to the Hebrews presents than Hartley Coleridge's:

> "Think not the faith by which the just shall live
> Is a dead creed, a map correct of heaven,
> Far less a feeling, fond and fugitive,
> A thoughtless gift, withdrawn as soon as given.
> It is an affirmation and an act
> That bids eternal truth be present fact."

How great are the mercies, O Lord, our God, which Thou hast prepared for all that put their trust in Thee! . . . Thou hast comfort for those that are in affliction; Thou hast strength for those that are weak; . . . Thou hast all blessings that are needed, and standest ready to be all things to all, and in all. And yet, with bread enough and to spare, with raiment abundant, and with all medicine, how many are there that go hungry, and naked, and sick, and destitute of all things! We desire, O Lord, that Thou wilt, to all Thine other mercies, add that gift by which we shall trust in Thee—faith that works by love; faith that abides with us; faith that transforms material things, and gives them to us in their spiritual meanings; faith that illumines the world by a light that never sets, that shines brighter than the day, and that clears the night quite out of our experience. This is the portion that Thou hast provided for Thy people. We beseech of Thee, grant us this faith, that shall give us victory over the world and over ourselves; that shall make us valiant in all temptation and bring us off conquerers and more than conquerors through Him that loved us. Amen.—Henry Ward Beecher.

COMMENT FOR THE WEEK

I

When Donald Hankey, who died in the trenches in the Great War (World War I), said that "true religion is betting one's life that there is a God," he not only gave expression to his own virile Christianity, but he gave a good description of all effective faith whatsoever. Faith is holding reasonable convictions, in realms beyond the reach of final demonstration, and, as well, it is thrusting out one's life upon those convictions as though they were surely true. *Faith is. vision plus valor*.

Our study may well begin by recognizing that, as it is exercised in the religious life, such faith is the supreme use of an attitude which we are employing in every other realm. No man can live without vision to see as true what as yet he cannot prove, or without valor to act on the basis of his insight. Our vocabulary in ordinary relationships, quite as much as in religion, is full of words involving faith. I believe, I feel sure, I am confident, I venture—such phrases express our common attitudes in work and thought. Each day we act on reasonable probabilities, hold convictions not yet verified, take risks whose outcome we cannot know, and trust people whom we have barely met. We may pride ourselves that our twentieth century's life is being built on scientifically demonstrable knowledge, but a swift review of any day's experience shows how indispensable is another attitude, without which our verifiable knowledge would be an unused instrument. In order to *live* we must have insight and daring. It is not alone the just who live by faith: lacking it, there is no real life anywhere.

To be sure, we may not leap from this general necessity of faith to the conclusion that therefore our religious beliefs are justified. Many men use faith in business and in social life who cannot find their way to convictions about God. But our desire to understand faith's meaning is quickened when we see how indispensable a place it holds, how tremendous an influence it wields, whether it be religiously applied or not. All sorts of human enterprise bear witness to its unescapable necessity. Haeckel, the biologist, describing science's method, says: "Scientific faith fills the gaps in our knowledge of natural laws with temporary hypotheses." Lincoln, the statesman, entreating the people, cries, "Let us have faith that right makes might and in that faith let us to the end dare to do our duty." Stevenson, the invalid, trying with fortitude to bear his trial, writes: "Whether on the first of January or the thirty-first of

27

December, faith is a good word to end on." And the Master states the substance of religion in a single phrase: "Have faith in God" (Mark 11:22). Scientific procedure, social welfare, personal quality, religion—the applications of our subject are as wide as life. Vision and valor are the dynamic forces in all achievement, intellectual as well as moral, and as for man's spiritual values and satisfactions, "It is faith in something," as Oliver Wendell Holmes put it, "which makes life worth living."

II

One major reason for this necessary place of faith in our experience is clear. *Life is an adventure and adventure always demands insight and daring.* That "Chinese" Gordon, on his hazardous expedition into the Soudan, should be thrown back on undiscourageable faith in himself, in the justice of his cause, in the bravery of his men, and in God; that he should even speak of praying his boats up the Nile, seems to us natural; for some kind of faith is obviously necessary to any great adventure. But men often forget that all ordinary living is essentially adventurous and that by this fact the need of faith is woven into the texture of every human life. It is an amazing adventure to be born upon this wandering island in the sky and it is an adventure to leave it when death calls. To go to school, to make friends, to marry, to rear children, to face through life the swift changes of circumstance that no man can certainly predict an hour ahead, these are all adventures. Each new day is an hitherto unvisited country, which we enter, like Abraham leaving Ur for a strange land, "not knowing whither he went" (Heb. 11:8), and every New Year we begin a tour of exploration into a twelvemonth where no man's foot has ever walked before. If we all love tales of pioneers, it is because from the time we are weaned to the time we die, life is pioneering. Of course we cannot live by verifiable knowledge only. Imagine men, equipped with nothing but powers of logical demonstration, starting on such an enterprise as the title of Sebastian Cabot's joint stock company suggests: "Merchants Adventurers of

England for the discovery of lands, territories, isles and seignories, unknown."

Indeed no knowledge of the sort that our scientific inductions can achieve ever will take from life this adventurous element. Scientific knowledge in these latter decades has grown incalculably; yet for all that, every child's life is a hazardous experiment, every boy choosing a calling takes his chances, every friendship is a risky exploration in the province of personality, and all devotion to moral causes is just as much a venturesome staking of life on insight and hope as it was when Garrison attacked slavery or Livingstone landed in Africa. To one who had acquired not only all extant but all possible knowledge, as truly as any man who ever lived, life would be full of hazard still. He could not certainly know in advance the outcome of a single important decision of his life. He could not at any moment tell in what new, strange, challenging, or terrific situation the next hour might find him. With all his science, he must face each day, as Paul faced his journey to Rome, "not knowing the things that shall befall me there" (Acts 20:22).

The reason for this is obvious. Our systematized knowledge is the arrangement under laws of the experiences which we have already had. It furnishes invaluable aid in guiding the experiments and explorations which life continuously forces on us. In every enterprise, however, we must use not only legs to stand on, but tentacles as well with which to feel our way forward—intuitions, insights, hopes, unverified convictions, faith. We project our life forward as we build a cantilever bridge. Part of the structure is solidly bolted and thoroughly articulated in a system; but ever beyond this established portion we audaciously thrust out new beginnings in eager expectation that from the other side something will come to meet them. Without this no progress ever would be possible.

Every province of life illustrates this necessity of adventure. In *science,* the established body of facts and laws is only the civilized community of knowledge from whose frontiers new guesses and intuitions start. Says Sir Oliver Lodge about the great Newton: "He had an extraordinary faculty for guessing correctly, sometimes with no apparent data—as for instance, his intuition that the mean density of the earth was probably between five and six times that of water, while we now know it is really about five and one half." In *personal character*, our habits are basic, but our ideals in which, despite ourselves, we must believe, are pioneers that push out into new territory and call our habits after them to conquer the promised land. In *social advance*, some Edmund Burke, statesman of the first magnitude, basing his judgment on the established experience of the race, can call slavery an incurable evil and say that there is not the slightest hope that trade in slaves can be stopped; and yet within eighty-two years the race can feel its way forward to Lincoln's Emancipation Proclamation. As for *daily business*, adventurous daring is there the very nerve of enterprise. Says a newspaperman: "There are plenty of people to do the possible; you can hire them at minimum wage. The prizes are for those who perform the impossible. If a thing can be done, experience and skill can do it; if a thing cannot be done, only faith can do it." Great in human life is this adventurous element, and, therefore, great in human life is the necessity of faith. To chasten and discipline, to make reasonable and stable the faiths by which we live is a problem unsurpassed in importance for every man.

III

One result of special interest follows from this truth. It is commonly suspected that as mankind advances, the function of faith proportionately shrinks. It is even supposed that the place of faith in human life has sensibly diminished with our growing knowledge, and that Matthew Arnold told the truth:

> "The sea of faith
>   Was once, too, at the full, and round earth's shore
> Lay like the folds of a bright girdle furl'd.
>   But now I only hear
>   Its melancholy, long, withdrawing roar,
>   Retreating, to the breath
> Of the night-wind, down the vast edges drear
>   And naked shingles to the world."

Accordingly by custom we call the medieval centuries the "Age of Faith." But even a cursory comparison between the medieval people and ourselves reveals that among the many differences that distinguish us from them, none is more marked than the diversity and range of our faiths. One considers in surprise the things which they did not believe. That the world would ever grow much better, that social abuses like political tyranny and slavery could be radically changed, that man could ever master nature by his inventions until her mighty forces were his servants, that the whole race could be reached for Christ, that war could be abolished and human brotherhood in some fair degree established, that common men could be trusted with responsibility for their own government or with freedom to worship God according to the dictates of their own consciences—none of these things did the medieval folk believe. One of the most distinguishing characteristics of the so-called "Age of Faith" was its lack of faith. It lived in a static world; it was poor in possibilities except in heaven; it pitiably lacked those most certain signs of vital faith, the open mind eager for new truth and the ardent, vigorous life seeking new conquests. In comparison with such an age our generation's faiths are rich and manifold. To call our time an "Age of Doubt" because of its free spirit of critical inquiry, is seriously to misunderstand its major drift. Bunyan's Pilgrim found Doubting Castle kept by Giant Despair and his wife Diffidence and in any Doubting Castle these two always dwell. But who, considering our generation's life as a whole, would call it diffident or desperate? It is rather robust and confident; its social faiths, at least, are unprecedented in their sweep and certainty. Even the Great War is the occasion of such organized faith in a federated and fraternal world as mankind has never entertained before.

The truth is that with the progress of the race the adventure of life is elevated and enlarged, and in consequence faith grows not less but more necessary. *The faiths of a savage are meager compared with a modern man's.* The Australian bushman never dreams of laboring for social ideals even a few years ahead. What can he know of those superb faiths in economic justice and international brotherhood, which even in the face of overwhelming difficulty, master the best of modern men? The primitive mind was not curious enough to wonder whether the sun that rises in the morning was the same sun that set the night before. What could such a mind understand of modern science's faith in the universal regularity of law? Put a Moro head hunter beside Mr. Edison, and see how incalculable the difference between them, not simply in their knowledge, but in their faith as to what it is possible for humanity to do with nature! Or put a fetish worshiper from Africa beside Phillip Brooks and compare the faith of the one in his idol with the faith of the other in God. Faith does not dwindle as wisdom grows; vision and valor are not less important. *The difference between the twentieth century and the savage is quite as much in the scope and quality of their faith as in the range and certainty of their knowledge.*

Faith, therefore, is not a transient element in human life to be evicted by growing science. For whatever life may *know,,* life *is* adventure; and as the adventure widens its horizons, the demand for faith is correspondingly increased. If one tries to imagine the world with all faith gone—knowledge supposedly having usurped its place—he must conceive a world where no conscious life and effort remain at all. Take trust in testimony away from courts of law, and unsure experiments from the physician's practice; refuse the teacher his confidence in growing minds and the businessman his right to ventures that involve uncertainty; abstract from civic reforms all faith in a better future, from science all unproved postulates, from society all mutual trust and from religion all belief in the Unseen, and life would become an "inane sand heap." A man who tries to live without faith will die of inertia. A society that makes the attempt will be paralyzed within an hour. The question is not whether or no we shall live by faith. The question is rather, By what faiths shall we live? What range and depth and quality shall they have? How reasonable and how assured shall they be?

IV

Among all the faiths which mankind has cherished and by which it has been helped in life's adventure, none have been more universally and more passionately held than those associated with religion. In the daring experiment of living, men naturally have sought by faith interpretation not only of life's details but of life itself—its origin, its meaning, and its destiny. Australian bushmen, unable to count above four on their fingers, have been heard discussing in their huts at night whence they came, whither they go, and who the gods are anyway. And when one turns to modern manhood in its finest exhibitions of intelligence and character, he sees that Professor Ladd, of Yale, speaks truly: "The call of the world of men today, which is most insistent and most intense, if not most loud and clamorous, is the call for a rehabilitation of religious faith."

For it does make a prodigious difference to the spirit of our adventure in this world, whether we think that God is good or on the other hand see the universe as Carlyle's terrific figure pictures it—"one huge, dead, immeasurable Steam-engine, rolling on, in its dead indifference, to grind me limb from limb." It does make a difference of quite incalculable magnitude whether we think that our minds and characters are an evanescent product of finely wrought matter which alone is real and permanent, or on the contrary with John believe that "Now we are children of God and it is not yet made manifest what we shall be" (I John 3:2).

How great a difference in life's adventure religious faith does make is better set forth by concrete example than by abstract argument. On the one side, how radiant the spirit of the venture as the New Testament depicts it! The stern, appealing love of God behind life, his good purpose through it, his victory ahead of it, and man a fellow worker, called into an unfinished world to bear a hand with God in its completion—here is a game that indeed is worth the candle. On the other side is Bertrand Russell's candid disclosure of the consequences of his own scepticism: "Brief and powerless is man's life; on him and all his race the slow sure doom falls pitiless and dark. Blind to good and evil, reckless of destruction, omnipotent matter rolls on its relentless way; for Man condemned today to lose his dearest, tomorrow himself to pass through the gate of darkness, it remains only to cherish, ere yet the blow falls, the lofty thoughts that ennoble his little day—proudly defiant of the irresistible forces that tolerate for a moment his knowledge and his condemnation, to sustain alone, a weary but unyielding Atlas, the world that his own ideals have fashioned despite the trampling march of unconscious power.''

Man's life, interpreted and motivated by religious faith, is glorious, but shorn of faith's interpretations life loses its highest meaning and its noblest hopes. Let us make this statement's truth convincing in detail.

When faith in God goes, man the thinker loses his greatest thought. Man's mind has ranged the universe, has woven atoms and stars into a texture of law; his conquering thoughts ride out into every unknown province of which they hear. But among all the ideas on which the mind of man has taken hold, incomparably the greatest is the idea of God. In sheer weight and range no other thought of man compares with that. Amid the crash of stars, the reign of law, the vicissitudes of human history, and the griefs that drive their ploughshares into human hearts, to gather up all existence into spiritual unity and to believe in God, is the sublimest venture of the human mind.

When faith in God goes, man the worker loses his greatest motive. Man masters nature until the forces that used to scare him now obey; in society he labors tirelessly that his children may have a better world. Wars come, destroying the achievements of ages; yet when war is over, man rebuilds his cities, recreates his commerce, dreams again his human brotherhoods, and toils on. Many motives, deep and shallow, fine and coarse, have sustained him in this tireless work, but when one seeks the fountain of profoundest hope in mankind's toil he finds it in religious faith. To believe that we do not stand alone, hopelessly pitted against the dead apathy of cosmic forces which in the end will crush us in some solar wreck and bring our work to naught; to believe that we are fellow-laborers with God, our human purposes comprehended in a Purpose, God behind us, within us, ahead of us—this incomparably has been the master-faith in man's greatest work.

When faith in God goes, man the sinner loses his strongest help. For man is a sinner. He tears his spiritual heritage to shreds in licentiousness and drink. He wallows in vice, wins by cruelty, violates love, is treacherous to trust. His sins clothe the world in lamentation. Yet in him is a protest that he cannot stifle. He is the only creature whom we know whose nature is divided against itself. He hates his sin even while he commits it. He repents, tries again, falls, rises, stumbles on—and in all his best hours cries out for saviorhood. No message short of religion has ever met man's need in this estate. That God himself is pledged to the victory of righteousness in men and in the world, that he cares, forgives, enters into man's struggle with transforming power, and crowns the long endeavor with triumphant character—such faith alone has been great enough to meet the needs of man the sinner.

When faith in God goes, man the sufferer loses his securest refuge. One who has walked with families through long illnesses where desperate prayers rise like a fountain day and night, who has seen strong men break down in health or lose the fortune of a lifetime, who has stood at children's graves and heard mothers cry, "How empty are my arms!" does not need long explication of life's tragic suffering. The staggering blows shatter the hopes of good and bad alike. Whether one's house be built on rock or sand, on both, as Jesus said, the rains descend and the floods come and the winds blow. In this experience of crushing trouble nothing but religious faith has been able to save men from despair or from stoical endurance of their fate. To face the loom of life and hopefully to lay oneself upon it, as though the dark threads were as necessary in the pattern as the light ones are, we must believe that there is a purpose running through the stern, forbidding process. What men have needed most of all in suffering is not to know the explanation, but *to know that there is an explanation.* And religious faith alone gives confidence that human tragedy is not the meaningless sport of physical forces, making our life what Voltaire called it, "a bad joke," but is rather a school of discipline, the explanation of whose mysteries is in the heart of God. No one who has lived deeply can ever call such faith a "matter of words and names." To multitudes it is a matter of life and death.

When faith in God goes, man the lover loses his fairest vision. When we say our worst about mankind, this redeeming truth remains, that each of us has some one for whose sake he willingly would die. The very love lyrics of

35

the race are proof of this human quality, from homely folk songs like "John Anderson, My Jo, John" to great poetry like Mrs. Browning's sonnets. We call them secular, but they are ineffably sacred. And when one seeks the faith that has made these loves of men radiant with an illumination which man alone cannot create, he finds it in religion. Love is not a transient fragrance from matter finely organized—so men have dared believe; love is of kin with the Eternal, has there its source and ground and destiny; love is the very substance of reality. "God is love, and he that abideth in love, abideth in God, and God abideth in him" (I John 4:16). Man the lover is bereft of his finest insight and love's inner glory has departed, when that faith has gone.

When faith in God goes, man the mortal loses his only hope. Man's nature, like a lighthouse, combines two elements. At the foundation of the beacon all is stone; as one lifts his eyes, all is stone still; but at the top is something new and wonderful. It is the thing for which the rock was piled. Its laws are not the laws of stone nor are its ways the same. For while the stolid rock stands fast, this miracle of light with speed incredible hurls itself out across the sea. Two worlds are here, the one cold and stationary, the other full of the marvel and mystery of fire. So man has in him a miracle which he cannot explain; he "feels that he is greater than he knows"; and he never has been able to believe that the mystery of spirit was given him in vain, had no reality from which it came, and no future beyond death. The finest thing ever said of Columbus is a remark of his own countryman, "The instinct of an unknown continent burned in him." That is the secret of Columbus' greatness. All the arguments by which he attempted to convince the doubters were but afterthoughts of this; all the labors by which he endeavored to make good his hopes were but its consequence. And if we ask of man why so universally he has believed in life to come, the answer leaps not superficially from the mind, but out of the basic intuitions of man's life. We know that something is now ours which ought not to die; the instinct of an unknown continent burns in us. But all the hopes, the motives, the horizons that immortality has given man must go, if faith in God departs. In a godless world man dies forever.

One, therefore, who is facing loss of faith may not regard

it as a light affair. To be sure, some denials of religion, even a Christian must respect. Huxley, for example, at the death of his little boy, wanting to believe in immortality as only a father can whose son lies dead, yet, for all that, disbelieving, wrote to Charles Kingsley, "I have searched over the grounds of my belief, and if wife and child and name and fame were all to be lost to me one after another as the penalty, still I will not lie." One respects *that*. When George John Romanes turned his back for a while on the Christian faith, he wrote out of his agnosticism, "When at times I think, as think at times I must, of the appalling contrast between the hallowed glory of that creed which once was mine, and the lonely mystery of existence as now I find it—at such times I shall ever feel it impossible to avoid the sharpest pang of which my nature is susceptible." One respects *that*. But some discard religion from their life's adventure with no such serious understanding of the import of their denial. They are pert disbelievers. They toss faith facilely aside in a light mood. Such frivolous sceptics indict their own intelligence. Whoever discards religious faith should appoint a day of mourning for his soul, and put on sackcloth and ashes. He must take from his life the greatest thought that man the thinker ever had, the finest faith that man the worker ever leaned upon, the surest help that man the sinner ever found, the strongest reliance that man the sufferer ever trusted in, the loftiest vision that man the lover ever saw, and the only hope that man the mortal ever had. So he must deny his faith in God. Before one thus leaves himself bereft of the faith that makes life's adventure most worth while he well may do what Carlyle, under the figure of Teufelsdröckh, says that he did in his time of doubt: "In the silent night-watches, still darker in his heart than over sky and earth, he has cast himself before the All-seeing, and with audible prayers cried vehemently for Light."

V

If minimizing the importance of religious faith is unintelligent, so is avoiding some sort of decision about religious faith impossible. Most of those into whose hands these studies fall will grant readily faith's incalculable importance. Some, however, will not be helped but plunged into deeper trouble by their consent. For they feel themselves unable to decide about a matter which they acknowledge to be the most important in the world. Asked whether they believe in God, they would reply with one of Victor Hugo's characters, "Yes—No— Sometimes." They grant that to be steadily assured of God would be an invaluable boon, but for themselves, how can they balance the opposing arguments and find their way to confidence? All our studies are intended for the help of such, but at the beginning one urgent truth may well be plainly put. However undecided they may appear, men cannot altogether avoid decision on the main matters of religion. Life will not let them. For while the mind may hold itself suspended between alternatives, the adventure of life goes on, and men inevitably tend to live either as though the Christian God were real or as though he were not.

Some questions allow a complete postponement of decision. As to which of several theories about the Northern Lights may be true, a man can hold his judgment in entire suspense. Life does not require from him any action that depends on what he thinks of the Aurora Borealis; and whether a man think one thing or another, no conceivable change would be the consequence in anything he said or did. But there is another kind of question, where, however much the mind may waver between opinions and may resolve on indecision, life itself compels decision. A man cannot really be agnostic and neutral on a question like the moral law of sexual purity, for, by an irrevocable necessity, he has to act one way or another. He may stop thinking, but he cannot stop living. With tremendous urgency the adventure of life insistently goes on, and it never pauses for any man to make up his mind on any question. Therefore while a man may theoretically suspend his judgment as to the requirements of the moral law, his life will be a loud, convincing advertisement to all who know him that he has vitally decided. *A man can avoid making up his mind, but he cannot avoid making up his life.*

Quite as truly, though, it may be, not quite as obviously, religious questions belong to this second class. Not all questions that are called religious belong there. With fatal pettiness religious men have reduced the great faiths to technicalities and some beliefs called religious a man may hold or not, with utter indifference to anything he is or does. But on the basic attitudes of religion such as we have just rehearsed, a man cannot be completely neutral, no matter how he tries. Bernard Shaw's remark, "What a man believes may be ascertained not from his creed, but from the assumptions on which he habitually acts," should be taken to heart by any one trying to remain religiously neutral. For one cannot by any possibility avoid "assumptions on which he habitually acts." He tends to undertake social service either as confident cooperation with God's purpose or as an endeavor to make one corner of an unpurposed world as decent as possible. He tends to follow his ideals, either as the voice of God calling him upward, or as the work of natural selection, adjusting him to a temporary environment. He tends to face suffering either hopefully as a school of moral discipline, in a world presided over by a Father, or grimly as a hardship in which there is no meaning. He tends to face death either as the supreme adventure, full of boundless hope, or as a final exit that leads nowhere. He may never consciously formulate his ideas on any of these matters, he may maintain an intellectual agnosticism, genuine and complete, but his living subtly involves the confession of some faith. "A man's action," said Emerson, "is only the picture-book of his creed." And the more thoughtful he is, the more he will be aware of that unescapable tendency to confess in his living an inward faith about life.

Once practical result of this urgent truth is too frequently seen to be doubtful. *Those who in religion do not decide, thereby decide against religion.* Religious faith is a positive achievement, and he who does not deliberately choose it, loses it. A man who, rowing down Niagara River, debates within himself whether or not he will stop at Buffalo, and who cannot decide, thereby has decided. His irresolution has not for a moment interfered with the steady flow of the river, and if he but debate long enough concerning his stop at Buffalo, he will awake to discover that he has finally decided not to stop there. As much beyond the control of man's volition is the steady flow of life. It pauses for no man's indecision, and if one is irresolute about any positive, aspiring faith in any realm, his indecisiveness is decision of a most final sort.

This, then, is the summary of the matter. Life is a great adventure in which faith is indispensable; in this adventure faith in God presents the issues of transcendent import; and on these issues life itself continuously compels decision. Our obligation is obvious—since willy-nilly the decision must be made—to make it consciously, to reach it by reason, not by chance, by thinking, not by drifting. If a man is to be irreligious, let him at least know why, and not slip into this estate, as most irreligious men do, by careless living and frivolous thought. If a man is to be religious, let him have reason for his choice; let his faith be founded not on credulity and chance, but on real experience and reasonable thought. So his faith shall be good not only for domestic consumption, but for export too—clear in his own mind and convincing to his friends. The forms of thought shift with the centuries and old situations cannot be repeated in detail, but one crisis in its essential meaning is perennial: "Elijah came near unto all the people, and said, How long go ye limping between the two sides? If Jehovah be God follow him; but if Baal then follow him" (I Kings 18:21).

CHAPTER II

Faith a Road to Truth

DAILY READINGS

Many minds are prevented from even a fair consideration of religious faith by prejudices which spring, not from reasoned argument, but from practical experience. They are biased before argument has begun; they *feel* that faith means credulity, and that religious faith in particular is a surrender of reason. Before we positively present faith as an indispensable means of dealing with reality in any realm, let us, in the daily readings, consider some of the practical experiences and attitudes that thus prejudice men against religion.

Second Week, First Day

Many men are biased in advance by the *unwise treatment to which in their childhood they were subjected.* Paul pictures the home life of Timothy as ideal:

I thank God, whom I serve from my forefathers in a pure conscience, how unceasing is my remembrance of thee in my supplications, night and day longing to see thee, remembering thy tears, that I may be filled with joy; having been reminded of the unfeigned faith that is in thee; which dwelt first in thy grandmother Lois, and thy mother Eunice; and, I am persuaded, in thee also.—II Tim. 1:3-5.

"Unfeigned faith" is often thus a family heritage, handed down by vital contagion. But in many homes religion is not thus beautifully presented to the children; it is a hard and rigorous affair of dogma and restraint. "Oh, why," said a young professional man, whom Professor Coe quotes, "why did my parents try to equip me with a doctrinal system in childhood? I supposed that the whole system must be believed on pain of losing my religion altogether. And so, when I began to doubt some points, I felt obliged to throw all overboard. I have found my way back to positive religion, but by what a long and bitter struggle!" If, however, one has been so unfortunate as to be hardened in youth by unwise training, is it reasonable on that account forever to shut himself out from the most glorious experience of man? This complaint about mistreatment in youth is often an excuse, not a reason for irreligion. Says Phillips Brooks: "I have grown familiar to weariness with the self-excuse of men who say, 'Oh, if I had not had the terrors of the law so preached to me when I was a boy, if I had not been so confronted with the woes of hell and the awfulness of the judgment day, I should have been religious long ago.' My friends, I think I never hear a meaner or a falser speech than that. Men may believe it when they say it—I suppose they do—but it is not true. It is unmanly, I think. It is throwing on their teaching and their teachers, or their fathers and their mothers, the fault which belongs to their own neglect, because they have never taken up the earnest fight with sin and sought through every obstacle for truth and God. It has the essential vice of dogmatism about it, for it claims that a different *view* of God would have done for them that which no view of God can do, that which must be done, *under any system, any teaching,* by humility and penitence and struggle and self-sacrifice. Without these no teaching saves the soul. With these, under any teaching, the soul must find its Father."

O Thou, who didst lay the foundations of the earth amid the singing of the morning stars and the joyful shouts of the sons of God, lift up our little life into Thy gladness. Out of Thee, as out of an overflowing fountain of Love, wells forth eternally a stream of blessing upon every creature Thou hast made. If we have thought that Thou didst call into being this universe in order to win praise and honor for Thyself, rebuke the vain fancies of our foolish minds and show us that Thy glory is the joy of giving. We can give Thee nothing of our

*own. All that we have is Thine. Oh, then, help us to glorfy
Thee by striving to be like Thee. Make us just and pure and
good as Thou art. May we be partakers of the Divine Nature,
so that all that is truly human in us may be deepened,
purified, strengthened. And so may we be witnesses for Thee,
lights of the world, reflecting Thy light.*

*Help us to make religion a thing so beautiful that all men
may be won to surrender to its power. Let us manifest in our
lives its sweetness and excellency, its free and ennobling
spirit. Forbid that we should go up and down the world with
melancholy looks and dejected visage, lest we should repel
men from entering Thy Kingdom. Rather, may we walk in
the freedom and joy of faith, and with Thy new song in our
mouths, so that men looking on us may learn to trust and to
love Thee. Amen.*—Samuel McComb.

Second Week, Second Day

Many men are prejudiced against religion during their
youthful *period of revolt against authority.* Listen to an
ancient father talking with his sons:

Hear, my sons, the instruction of a father,
And attend to know understanding:
For I give you good doctrine;
Forsake ye not my law.
For I was a son unto my father,
Tender and only beloved in the sight of my mother.
And he taught me, and said unto me:
Let thy heart retain my words;
Keep my commandments, and live;
Get wisdom, get understanding;
Forget not, neither decline from the words of my mouth;
Forsake her not, and she will preserve thee;
Love her, and she will keep thee.
Wisdom is the principal thing; therefore get wisdom;
Yea, with all thy getting get understanding.
Exalt her, and she will promote thee;
She will bring thee to honor, when thou dost embrace her.
She will give to thy head a chaplet of grace;
A crown of beauty will she deliver to thee.

—Prov. 4:1-0.

No father can read this urgent, anxious plea without understanding the reason for its solicitude. Every boy comes to the time when he breaks away from parental authority and begins to take his life into his own hands. It is one of youth's great crises, and the spirit of it is sometimes harsh and rebellious. So Carlyle describes his own experience: "Such transitions are ever full of pain: thus the Eagle when he moults is sickly; and, to attain his new beak, must harshly dash-off the old one upon rocks." For religious faith this period of life is always critical. Stevenson in his revolt, when he called respectability "the deadliest gag and wet-blanket that can be laid on man," also became, as he said, "a youthful atheist." How many have traveled that road and stopped in the negation! Stevenson did not stop, and years afterward wrote of his progress: "Because I have reached Paris, I am not ashamed of having passed through Newhaven and Dieppe." Surely if anyone has been a "a youthful atheist," it was an experience to be "passed through."

O God, we turn to Thee in the faith that Thou dost understand and art very merciful. Some of us are not sure concerning Thee; not sure what Thou art; not sure that Thou art at all. Yet there is something at work behind our minds, in times of stillness we hear it, like a distant song; there is something in the sky at evening-time; something in the face of man. We feel that round our incompleteness flows Thy greatness, round our restlessness Thy rest. Yet this is not enough.

We want a heart to speak to, a heart that understands; a friend to whom we can turn, a breast on which we may lean. O that we could find Thee! Yet could we ever think these things unless Thou hadst inspired us, could we ever want these things unless Thou Thyself wert very near?

Some of us know full well; but we are sore afraid. We dare not yield ourselves to Thee, for we fear what that might mean. Our foolish freedom, our feeble pleasures, our fatal self-indulgence suffice to hold us back from Thee, though Thou art our very life, and we so sick and needing Thee. Our freedom has proved false, our pleasures have long since lost their zest, our sins, oh how we hate them!

Come and deliver us, for we have lost all hope in ourselves. Amen. —W. E. Orchard.

Second Week, Third Day

Some men—often the precocious, clever ones—are biased against religion because *in youth they accepted an immature philosophy of life and have never changed it.* The crust forms too soon on some minds, and if it forms during the period of youthful revolt, they are definitely prejudiced against religious truth. The difference between such folk and the great believers is not that the believers had no doubts, but that they did not fix their final thought of life until more mature experience had come. They fulfilled the admonition of a wise father to keep up a tireless search for truth:

My son, if thou wilt receive my words,
And lay up my commandments with thee;
So as to incline thine ear unto wisdom,
And apply thy heart to understanding;
Yea, if thou cry after discernment,
And lift up thy voice for understanding;
If thou seek her as silver,
And search for her as for hid treasures:
Then shalt thou understand the fear of Jehovah,
And find the knowledge of God.

—Prov. 2:1-5.

Mrs. Charles Kingsley, for example, says of her husband that at twenty "He was full of religious doubts; and his face, with its unsatisfied, hungering, and at times defiant look, bore witness to the state of his mind." At twenty-one Kingsley himself wrote: "You believe that you have a sustaining Hand to guide you along that path, an Invisible Protection and an unerring Guide. I, alas! have no stay for my weary steps, but that same abused and stupefied reason which has stumbled and wandered, and betrayed me a thousand times ere now, and is every moment ready to faint and to give up the unequal struggle." If Kingsley had framed his final philosophy then, what a loss to the world of an inspiring life transfigured by Christian faith! He cried after discernment, lifted up his voice for understanding, and he found the knowledge of God. Many a man ought to revise in the light of mature experience and thought a hasty irreligious guess at life's meaning which he made in youth.

Our Father, we turn to Thee because we are sore vexed with our own thoughts. Our minds plague us with questionings we cannot answer; we are driven to voyage on strange seas of thought alone. Dost Thou disturb our minds with endless questioning, yet keep the answers hidden in Thy heart, so that away from Thee we should always be perplexed, and by thoughts derived from Thee be ever drawn to Thee? Surely, our God, it must be so.

But still more bitter and humbling, O Father, is our experience of failure, so frequent, tragic, and unpardonable. We have struggled on in vain, resolves are broken ere thy pass our lips; we can see no hope of better things, we can never forgive ourselves; and after all our prayers our need remains and our sense of coming short but deepens. Yet, at least we know that we have failed, and how, if something higher than ourselves were not at work within?

Our desperate desires have driven us at last to Thee, conscious now, after all vain effort, that it is Thyself alone can satisfy, and now at peace to know that Thou it is who art desired, because Thou it is who dost desire within us. Beyond our need reveal Thyself, its cause and cure; in all desire teach us to discern Thy drawing near. Amen.—W. E. Orchard.

Second Week, Fourth Day

Men are often prejudiced against religion because *the churches which they happen to attend in youth urged on them an irrational faith.* Some men never recover from the idea that all religion everywhere must always be the same kind of religion against which in youth their good sense rose in revolt; they are in perpetual rebellion against religion as it was when they broke with it a generation ago. But if one thing more than another grows, expands, becomes in the intelligent and pure increasingly pure and intelligent, it is religion.

Consider an early Hebrew idea of God:

And it came to pass on the way at the lodging-place, that Jehovah met him, and sought to kill him. Then Zipporah

took a flint, and cut off the foreskin of her son, and cast it at his feet; and she said, Surely a bridegroom of blood art thou to me. So he let him alone. Then she said, A bridegroom of blood art thou, because of the circumcision.—Exod. 4:24-26.

Over against so abhorrent a picture of a deity who would have committed murder, had not a mother swiftly circumcised her son, consider a later thought of God:

How think ye? if any man have a hundred sheep, and one of them be gone astray, doth he not leave the ninety and nine, and go unto the mountains, and seek that which goeth astray? And if so be that he find it, verily I say unto you, he rejoiceth over it more than over the ninety and nine which have not gone astray. Even so it is not the will of your Father who is in heaven, that one of these little ones should perish.—Matt. 18:12-14.

So religion grows with man's capacity to receive higher, finer revelations of the divine. And in no age of the world has so great a change passed over the intellectual framework of faith as in the generation just gone. To live in protest against forms of belief a generation old is fighting men of straw; the vanguard of religious thought and life has pushed ahead many a mile beyond the point of such attack. Men who threw away the living water of the Gospel because they disliked the water buckets in which their boyhood churches presented it, are living spiritually thirsty lives when there is no reasonable need of their doing so. There is many an unbeliever with a "God-shaped blank" in his heart, who could be a confident and joyful believer if he only knew what religion means to men of faith today.

O God, who hast formed all hearts to love Thee, made all ways to lead to Thy face, created all desire to be unsatisfied save in Thee; with great compassion look upon us gathered here. Our presence is our prayer, our need the only plea we dare to claim, Thy purposes the one assurance we possess.

Some of us are very confused; we do not know why we were ever born, for what end we should live, which way we should take. But we are willing to be guided. Take our trembling hands in Thine, and lead us on.

Some of us are sore within. We long for love and friendship, but we care for no one and we feel that no cares for us. We are misunderstood, we are lonely, we have been disappointed, we have lost our faith in man and our faith in life. Wilt Thou not let us love Thee who first loved us?

Some of us are vexed with passions that affright us; to yield to them would mean disaster, to retrain them is beyond our power, and nothing earth contains exhausts their vehemence or satisfies their fierce desire.

And so because there is no answer, no end or satisfaction in ourselves; and because we are what we are, and yet long to be so different; we believe Thou art, and that Thou dost understand us. By faith we feel after Thee, through love we find the way, in hope we bring ourselves to Thee. Amen.—W. E. Orchard.

Second Week, Fifth Day

Many minds are prejudiced against religion because, having gone so far as to feel the credulity of religious belief, they have never gone further and *seen the credulity of religious unbelief*. Irreligion implies a creed just as surely as religion does; and many a man's return to faith has begun when his faculties of doubt, which hitherto had been used only against belief in God, became active against belief in no-God. Mr. Gilbert Chesterton, with his characteristic vividness and exaggeration, narrates such an experience: "I never read a line of Christian apologetics. I read as little as I can of them now. It was Huxley and Herbert Spencer and Bradlaugh who brought me back to orthodox theology. They sowed in my mind my first wild doubts of doubt. Our grandmothers were quite right when they said that Tom Paine and the free-thinkers unsettled the mind. They do. They unsettled mine horribly. The rationalist made me question whether reason was of any use whatever; and when I had finished Herbert Spencer I had got as far as doubting (for the first time) whether evolution had occurred at all. As I laid down the last of Colonel Ingersoll's atheistic lectures the dreadful thought broke across my mind, 'Almost thou persuadest me to be a Christian.' I was in a desperate way." Lest Mr. Chesterton's whimsicality may hide the seriousness of such an experience, we may add that Robert Louis Stevenson's first break with his "youthful atheism" came when, under the influence of Professor Fleeming Jenkin, he too began to have his "first wild doubts of doubt." He began thinking, as he says, that "certainly the church was not right, but certainly not the anti-church either." Many a man has played unfairly with his doubts; he has used them against religion, but not against irreligion. When he is thorough with his doubts he may join the many who understand what the apostle meant when he wrote to Timothy:

O Timothy, guard that which is committed unto thee, turning away from the profane babblings and oppositions of the knowledge which is falsely so called; which some professing have erred concerning the faith.

Grace be with you.—1 Tim. 6:20-21.

O God, too near to be found, too simple to be conceived, too good to be believed; help us to trust, not in our knowledge of Thee, but in Thy knowledge of us; to be certain of Thee, not because we feel our thoughts of Thee are true, but because we know how far Thou dost transcend them. May we not be anxious to discern Thy will, but content only with desire to do it; may we not strain our minds to understand Thy nature, but yield ourselves and live our lives only to express Thee.

Shew us how foolish it is to doubt Thee, since Thou Thyself dost set the questions which disturb us; reveal our unbelief to be faith fretting at its outworn form. Be gracious when we are tempted to cease from moral strife: reveal what it is that struggles in us. Before we tire of mental search enable us to see that it was not ourselves but Thy call which stirred our souls.

Turn us back from our voyages of thought to that which sent us forth. Teach us to trust not to cleverness or learning, but to that inward faith which can never be denied. Lead us out of confusion to simplicity. Call us back from wandering without to find Thee at home within. Amen.—W. E. Orchard.

Second Week, Sixth Day

Many men are biased in favor of their habitual doubt because they do not see that *positive faith is the only normal estate of man.* We live not by the things of which we are uncertain, but by the things which we verily believe. Columbus doubted many of the old views in geography, but these negations did not make him great; his greatness sprang from the positive beliefs which he confidently held and on which he launched his splendid adventure. Goethe is right whan he makes Mephistopheles, his devil, say, "I am the spirit of negation," for negation, save as it paves the way for positive conviction, always bedevils life. The psalmist reveals the ideal experience for every doubter.

First, *uncertainty:*

But as for me, my feet were almost gone;
My steps had well nigh slipped.
For I was envious at the arrogant,
When I saw the prosperity of the wicked.

—Ps. 73:2-3.

Then *vision:*

When I thought how I might know this,
It was too painful for me;
Until I went into the sanctuary of God,
And considered their latter end.

—Ps. 73:16-17

Then, *positive assurance:*

Thou wilt guide me with thy counsel,
And afterward receive me to glory.
Whom have I in heaven but thee?
And there is none upon earth that I desire besides thee.
But God is the strength of my heart and my portion for ever.

—Ps. 73:24-26.

Doubt, therefore, does have real value in life; it clears away rubbish and stimulates search for truth; but it has no value unless it is finally swallowed up in positive assurance. So Tennyson pictures the experience of his friend, Arthur Hallam:

> "One indeed I knew
> In many a subtle question versed,
> Who touch'd a jarring lyre at first,
> But ever strove to make it true:
>
> Perplext in faith, but pure in deeds,
> At last he beat his music out.
> There lives more faith in honest doubt,
> Believe me, than in half the creeds.
>
> He fought his doubts and gather'd strength,
> He would not make his judgment blind,
> He faced the spectres of the mind
> And laid them: thus he came at length
>
> To find a stronger faith his own."

O Most Merciful, whose love to us is mighty, long-suffering, and infinitely tender; lead us beyond all idols and imaginations of our minds to contact with Thee the real and abiding; past all barriers of fear and beyond all paralysis of failure to that furnace of flaming purity where falsehood, sin, and cowardice are all consumed away. It may be that we know not what we ask; yet we dare not ask for less.

Our aspirations are hindered because we do not know ourselves. We have tried to slake our burning thirst at broken cisterns, to comfort the crying of our spirits with baubles and trinkets, to assuage the pain of our deep unrest by drugging an accusing conscience, believing a lie, and veiling the naked flame that burns within. But now we know Thou makest us never to be content with aught save Thyself, in earth, or heaven, or hell.

Sometimes we have sought Thee in agony and tears, scanned the clouds and watched the ways of men, considered the stars and studied the moral law; and returned from all our search no surer and no nearer. Yet now we know that the impulse to seek Thee came from Thyself alone, and what we sought for was the image Thou hadst first planted in our hearts.

We may not yet hold Thee fast or feel Thee near, but we know Thou holdest us. All is well. Amen.—W. E. Orchard.

Second Week, Seventh Day

Men are often prejudiced against religion or any serious consideration of it, because they *never have felt any vital need of God*. To study wireless telegraphy in the safe seclusion of a college laboratory is one thing; to hear the wireless apparatus on a floundering ship send out its call for help across a stormy sea is quite a different matter. Many folk have never thought of faith in God save with a mild, intellectual curiosity; they do not know those deep experiences of serious souls with sin and sorrow and anxiety, with burden for great causes and desire for triumphant righteousness in men and nations—experiences that throw men back on God as their only sufficient refuge and hope. *Men never really find God until they need him;* and some men never feel the need of him until life plunges them into a shattering experience. Even in scientific research new discoveries are made because men *want* them, and Mayer, lighting on a theory that proved to be of great value, says, "Engaged during a sea voyage almost exclusively with the study of physiology, I discovered the new theory, for the sufficient reason that I *vividly felt the need of it.*" How much more must the vital discovery of God depend on life's conscious demand for him! And how certainly a shallow, frivolous nature, unstirred by the deep concerns of life, is biased against any serious interest in religious faith! Great believers have first of all *thirsted* for God.

Ho, every one that thirsteth, come ye to the waters, and he that hath no money; come ye, buy, and eat; yea, come, buy wine and milk without money and without price. Wherefore do ye spend money for that which is not bread? and your labor for that which satisfieth not? hearken diligently unto me, and eat ye that which is good and let your soul delight itself in fatness. Incline your ear, and come unto me; hear, and your soul shall live: and I will make an everlasting covenant with you, even the sure mercies of David. . . . Seek ye Jehovah while he may be found; call ye upon him while he is near: let the wicked forsake his way, and the unrighteousness man his thoughts; and let him return unto Jehovah, and he will have mercy upon him; and to our God, for he will abundantly pardon.—Isa. 55:1-3, 6-7.

Grant unto us, we pray Thee, the lost hunger and thirst after righteousness—the longing for God. Grant unto us that drawing power by which everything that is in us shall call out for Thee. Become necessary unto us. With the morning and evening light, at noon and at midnight, may we feel the need of Thy companionship. . . . Though Thou dost not speak as man speaks, yet Thou canst call out to us; and the soul shall know Thy presence, and shall understand by its own self what Thou meanest. Grant unto us this witness of the Spirit, this communion of the soul with Thee—and not only once or twice: may we abide in the light.

Thou hast come unto Thine own; and even as of old, Thine own know Thee not, and believe Thee not. How many are there that have learned Thy name upon their mother's knee, but have forgotten it! How many are there that grew up into the happiness of a childhood in which piety presided, but have gone away, and have not come back again to their first love and to their early faith! How many are there marching on now in the Sahara of indifference and in the wilderness of unbelief! . . . Lord, look upon them; have merciful thoughts toward them, and issue those gracious influences of power by which what is best in them shall lift itself up and bear witness against that which is worst. Amen.—Henry Ward Beecher.

COMMENT FOR THE WEEK

I

We are to deal in this chapter with one of the most common experiences of doubt and are to attempt the statement of a truth useful in meeting it. Many minds are undone at the first symptoms of religious uncertainty, because they suppose that their doubt is philosophical, and they feel a paralyzing inability to deal with philosophy at all. As men have been known to take to their beds at hearing the scientific names of illnesses which hitherto they had patiently endured, so minds are sometimes overwhelmed by an unsettlement of faith that takes the name of philosophic doubt. It is well, then, early in our study, to note the homely, familiar experience, which in most cases underlies and helps to explain the problem of theological unrest.

We all began, as children, with an unlimited ability to believe what we were told. We were credulous long before we became critical. God and Santa Claus, fairy stories and life after death—in what beautiful, unquestioning confusion we received them all! Our thinking was altogether imitative, as our talking was. From the existence of Kamchatka to the opinion that it was wrong to lie, we had no independent knowledge of our own. Reliance on authority was our only road to truth. One prescription was adequate for every need of information: ask our parents and be told.

This situation was the occasion of our first unsettlement of faith: we discovered the fallibility of our parents. They failed to tell us what we asked, or we found to be untrue what they had said, or they themselves confessed how much they did not know. To some this was a shock, the memory of which has never been forgotten. Edmund Gosse, the literary critic, tells us that up to his sixth year he thought that his father knew everything. Then came the fateful crisis when his father wrongly reported an incident which Edmund himself had witnessed. "Nothing could possibly have been more trifling to my parents," he writes, "but to me it meant an epoch. Here was the appalling discovery never suspected before that my father was not as God and did not know everything. The shock was not caused by any suspicion that he was not telling the truth, as it appeared to him, but by the awful proof that he was not, as I had supposed, omniscient." By most of us, however, the transfer of our faith from our parents' authority to some other basis of belief was easily accomplished. We found ourselves resting back on the priest or the church or the creed or the Bible. Still our convictions were not independently our own; we had never fought for them or thought them through; they were founded on the say-so of authority. What we wished to know we asked another, and what was told us we implicitly believed.

The time inevitably comes, however, to a normally developing mind, when such an attitude of unquestioning credulity becomes impossible. The curious "Why?" of the growing child, that began in early years to besiege all statements of fact, now ranges out to call in question the propositions of religious faith. For long-accepted truths, from the rotundity of the earth to the existence of God, the enlarging intellect wants reasons rather than dogmas. So normal is this period of interrogation that it is regularly slated on the timetables of psychological development. Starbuck fixes the average age of the doubt period at about eighteen years for boys and about fifteen for girls.

At whatever time and in whatever special form this period of doubt arises, the characteristic quality of its outcome is easily described. In the end the fully awakened mind is ill content to accept any authoritative statements that he dare not question or deny. He resents having a quotation from any source waved like a revolver in his face with the demand that he throw up his intellectual hands. No more in religion than in politics does he incline to stand before infallibility, like the French peasants before Louis XI, saying, "Sire, what are our opinions?" He claims his right to question everything, to make every truth advance and give the countersign of reasonableness, to weigh all propositions in the scales of his own thinking, and if he is to love the Lord his God at all, to do it, not with all his credulity, but, as Jesus said, with all his mind.

Biography reveals how many of the great believers have passed through this youthful period of rebellion against accepted tradition and have suffered serious religious unsettlement in the process. Robert Browning tells us that as a boy he was "passionately religious." When his period of questioning and revolt arrived, however, it carried him so far that he was publicly rebuked in church for intentional misbehavior, and in his sixteenth year, under the influence of Shelley's "Queen Mab," he declared himself an atheist. But in his "Pauline," written when he was twenty-one, the direction in which his quest was leading him was plain:

> "I have always had one lode-star; now
> As I look back, I see that I have halted
> Or hastened as I looked towards that star—
> A need, a trust, a yearning after God."

And when he grew to his maturity, had left his early credulousness with the revolt that followed it far behind and had used his independent thinking to productive purpose, from what a height of splendid faith did he look back upon that youthful period of storm and stress which he called "the passionate, impatient struggles of a boy toward truth and love"!

Henry Ward Beecher's intellectual revolution was postponed until he had entered the theological seminary. "I was then twenty years old," he writes, "and there came a great revulsion in me from all this inchoate, unregulated, undirected experience. My mind took one tremendous spring over into scepticism, and I said: 'I have been a fool long enough—I will not stir one step further than I can see my way, and I will not stand a moment where I cannot see the truth. I will have something that is sure and steadfast.' Having taken that ground, I was in that state of mind for the larger part of two years." A wholesome restraint upon the wild perversions, the anarchic denials, the abysmal despairs of this period of life is the clear recognition that in some form it is one of the commonest experiences of man.

II

The treatment accorded to a youth who is passing through this difficult adjustment often determines, in a fine or lamentable way, his subsequent attitude toward religion. *Negative repression of real questions is of all methods the most fatal, whether it be practiced on the youth by others or by the youth upon himself.* "I have not been in church for twenty years," said a college graduate. "Why?" was the inquiry. "Because in college I learned from geology through how many ages this earth was slowly being built. Troubled by the conflict between this new knowledge and my early training, I went to my minister. He said that the Bible told us the earth was made in six days and that I must accept that on faith. That's why." Thousands of men are religious wrecks today because, when the issue was raised in their thinking between their desire for a reason and their traditional beliefs, they were told that to ask a reason is sin. George Eliot's experience unhappily is not unique. Just when in girlhood her mind was waking to independent thought, a book now long unread, Hennell's "Inquiry Concerning the Origin of Christianity," convinced her immature judgment that her early credulity had been blind. No one was at hand to state the faith in a reasonable way or to meet, not by denying but by using her right to think, the attacks of Hennell, which now are forgotten in their futility. She never came through her youthful unsettlement. Years after, F. W. H. Myers wrote: "I remember how at Cambridge I walked with her once in the Fellows' Garden of Trinity, on an evening of rainy May, and she, stirred somewhat beyond her wont, and taking as her text the three words which have been used so often as the inspiring trumpet calls of men—the words God, Immortality, Duty—pronounced with terrible earnestness, how inconceivable was the first, how unbelievable was the second, and how peremptory and absolute the third. Never, perhaps, had sterner accents affirmed the sovereignty of impersonal and unrecompensing law. I listened and night fell; her grave, majestic countenance turned toward me like a Sibyl's in the gloom; it was as though she withdrew from my grasp one by one the two scrolls of promise, and left me the third scroll only, awful with inevitable fate."

In this period of readjustment, whether one is the youth in the midst of the struggle or the solicitous friend endeavoring to help, one most needs a clear perception of the ideal outcome of such intellectual unrest. Let us attempt a picture of that ideal. The youth who long has taken on his parents' say-so the most important convictions that the soul can hold, or who, with no care to think or question for himself, has looked to Book or Church for all that he believed about God, now feels within him that intellectual awakening that cannot be quieted by mere authority. He long has taken his truth preserved by others' hands; now he desires to pick it for himself, fresh from the living tree of knowledge. His declaration of independence from subjection to his parents or his Church is not at first irreverent desire to disbelieve; it is rather desire to enter into the Samaritans' experience when they said to the woman who first had told them about Jesus: "Now we believe, not because of *thy* speaking; for we have *heard for ourselves,* and know that this is indeed the Saviour of the world" (John 4:41). The youth turns from second-hand rehearsal of the truth to seek a first-hand, original acquaintance with it. As he began in utter financial dependence on his father, then made a bit of spending money of his own, and at last moved out to make his living, ashamed to be a pensioner and parasite when he should be carrying himself, so from his old, intellectual dependence the youth passes to a fine responsibility for his own thinking and belief. He knows that such transitions, whether financial or intellectual, generally mean stress and perplexity, but if he is to be a man the youth must venture.

In this transition beliefs will certainly be modified. Not only do forms of religious thinking shift and change with the passing generations, but individuals differ in their powers to see and understand. Religious faith, like water, takes shape from the receptacles into whose unique nooks and crannies it is poured. If the truth which the youth possesses is to be indeed his own, it will surely differ from the truth which once he learned, by as much as his mind and his experience differ from his father's. Even in the New Testament one can easily distinguish James' thought from Paul's and John's from Peter's. But change of form need not mean loss of value. To pass by fine gradations from unquestioning credulity to thoughtful faith is not impossible. Thus a boy learns to swim with his father's hands beneath him and passes so gradually from reliance upon another to independent power to swim alone that he cannot tell when first the old support was quietly withdrawn.

Thus ideally pictured, this transition is nothing to be feared; it is one of life's steps to spiritual power. This period of questioning and venture we have called the passage from credulity to independence, but its significance is deeper than those words imply. *It is the passage from hearsay to reality.* Of all inward intimate experiences, religion reaches deepest and is least transferable. It is as incommunicable as friendship. A father may commend a comrade to his son and lay bare his own deep friendship with the man, but if the son himself does not see the value there nor for himself in loyalty and love make self surrender, the father can do nothing more. Friendship cannot be carried on by proxy. One can as easily breathe for another as in another's place be loyal to a friend or trust in God.

When, therefore, the youth moves out from mere dependence on his father, his Bible, or his Church to see and know God in his own right, he is fulfilling the end of all religion. *For this his father taught him, for this the Book was written and the Church was founded.* As George Macdonald put it, "Each generation must do its own seeking and finding. The father's having found is only the warrant for the children's search." Said Goethe: "What you have inherited from your fathers you must earn for yourself before you can call it yours." This individual experience makes religion real, and the "awkward age" of the spirit when the old security of credulous belief has gone and the new assurance of personal conviction has not yet fully come, is a small price to pay for the sense of reality that enters into religion when a man for himself knows God. Such is the ideal transition from credulity to independence, from hearsay to reality.

III

One fallacy which disastrously affects many endeavors after this ideal transition is the prejudice that, since faith has hitherto in the youth's experience meant credulous acceptance of another's say-so, faith always must mean that. Faith and credulity appear to him identical. In *Alice Through the Looking Glass* the Queen asserts that she is a hundred and one years, five months, and one day old. "I can't believe that," said Alice. "Can't you?" said the Queen. "Try again, draw a long breath and shut your eyes." So blind, irrational, and willful does faith seem to many! So far from being an essential part of all real knowledge, therefore, faith seems to stand in direct contrast with knowledge, and this impression is deepened by our common phraseology. Tennyson, for example, sings:

"We have but faith: we cannot know;
    For knowledge is of things we see."

Before there can be any profitable discussion of religious belief, therefore, we need to see that faith is one of the chief ways in which continually we deal with reality; it is a road to truth, without which some truth never can be reached at all. The reason for its inevitableness in life is not our lack of knowledge, but rather that faith is as indispensable as logical demonstration in any real knowing of the world. Behind all other words to be said about our subject lies this fundamental matter: *faith is not a substitute for truth, but a pathway to truth; there are realities which without it never can be known.*

For one thing, no one can know *persons* without faith. The world of people, without whom if a man could live, he would be, as Aristotle said, either a brute or a god, is closed in its inner meaning to a faithless mind. Entrance into another life with insight and understanding is always a venture of trust. We cry vainly like Cassim before the magic cave, "Open, Barley," if we try to penetrate the secrets of a human personality without sympathy, loyalty, faith. These alone cry, "Open, Sesame."

Surely this knowledge of persons, impossible without faith, is as important as any which we possess. While the physical universe furnishes the general background of our existence, the immediate world in which we really live is personal, made up of people whom we fear or love, by whom we are cheered, admonished, hurt, and comforted. "The world is so waste and empty," cried Goethe, "when we figure but towns and hills and rivers in it, but to know that someone is living on it with us, even in silence—this makes our earthly ball a peopled garden." A solitary Robinson Crusoe would give up any other knowledge, if in return he could know even a benighted savage like Friday. But even a savage cannot be known by logical demonstration. Crusoe could so have learned some things, but when he wanted to know Friday, he came by way of adventures in confidence, personal trust and self-commitment, growing reliance and appreciative insight, assured loyalty and faith. He *knew* whom he had *believed.*

Moreover, such knowledge of persons is as solid as it is

important. That two plus two make four cannot be gain-said, and doubtless no other kinds of information can be quite so absolute as mathematical theorems. But when one thinks of a comrade, long loved and trusted until he is known through and through, for practical purposes one can think of nothing more stable than his knowledge of his friend. The plain fact is that we *do* know people, know them well, and that this knowledge never has been or can be a matter of logical demonstration. By taking Arthur Hallam to pieces and analyzing him, the inductive mind might work out all the laws that are involved in Arthur Hallam's constitution; but that mind with all its knowledge would not know Arthur Hallam. Tennyson's "In Memoriam," however, makes clear that knowledge of a friend is not interdicted because scientific demonstration cannot supply it. Tennyson knew Hallam well, and this knowledge, far more solid and significant than most other information he possessed, was not achieved by grinding laws out of facts; it came, as all such knowledge comes, by faith.

As one considers what this understanding of the personal world, seen with the open eyes of trust and loyalty, means to us, how assured it is, how it enriches and deepens life, he perceives that here at least faith is something far more than a stop-gap for ignorance, a dream, a fantasy. It is positively a pathway to truth.

There is another realm where faith is our only way of dealing with reality; by it alone can we know *the possibilities of individuals and of society*. We are well assured now in the United States that the nation can be economically prosperous without slavery. But many years ago plenty of people were assured of the contrary, were convinced that if the abolitionists succeeded we could not economically endure. How did we come by this significant knowledge that the immoral system was dispensable? Not by logical demonstration. The economists of most of our universities logically demonstrated that slavery was essential. *Faith was the pathway to the truth.* Faith that a new order minus slavery was possible gained adherents, grew in certainty with access of new believers, fed its followers on hopes unrealized but passionately believed in, until *faith became experiment, and experiment became experience, and experience brought forth knowledge.* The nation trusted and tried.

This is the only way to truth in the realm of moral possibilities. If the world were finished, its *i*'s all dotted and its *t*'s all crossed, we might exist on the sort of descriptive science that finds the facts and plots their laws. But the world is in the making; what is *actual* is not quite so important to us as what is *possible;* we live, as Wordsworth sings, in

> "Hope that can never die,
> Effort and expectation and desire,
> And something evermore about to be."

To endeavor to satisfy man, therefore, with descriptions of the actual is preposterous. The innermost meaning of personal and social life lies in the contrast between what we are and what we may become. Beyond the achieved present and the demonstrable future, stands the ideal, whose possibility we can never know as a truth without faith enough to try.

When, therefore, one hears disparagement of faith as a poor makeshift for knowledge, he may be pardoned a sharp rejoinder. When has man ever found solid knowledge in this most important realm of human possibilities, without faith as the pioneer? We do not know first and then supply by belief what knowledge lacks. *We believe first, as Columbus did, and then find new continents because what faith first suggested a great venture has confirmed.* When Stephenson proposed to run a steam car forty miles an hour, a host of wise-acres proved the feat impossible on the ground that no one could move through the air so rapidly and still survive. If now we know that one easily survives a speed of over a hundred miles an hour in an airplane, it is because a faith that *saw* and *dared* introduced us to the information. We know now that democracy is not a futile dream, nor the conquest of the air by wireless and of the land by electricity a madman's frenzy; we know truths of highest import and certainty from the usefulness of radium to the wisdom of religious liberty, and all this knowledge existed as belief in possibility before it became truth in fact. Faith was "assurance of things hoped for, a conviction of things not seen" (Heb. 11:1). Faith is no makeshift. Its power is nowhere felt more effectively than in the achievement of knowledge.

IV

So far is faith then, from being blind credulity, that it alone deserves to be called the Great Discoverer. Everywhere faith goes before as a pioneer and the more prosaic faculties of the mind come after to civilize the newly opened territory. In the evolution of the senses touch developed first. All the knowledge that any creature had, concerned the tangible. But in time other senses came. Dimly and uncertainly creatures discerned by hearing and seeing the existence of distant objects. They became aware of presences which as yet they could not touch; they were furnished with clues, in following which they found as real what at first had been intangible. Such a relation faith bears to knowledge. Faith, said Clement of Alexandria, is the "ear of the soul." Said Ruskin, faith is "veracity of insight." By it we hear what as yet we cannot touch and see what the arms of our logic are not long enough to reach.

All the elemental, primary facts of life are faith's discoveries; we have no other means of finding them. By faith we discover our *selves*. We do not hold back from living until we can prove that we exist. We never can strictly prove that we exist. The very self that we are trying to demonstrate would have to be used in the demonstration. We have no other way of getting at ourselves except to take ourselves for granted—accepting

> "This main miracle that you are you,
>   With power on your own act and on the world."

As Mr. Chesterton remarked, "You cannot call up any wilder vision than a city in which men ask themselves if they have any selves." By faith all men go out to live as though their selves were real.

By faith we accept the existence of the *outer world*. We do not restrain ourselves from acting as though the physical world were really there, until we can prove it. We never can strictly prove it; perhaps it is not there at all. When through a microscope an Indian was shown germs in the Ganges' water, to convince him of the peril of its use, he broke the instrument with his cane, as though when the microscope was gone, the facts had vanished too. In his philosophy all that we see is illusion. Perhaps this is true—the world a phantasm and our minds fooling us. But none of us believes it. And we do not believe it because we live by faith—the elemental faith on which all common sense and science rest and without which man's thought and work would halt—that our senses and our minds tell us the truth. "It is idle to talk always of the alternative of reason and faith. *Reason itself is a matter of faith.* It is an act of faith to assert that one's thoughts have any relation to reality at all."

By faith we even discover the *universe*. We cannot think of the world as a multiverse; we always think of it as having unity, and we do so whether as scientists we talk about the uniformity of nature, or as Christians we speak of one Creator. Not only, however, can no one demonstrate that this is a universe; *it positively does not look as though it were.* Opposing powers snarl at each other and clash in a disorder that gives to the casual observer not the slightest intimation that any unity is there. Thunderstorms and little babies, volcanoes and Easter lilies, immeasurable nebulae in the heavens and people getting married on the earth—what indescribable contrasts and confusions! Still we insist on thinking unity into this seeming anomaly, and out of it we wrest scientific doctrines about the uniformity of law. As Professor James, of Harvard, put it, "The principle of uniformity in nature has to be *sought* under and in spite of the most rebellious appearances; and our conviction of its truth is far more like religious faith than like assent to a demonstration."

One might suppose that beliefs so assumed and so incapable of adequate demonstration would make the knowledge based upon them insecure. *But the fact is that all our surest knowledge is thus based on assumptions that we cannot prove.* "As for the strong conviction," Huxley says, "that the cosmic order is rational, and the faith that throughout all duration, unbroken order has reigned in the universe, I not only accept it, but I am disposed to think it the most important of all truth." Faith then, in Huxley's thought, is not a makeshift when knowledge fails. Rather by faith we continually are getting at the most important realities with which we deal. As Prof. Ladd, of Yale, impatiently exclaims: "The rankest agnostic is shot through and through with all the same fundamental intellectual beliefs, all the same unescapable rational faiths, about the reality of the self and about the validity of its knowledge. You cannot save science and destroy all faith. You cannot sit on the limb of the tree while you tear it up by the roots."

V

If faith is thus the pioneer that leads to knowledge of persons and of moral possibilities; if by faith we discover ourselves, the outer world's existence and its unity, why should we be surprised that faith is our road to God? Superficial deniers of religion not infrequently seek the discredit of a Christian's trust by saying that God is only a matter of faith. To which the Christian confidently may answer: of course God is a matter of faith. Faith is always the Great Discoverer.

A man finds God as he finds an earthly friend. He does not go apart in academic solitude to consider the logical rationality of friendship, until, intellectually convinced, he coolly arms himself with a Q.E.D. and goes out to hunt a comrade. Friendship is never an adventure of logic; it is an adventure of life. It is arrived at by what Emerson called the "untaught sallies of the spirit." We fall in love, it may be with precipitant emotion; our instincts and our wills are first engaged; the whole personality rises up in hunger to claim the affection that it needs and without which life seems unsupportable; faith, hope, and love engage in a glorious venture, where logic plays a minor part. But to make friendship rational, to give it poise, to trace its origins and laws, to clarify, chasten, and direct—this is the necessary work of thought. Faith discovers and reveals; reason furnishes criticism, confirmation, and discipline.

So men find God. They are hungry for him not in intellect alone, but with all their powers. They feel with Tolstoi: "I remembered that I only *lived* at those times when I believed in God." They need him to put sense and worth and hope into life. As with the reality of persons, the validity of knowledge, the unity of the world, so in religion the whole man rises up to claim the truth without which life is barren, meaningless. His best convictions at the first are all of them insights of the spirit, affirmations of the *man*. But behind, around and through them all play clarifying thoughts, and reasons come to discipline and to confirm. But the reasons by themselves could not have found God. Faith is the Great Discoverer.

> "Oh! world, thou choosest not the better part,
> It is not wisdom to be only wise,
> And on the inward vision close the eyes;
> But it is wisdom to believe the heart.
> Columbus found a world and had no chart.
> Save one that Faith deciphered in the skies;
> To trust the soul's invincible surmise
> Was all his science and his only art.
> Our knowledge is a torch of smoky pine
> That lights the pathway but one step ahead
> Across the void of mystery and dread.
> Bid then the tender light of Faith to shine
> By which alone the mortal heart is led
> Into the thinking of the thought Divine."[1]

---

[1]Professor Santayana, of Harvard.

CHAPTER III

Faith in the Personal God

DAILY READINGS

We are to consider this week the Christian faith that God is personal. Before, however, we deal with the arguments which may confirm our confidence in such a faith, or even with the explanations that may clarify our conception of its meaning, let us, in the daily readings, consider *some of the familiar attitudes in every normal human life, that require God's personality for their fulfillment.* Men have believed in a personal God because their own nature demanded it.

Third Week, First Day

Men have believed in a personal God because of a *deep desire to think of creation as friendly.* F. W. Myers, when asked what question he would put to the Sphinx, if he were given only one chance, replied that he would ask, "Is the universe friendly?" Some have tried to think of creation as an enemy which we must fight, as though in Greenland we strove to make verdure grow, although the soil and climate were antagonistic. Some have tried to think creation neutral, an impersonal system of laws and forces, which we must impose our will upon as best we can, although in the end the system is sure to outlast all our efforts and to bring our gains to naught. But at the heart of man is an irresistible desire to think creation a friend, with whose good purposes our wills can be aligned, and whose power can carry our efforts to victorious ends. Says Gilbert Murray, of Oxford University, "As I see philosophy after philosophy falling into this unproven belief in the Friend behind phenomena, as I find that I myself cannot, except for a moment and by an effort, refrain from making the same assumption, it seems to me that perhaps here too we are under the spell of a very old ineradicable instinct." *But friends are always persons, and if creation is friendly then God is in some sense personal.* This faith is the radiant center of the Gospel.

But thou, when thou prayest, enter into thine inner chamber, and having shut thy door, pray to thy Father who is in secret, and thy Father who seeth in secret shall recompense thee. And in praying use not vain repetitions, as the Gentiles do: for they think that they shall be heard for their much speaking. Be not therefore like unto them: for your Father knoweth what things ye have need of, before ye ask him. After this manner therefore pray ye: Our Father who art in heaven, Hallowed be thy name. Thy kingdom come. Thy will be done, as in heaven, so on earth. Give us this day our daily bread. And forgive us our debts, as we also have forgiven our debtors. And bring us not into temptation, but deliver us from the evil one. For if ye forgive men their trespasses, your heavenly Father will also forgive you.— Matt. 6:6-14.

O Lord, we would rest in Thee, for in Thee alone is true rest to be found. We would forget our disappointed hopes, our fruitless efforts, our trivial aims, and lean on Thee, our Comfort and our Strength. When the order of this world bears cruelly upon us; when Nature seems to us an awful machine, grinding out life and death, without a reason or a purpose; when our hopes perish in the grave where we lay to rest our loved dead: O what can we do but turn to Thee, whose law underlieth all, and whose love, we trust, is the end of all? Thou fillest all things with Thy presence, and dost press close to our souls. Still every passion, rebuke every doubt, strengthen every element of good within us, that nothing may hinder the outflow of Thy life and power. In Thee, let the weak be full of might, and let the strong renew their strength. In Thee, let the tempted find succor, the sorrowing consolation, and the lonely and the neglected their Supreme Friend, their faithful Companion.

O Lord, we are weary of our old, barren selves. Separate

*us from our spiritual past, and quicken within us the seeds of
a new future. Transform us by the breath of Thy regenerating
power, that life may seem supremely beautiful and duty our
highest privilege, and the only real evil a guilty conscience.
Let us be no longer sad, or downcast, or miserable, or
despairing, vexed by remorse, or depressed by our failures.
Take from us the old self. Give us a new self, beautiful,
vigorous, and joyous. Let old things pass away and let all
things become new. Kindle within us a flame of heavenly
devotion, so that to us work for Thee shall become a
happiness, and rest in Thee shall become an energy,
unchecked by fears within and foes without. Give us love,
and then we shall have more than all we need, for Thou art
Love, Thyself the Giver and the Gift. Amen.*—Samuel
McComb.

Third Week, Second Day

Bless Jehovah, O my soul;
And all that is within me, bless his holy name.
Bless Jehovah, O my soul,
And forget not all his benefits:
Who forgiveth all thine iniquities;
Who healeth all thy diseases;
Who redeemeth thy life from destruction;
Who crowneth thee with lovingkindness and tender mercies;
Who satisfieth thy desire with good things,
So that thy youth is renewed like the eagle.

—Ps. 103:1-5.

Such an attitude of thankfulness as this psalm represents
is native to man's heart. When he is glad he feels grateful;
he has an irrepressible impulse to thank somebody. As
between a boastful Nebuchadnezzar—"This great Babylon
which I have built . . . by the might of my power and for the
glory of my majesty" (Dan. 4:30)—and the Master, grateful
for the dawning success of his cause—"I thank Thee, O
Father, Lord of heaven and earth" (Matt. 11:25)—we can
have no doubt which is the nobler attitude. Man at his best
always looks upon his blessings as gifts, his powers as
entrustments, his service as a debt which he owes, and his

success as an occasion of gratitude rather than pride. *But we cannot be really thankful to impersonal power.* Little children blame chairs for their falls and thank apple trees for their apples, but maturity outgrows the folly of accusing or blessing impersonal things. Thankfulness, in any worthy interpretation of the term, can never be felt except toward friendly persons who *intended the blessing* for which we are glad. A thoughtful man, therefore, cannot be grateful to a godless world-machine, even though it has treated him well, for the world-machine never purposed to treat him well and his happiness is a lucky accident, with no good will to thank for it. Haeckel says that there is no God—only "mobile, cosmic ether." Imagine a congregation of people, under Haeckel's leadership, rising to pray, "O Mobile Cosmic Ether, blessed be thy name!" It is absurd. *Unless God is personal, the deepest meanings of gratitude in human hearts for life and its benedictions have no proper place in the universe.*

O God above all, yet in all; holy beyond all imagination, yet friend of sinners; who inhabitest the realms of unfading light, yet leadest us through the shadows of mortal life; how solemn and uplifting it is even to think upon Thee! Like sight of sea to wearied eyes, like a walled-in garden to the troubled mind, like home to wanderer, like a strong tower to a soul pursued; so to us is the sound of Thy name.

But greater still to feel Thee in our heart; like a river glorious, cleansing, healing, bringing life; like a song victorious, comforting our sadness, banishing our care; like a voice calling us to battle, urging us beyond ourselves.

But greater far to know Thee as our Father, as dear as Thou art near; and ourselves begotten of Thy love, made in Thy image, cared for through all our days, never beyond Thy sight, never out of Thy thought.

To think of Thee is rest; to know Thee is eternal life; to see Thee is the end of all desire; to serve Thee is perfect freedom and everlasting joy. Amen.—W. E. Orchard.

Third Week, Third Day

Have mercy upon me, O God, according to thy loving-kindness:

According to the multitude of thy tender mercies blot out my
transgressions.
Wash me thoroughly from mine iniquity,
And cleanse me from my sin.
For I know my transgression;
And my sin is ever before me.
Against thee, thee only, have I sinned,
And done that which is evil in thy sight.

—Ps. 51:1-4.

Penitence is one of the profoundest impulses in man's
heart. And man at his deepest always feels about his sin as
the psalmist did: he has wronged not only this individual or
that, but he has sinned against the whole structure of life,
against whatever Power and Purpose may be behind life,
and his penitence is not complete until he cries to the
Highest, "Against Thee, Thee only, have I sinned." While
men, therefore, have always asked each other for
forgiveness, they have as well asked God for it. *But such an
attitude is utterly irrational if God is not personal.* Persons
alone care what we do, have purposes that our sins thwart,
have love that our evil grieves, have compassion to forgive
the penitent; and to confess sin to a world-machine—careless, purposeless, loveless, and without compassion—is
folly. Yesterday we saw how impossible it was really to feel
grateful to a materialist's god; today imagine congregations
of people addressing to the Cosmic Ether any such penitent
confessions as Christians by multitudes continually address
to their Father: "We have erred and strayed from Thy ways
like lost sheep." *Plainly in a world where creative power is
impersonal the deepest meanings of penitence have no place.*
Read over the prayer that follows, considering the futility of
addressing such a penitent aspiration to anything impersonal; and then really pray it to the God whom Christ
revealed:

*We beseech Thee, Lord, to behold us with favor, folk of
many families and nations gathered together in the peace of
this roof, weak men and women subsisting under the covert
of Thy patience. Be patient still; suffer us yet awhile
longer—with our broken purposes of good, with our idle*

71

*endeavors against evil, suffer us awhile longer to endure and
(if it may be) help us to do better. Bless to us our
extraordinary mercies; if the day come when these must be
taken, brace us to play the man under affliction. Be with our
friends, be with ourselves. Go with each of us to rest; if any
awake, temper to them the dark hours of watching; and when
the day returns, return to us, our sun and comforter, and call
us up with morning hearts—eager to labor—eager to be
happy, if happiness shall be our portion—and if the day be
marked for sorrow, strong to endure it.*

*We thank Thee and praise Thee; and in the words of
him to whom this day is sacred, close our oblation. Amen.*
—Robert Louis Stevenson.[1]

Third Week, Fourth Day

**Now the God of hope fill you with all joy and peace in
believing, that ye may abound in hope, in the power of the
Holy Spirit.—Rom. 15:13.**

**For in hope were we saved: but hope that is seen is not
hope: for who hopeth for that which he seeth? But if we hope
for that which we see not, then do we with patience wait for
it. —Rom. 8:24-25.**

Hope is no fringe on the garment of human life; it is part
of the solid texture of our experience; without it men may
exist, but they cannot live. Now some minds live by hope
about tomorrow, or at the most, the day after tomorrow,
and do not take long looks ahead. But as men grow mature
in thoughtfulness, such small horizons no longer can
content their minds; they seek a basis for hope about the far
issue of man's struggle and aspiration. They cannot bear to
think that creation lacks a "far-off divine event"; they
cannot tolerate a universe that in the end turns out to be

> "An eddy of purposeless dust,
> Effort unmeaning and vain."

---

[1]Copyright, 1914, Charles Scribner's Sons. Used by permission.

But it is obvious that if God is not in control of creation, with personal purpose of good will, directing its course, there is no solid basis for hope. If the universe is in the hands of physical forces, then a long look ahead reveals a world collapsing about a cold sun, and humanity annihilated in the wreck. Some such finale is the inevitable end of a godless world. As another pictures it, mankind, like a polar bear on an ice floe that is drifting into warmer zones, will watch in growling impotence the steady dwindling of his home, until he sinks in the abyss. All optimistic philosophies of life have been founded on faith in a personal God, who purposes good to his children, and without such faith no hope, with large horizons, is reasonable. Paul is fair to the facts when he says, "Having no hope and without God in the world" (Eph. 2:12). When one asks why men have believed in a personal God, this clearly is part of the answer: only a personal God can be "the God of hope."

O God of heaven above and earth beneath! Thou art the constant hope of every age—the reliance of them that seek Thee with thoughtfulness and love. We own Thee as the guardian of our pilgrimage; and when our steps are weary we turn to Thee, the mystic companion of our way, whose mercy will uphold us lest we fall. Thou layest on us the burden of labor throughout our days; but in this sacred hour Thou dost lift off our load, and make us partakers of Thy rest. Thou ever faithful God, our guide by cloud and fire! without this blest repose our life were but a desert path; here we abide by the refreshing spring, and pitch our tents with joy around Thy holy hill. Yet when we seek to draw nigh to Thee, Thou art still above us, like the heavens. O Thou that remainest in the height, and coverest Thyself with the cloud thereof! behold, we stand around the mountain where Thou art; and if Thou wilt commune with us, the thunder from Thy voice of love shall not make us afraid. Call up a spirit from our midst to serve Thy will; and take away the veil from all our hearts, that with the eye of purity we may look on the bright and holy countenance of life. And when we go hence to resume our way, may it be with nobler spirits, with more faithful courage, and more generous will. For life and death we trust ourselves to Thee as disciples of Jesus Christ. Amen.—James Martineau.

Third Week, Fifth Day

Jehovah is the portion of mine inheritance and of my cup:
Thou maintainest my lot.
The lines are fallen unto me in pleasant places;
Yea, I have a goodly heritage.
I will bless Jehovah, who hath given me counsel;
Yea, my heart instructeth me in the night seasons.
I have set Jehovah always before me:
Because he is at my right hand, I shall not be moved.
Therefore my heart is glad, and my glory rejoiceth:
My flesh also shall dwell in safety.
For thou wilt not leave my soul to Sheol,
Neither wilt thou suffer thy holy one to see corruption.
Thou wilt show me the path of life:
In thy presence is fulness of joy;
In thy right hand there are pleasures for evermore.
—Ps. 16:5-11.

Many things in human life bring joy. From the sense of a
healthy body and the exhilaration of a sunshiny day to the
deep satisfactions of home and friends—there are numberless sources of happiness. But man has always been athirst
to find joy in thinking about the total meaning of life.
Lacking that, the details of life lose radiance, for, in spite of
himself, man

> "Hath among least things
> An undersense of greatest; sees the parts
> As parts, but with a feeling of the whole."

If when he thinks about God, he can, like this psalmist,
rejoice in the love behind life, the good purpose through it,
the glorious future ahead of it, then all his other blessings
are illumined. Not only are there happy things *in life,* but
life itself is fundamentally blessed. But if when he raises his
thought to the Eternal, he has no joyful thoughts about it,
sees no love or purpose there, then a pall falls on even his
ordinary happiness. Alas for that man who does not like to
think about life's origin and destiny and meaning, because
he has no joyful faith about God! Some men have what
Epictetus called "paralysis of the soul" every time they

think of creation, for to them it is a huge physical machine crashing on without reason or good will. But some men have such a joyful faith in the divine that their gladness about the whole of life redeems their sorrow about its details. So Samuel Rutherford in prison said, "Jesus Christ came into my room last night and every stone flashed like a ruby." For the thought of God in terms of friendly personality is the most joyful idea of him that man has ever had. Man's thirst for joy is one of the sources of his faith in a personal God. He has wanted what Paul called "joy and peace in believing" (Rom. 15:13).

We rejoice, O Lord our God, not in ourselves nor in the firm earth on which we tread, nor in the household, nor in the church, nor in all the procession of things where mankind moves with power and glory. We rejoice in the Lord. We rejoce in Thy strength. A strange joy it is. Day by day we find ourselves breaking out into gladness through the ministration of the senses, and by the play of inward thought; but Thou art never beheld by us. . . . Thou never speakest to us, nor do we feel Thy hand, nor do we discern Thy face of love and glory and power. We break away from all other experiences, and look up into the emptiness, as it seems to us, which yet is full of life; into that which seems cold and void, but wherein moves eternal power; into the voiceless and inscrutable realm where Thou dwellest, God over all, blessed forever. . . . O Lord our God, how near Thou art to us! and we do not know it. How near is the other life! and we do not feel it. It clothes us as with a garment. It feeds us. It shines down upon us. It rejoices over us. . . . Thither, out of narrow and anguishful ways, out of sorrows, out of regrets, out of bereavements, we look; and already we are rested before we reach it.

Grant unto us, today, we beseech Thee, this beatific vision. Amen.—Henry Ward Beecher.

Third Week, Sixth Day

For when one saith, I am of Paul; and another, I am of Apollos; are ye not men? What then is Apollos? and what is Paul? Ministers through whom ye believed; and each as the

Lord gave to him. I planted, Apollos watered; but God gave the increase. So then neither is he that planteth anything, neither he that watereth; but God that giveth the increase. Now he that planteth and he that watereth are one: but each shall receive his own reward according to his own labor. For we are God's fellow-workers: ye are God's husbandry, God's building. —I Cor. 3:4-9.

One of the profoundest motives that can grip man's heart is the conviction that he is a fellow-worker with the Divine. To feel that there is a great Cause, on behalf of which God himself is concerned, and in the furtherance of which we can be God's instruments and confederates, is the most exhilarating outlook on life conceivable. Even people who deny God try to get this motive for themselves. One such man hopes for the success of his favorite causes in "the tendency of the universe"; another talks about "the nature of things taking sides." *But nothing save personality has moral tendencies, and only persons take sides in moral issues.* If the guidance of the world is personal, then, and then only, can we rejoice with confidence in a great Ally, who has moral purposes and who has committed to us part of his work. This was the Master's motive when he said, "My Father worketh even until now, and I work" (John 5:17). But one clearly sees that such an inspiring consciousness of cooperation with the Eternal depended on the certainty with which the Master called the Eternal by a personal name—Father. When men like Livingstone have gone out in sacrificial adventure for the saving of men they have not banked on the "tendency of the universe," nor trusted in any abstract "nature of things taking sides"; they have been servants of a personal God, under orders from him, and they have counted on personal guidance in the service of a cause whose issue was safe in God's hands.

O God, we pray Thee for those who come after us, for our children, and the children of our friends, and for all the young lives that are marching up from the gates of birth, pure and eager, with the morning sunshine on their faces. We remember with a pang that these will live in the world we are making for them. We are wasting the resources of the earth in our headlong greed, and they will suffer want. We are building sunless houses and joyless cities for our profit, and they must dwell therein. We are making the burden heavy and the pace of work pitiless, and they will fall wan and sobbing by the wayside. We are poisoning the air of our land by our lies and our uncleanness, and they will breathe it.

O God, Thou knowest how we have cried out in agony when the sins of our fathers have been visited upon us, and how we have struggled vainly against the inexorable fate that coursed in our blood or bound us in a prison-house of life. Save us from maiming the innocent ones who come after us by the added cruelty of our sins. Help us to break the ancient force of evil by a holy and steadfast will and to endow our children with purer blood and nobler thoughts. Grant us grace to leave the earth fairer than we found it; to build upon it cities of God in which the cry of needless pain shall cease; and to put the yoke of Christ upon our business life that it may serve and not destroy. Lift the veil of the future and show us the generation to come as it will be if blighted by our guilt, that our lust may be cooled and we may walk in the fear of the Eternal. Grant us a vision of the far-off years as they may be if redeemed by the sons of God, that we may take heart and do battle for Thy children and ours. Amen.—
Walter Rauschenbusch.

Third Week, Seventh Day

I will extol thee, my God, O King;
And I will bless thy name for ever and ever.
Every day will I bless thee;
And I will praise thy name for ever and ever.
Great is Jehovah, and greatly to be praised;
And his greatness is unsearchable.
One generation shall laud thy works to another,
And shall declare thy mighty acts.
Of the glorious majesty of thine honor,
And of thy wondrous works, will I meditate.
And men shall speak of the might of thy terrible acts;
And I will declare thy greatness.
They shall utter the memory of thy great goodness,
And shall sing of thy righteousness.
Jehovah is gracious, and merciful;

Slow to anger, and of great lovingkindness.
Jehovah is good to all;
And his tender mercies are over all his works.
All thy works shall give thanks unto thee, O Jehovah;
And thy saints shall bless thee.

—Ps. 145:1-10.

Adoration springs from the deeps of man's spirit. We never can be content with looking down on things beneath us, nor with looking out on things that find our level. We always must look up to things above us. As a medieval saint said, *"The soul can never rest in things that are beneath itself."* Worship, therefore, is an undeniable impulse in man's heart. Poets worship Beauty; scientists worship Truth; every man of honor worships Right. That is, the good, true, and beautiful stand above us calling out our adoration, and all the best in us springs from our worshipful response to their appeal. But this impulse to adore is never fulfilled until we gather up all life into spiritual unity and bow down in awe and joy before God. That is adoration glorified, worship crowned and consummated. And the only God whom man can adore with awe and joy is personal. No impersonal thing is worshipful; however great a *thing* may be it still lies beneath our soul. No abstract Idea is worshipful; we still are greater than any *idea* that we can hold. Only God, thought of in personal terms but known to be greater than any terms which human life can use, is adorable. *Men have believed in Him because worship is man's holiest impulse.*

Such are the experiences of man, with which faith in a personal God is inseparably interwoven. Our demand for a friendly creation, our deepest impulses to thanksgiving, penitence, hope, joy, cooperation with the Eternal, and adoration of the highest—all require personality in God. As Professor William James said, "The universe is no longer a mere *It* to us, but a *Thou* if we are religious."

O Lord our God, Thy greatness is unsearchable, and the glory of Thy presence has overwhelmed us. Thou art hidden in excess of light; and if we were to behold Thee in the great sphere in which Thou art living, none of us would dare to draw near to Thee. Our imperfections, our transgressions, our secret thoughts, our wild impulses, that at times come surging in upon us, are such that we should be ashamed to stand before the All-searching Eye. Our lives are before Thee, open as a book, and Thou readest every word and every letter thereof. Blessed be Thy name, Thou has taught us to come to Thee through the Lord Jesus Christ as through a friend, and thou hast taught us to draw near to Thee in person through the familiar way of Fatherhood; from our childhood we have said, Our Father, and in this way we are not afraid, in this way we come familiarly and boldly: not irreverently, but with the familiarity which love gives. Thou hast poured the light of Thy love upon the path which we tread, and Thou has taught us to come rejoicing before Thee. . . . Open Thy hand and Thy heart, and say to everyone of us, Peace be unto you! Amen.—Henry Ward Beecher.

COMMENT FOR THE WEEK

I

We have been using freely the most momentous word in human speech as though we clearly understood its meaning. We have been speaking of God as though the import of the term were plain. But most of us, asked to state precisely what we mean by "God," would welcome such a refuge from our confusion as Joubert sought. "It is not hard to know God," said he, "provided one will not force oneself to define him." Many people who stoutly claim to believe in God live in perpetual vacillation as to what they mean by him. Writes one: "God to my mind is an impersonal being, but whether for convenience or through sheer impotence I pray to him as a personal being. . . . I know I talk on both sides of the fence, but that is just where I am."

At times, indeed, some question whether there is any need to think or say what "God" may signify. They call him by vague names—the All, the Infinite. In moods of exalted feeling, impatient of definition, they wish to be left alone with their experience of the Eternal; they resent the intrusion of theology, as a poet, lost in wonder at a landscape, might resent the coming of surveyors with their clanking chains. So Walt Whitman wanted to see the stars rather than hear the astronomer, and after listening to the learned lecture, with its charts and diagrams, he says,

"I became tired and sick,
  Till rising and gliding out I wandered off by myself,
  In the mystical moist night air, and from time to time
  Looked up in perfect silence at the stars."

But, for all that, we well may be thankful for astronomers. At times the "mystical, moist night air" is absent; we do not wish to "look up in perfect silence at the stars"; and, even though we know in advance that they are bound to be inadequate, we do want as clear and worthy ideas as possible about the universe. Moreover, when such ideas are ours, looking up in perfect silence at the stars is more impressive than it ever was before. No more can men content themselves with a vague consciousness of God. Spirits like Wordsworth have raptures of which they sing,

"In such access of mind, in such high hour
  Of visitation from the living God,
  Thought was not—in enjoyment it expired."

In communion with nature, in love for family, in fellowship with God, such hours may come, but nature, family, and God must also be the objects of understanding thought. Days of vital need, if not of mental doubt, inevitably come when it is impossible any longer to use a term like "God" without knowing what we mean.

The special urgency of this is felt by most of us because as children we were taught to picture the Divine in terms of personality. The God of the Bible is personal. Little that persons do, save sinning, is omitted from the catalogue of God's activities as he is pictured for us in the Scripture. He knows, loves, purposes, warns, rebukes, allures, rewards, and punishes, as only persons can. And all our relationships with him are clearly personal. When we pray we say "Our Father"; when we seek our duty we ask, "What wilt thou have me to do?" God is *He* and *Thou*, not *It*, and friendship is the ideal relation of all souls with him.

Moreover, in our maturity we are not likely to be

interested in a God who is not personal. Whoever curiously asks why he believes in God, will find not simply *reasons* but *causes* for his faith, and will perceive that the causes of faith lie back of the reasons for it. Vital need always precedes the arguments by which we justify its satisfaction. A man eats one thing and shuns another on principles of dietetics that can be defended before his intelligence; but behind all such sophisticated reasons stands the vital cause of eating—hunger. So back of intellectual arguments for belief in God lies the initial cause of faith: *men are hungry*. Men believe in God because they hunger for a world that is not chance and chaos, but that is guided by a Purpose. They believe in God, because in their struggles after righteousness they hunger for a Divine Ally in whom righteousness has its origin, its ground and destiny. They believe in God because they hunger for confidence that Someone cares about our race in its conflicts and defeats and because in their individual experience they want a friend. Without such faith man feels himself to be, in Goethe's phrase, "a troubled wanderer upon a darkened earth." Plainly this elemental human hunger for purpose, righteousness, and friendship calls for something akin to personality in God. *Only persons have purpose, character, and friendliness.* The vital motives which lead men to seek God's comfort, forgiveness, guidance, and cooperation plainly imply his personality. Things do not forgive us, love us, nor purpose good concerning us, nor can any thing be imagined so subtle and so powerful as to satisfy the needs on account of which men come to God. If God is not personal, he can feel no concern for human life and a God of no concern is of no consequence.

The philosophers of India, with a well-reasoned pantheistic system and centuries to make their philosophy effective, have failed to quell this deathless thirst for a God who counts. Every wayside shrine of Hinduism incarnates the old faith in gods conceived as friends, not things; and Buddha, who taught impersonal deity, is now himself adored as the Personal Lord of Love and Blessedness. Wherever one finds vital religion one finds that God is no dry impersonal abstraction, but man's friend. Boscamen, speaking of the Egyptian Book of the Dead and of the Chaldean Tablets, says: "Six thousand years ago in Egypt and Chaldea—it is not dread, but the grateful love of a child to his father, of friend to friend, that meets us in the oldest books of the world." And when one turns from the oldest to the newest books this inner demand of man's religious life has not ceased; it has been refined and confirmed. "The All would not be the All unless it contained a Personality," said Victor Hugo. "That Personality is God."

Biography is lavish in illustrations of this need in man's religious life. The biographer of Theodore Parker, the free-lance preacher of Boston, remarks: "In his *theology* God was neither personal nor impersonal, but a reality transcending these distinctions. In his *devotions* God was as personal as his own father or mother, and he prayed to him as such, daringly indifferent to the anthropomorphisms of his unfettered speech." When one passes from speculation to religion, he always comes into a realm where only a personal God will do. On this point even confessed unbelievers furnish confirmation. One who calls himself an agnostic writes: "At times in the silence of the night and in rare lonely moments, I experience a sort of communion of myself with Something Great that is not myself. Then the Universal Scheme of things has on me the effect of a sympathetic Person, and my communion therewith takes on a quality of fearless worship. These moments happen, and they are to me the supreme fact in my religious life." Always for the purposes of vital religion, God must have on us the "effect of a sympathetic Person."

II

When one, however, subjects this need of his religious life to searching thought, what difficulty he encounters! Multitudes, if they were candid, would confess what a college senior wrote: "When I am just thinking about God in a speculative or philosophical way, I generally think of him as impersonal, but for practical purposes I think of him as personal." Many folks feel thus distraught; at the heart of their religious life is the paralyzing doubt, that in a universe like this to think of God as personal is absurd. If a train moving a mile a minute should leave the earth, it must travel 40,000,000 years before it would reach the nearest star. The Creator of such a world is not readily reduced to the similitude of human life. Once men lived on a flat earth, small in compass and cosily tucked beneath the sky's coverlet, but now the world's vastness beggars imagination. As an astronomer remarked, coming from a session with his telescope, "This does away with a six-foot god; you cannot shake hands with the Creator of *this.*" Men used to suppose that Arcturus was a single star, but now new telescopes reveal Arcturus as a galaxy of stars, thousands in number, with interstellar spaces so immense that thought breaks down in spanning them and imagination even cannot make the leap. Is the God of such a universe to be conceived in terms of a magnified man?

So to picture deity seems at first sight a survival of mere childishness. Professor John Fiske, of Harvard, has told us that when he was a boy God always conjured up in his imagination the figure of a venerable bookkeeper, with white flowing beard, standing behind a high desk and writing down the bad deeds of John Fiske. How many of us can recall such early crude and childish thoughts of God! A mother asked her young daughter what she was drawing. "A picture of God," was the answer. "But no one knows what God looks like," the mother said. "They will," came the rejoinder, "when I get through." We all began with some such primitive idea of deity. Indeed, these early conceptions long persist in many minds, as the following statements, written by college students, indicate: "I think of God as real, actual skin and blood and bones, something we shall see with our eyes some day, no matter what lives we lead on earth." "It may be a remnant of youth, but anyhow, every time I think of God there appears a vague image of a man, with all members of the body, just enormously large." "I have always pictured him according to a description in *Paradise Lost* as seated upon a throne, while around are angels playing on harps and singing hymns." "I think of God as having bodily form and being much larger than the average man. He has a radiant countenance beaming with love and compassion. He is erect and upright, fearless and brave."[2]

---

[2]From a questionnaire, "Belief in God and Immortality," by Prof. James H. Leuba.

No one of us may be contemptuous of such crude ideas; we all possessed them once. Indeed the loss of them, with their picture of deity, clear in feature and distinct in outline, has been to some a shock from which faith has not recovered. When increasing knowledge discredited our immature theology, and our world immeasurably widened, the very human God of our first imaginations was lost among the stars. We learned that this is a universe where the light that falls upon our eyes tonight left the far heavens when Abraham was shepherding on Syrian hills. The Christian Gospel of the personal Father which once was good news became a serious problem. We still may cling to the old meanings of our religious faith; still we may pray in hours of need as though our childhood's God were really there; but at times we suspect that we are clinging to the beauty of an early memory while reluctantly we lose conviction of its truth. Many modern men and women can understand the plight of the famous Dr. Jowett of Oxford, who, so runs the tradition, inserted "used to" in a muffled voice, when he recited the creed: "I *used to* believe in God the Father Almighty."

With such misgivings, whether as habitual disturbers of our faith or as occasional moods of unbelief that come and go, most of us must be familiar. What Charles Darwin is reported to have said about himself, many if they spoke frankly would say too: "Sometimes I feel a warm sense of a personal God, and then"—with a shake of his head—"it goes away."

III

Whatever may be our theology, the fact is plain that the denial of a personal God solves no problem. For if we may not think of God in terms of personality, the query still remains, which was there before—*in what terms shall we conceive of the Eternal?* In a discussion on the nature of the sky, one boy, denying the idea of a solid canopy, exclaimed, "There ain't any sky." Said the other, seeing how little this negation solved the problem, "Well, what *is* it that ain't?" Some such inquiry one must put to his doubts about God's personality. Though we may deny a personal God, nevertheless in the place where he once stood, creator and sustainer of all existence, is Something that we do think of somehow. We may have but little of Carlyle's sublime imagination; may not easily transport ourselves to stand with him on the far northern cliff, "behind him all Europe and Africa fast asleep, except the watchmen, and before him the silent Immensity and Palace of the Eternal, whereof our sun is but the porch-lamp." Yet who of us, regarding the illimitable universe, on the far outskirts of which our little earth is whirling, so minute that through the strongest telescope from the nearest star its conflagration would be quite invisible, has escaped the sense of a Universal Power? And the human mind cannot so keep itself at home in little tasks and pleasures as to evade the question: How shall we think of the Power that made the universe? In what terms? By what analogies? Hours of revelation come in every serious life when no desire compares in urgency with the desire to know the character of the Eternal. It does make a prodigious difference what hands hold the leash of the universe.

This second fact is also clear, that if we are to think of the Eternal at all, we must think in terms of something drawn from our experience. When we sing of Paradise we speak of golden streets and gates of pearl, and Thoreau remarks that, arriving in heaven, he expects to find pine trees there. Such words we do not take literally, but such words we cannot utterly avoid, for it we are to speak at all of the unknown glory, we must use pictures from the known. So we think of God in human symbols. We cannot catch him in an abstract definition as though a boy with a butterfly net should capture the sun at noon. Our minds are not fitted for such enterprise. Of necessity we take something homely, familiar, close at hand, and lifting it up as far as we can reach, say *God is most like that.* No one who thinks at all of the Eternal escapes this necessity.

By this method the *materialist* reaches his philosophy. Haeckel laughs to scorn the opening clause of the "Apostles' Creed." "I believe in God the Father Almighty, maker of heaven and earth"—for such faith no words are contemptuous enough. This denial does not mean however that Haeckel has no faith; he deliberately offers a creedal substitute which runs in part: I believe in a "chemical substance of a viscous character, having albuminous matter and water as its chief constituents." In such terms does Haeckel think of the Eternal. A professor of medicine has remarked that such a theory reduces all reality to "phosphorus and glue." When some psalmist cries, "Bless the Lord, O my soul," nothing substantial is speaking or is being spoken to save phosphorus and glue! When an Italian patriot cries, "The time for dying comes to all, but the time for dishonoring oneself ought never to come," nothing is real and causal save phosphorus and glue! And every gracious and redeeming deed in history from the love of mothers to the cross of Christ has been a complicated working out of phosphorus and glue! In whatever labored phrases he may state his case, the materialist's method there is obvious; he has taken physical energy, of whose presence in his own body he is first assured, and whose reality he has then read out into the world, and this homely and familiar experience he has lifted up as far as he can reach to say, the Eternal is most like that.

So far as method is concerned, the *theist* of necessity travels the same road; only he insists on a nobler symbol than physical energy in terms of which to think of God. He takes *mind*. He says in effect: there may be wide stretches of the universe where our intellects meet no answer and find no meaning. But in much of the universe we do see meaning; and how can intelligence find sense where intelligence has not put sense? A few scratches on a cliff's face in Assyria, after centuries of neglect, rendered up their meaning to the mind of Rawlinson. They were themselves the work of intelligence, and intelligence could read them. So, the theist continues, the universe is in part at least intelligible. Our minds fit into it and are answered by it. We can trace its laws and predict its movements. Man first worked out the nature of the ellipse in theoretical geometry, and then telescopes later showed the gigantic ellipses of planetary orbits in the heavens. Can it be that this intelligible world, readable by mind, is itself essentially mindless? As easily believe that the notes of Wagner's operas were accidentally blown together by a whirlwind and yet are playable by man! Therefore the theist believes the universe to be rational; he takes mind as he has known it in himself, and lifting it as high as he can reach, cries, God is most like that.

So far as the general method of approach is concerned, the Christian travels the same road to his idea of God. Only he cannot believe that the best he knows is too good or too great to be a symbol in terms of which to think of the Eternal. Therefore he will not take a by-product of experience such as physical energy, nor a section of personality such as mind; he takes the full orb of personality, *self-conscious being that knows and purposes and loves,* and he affirms that God is most like this. Such in its simplest form is the Christian assertion of God's personality.

In one of his noblest passages Martineau has put into classic form this necessity, which we have been discussing, of thinking about God in terms of human experience: "God, being infinite, can never be fully comprehended by our minds; whatever thought of him be there, his real nature must still transcend: there will yet be deep after deep beyond, within that light ineffable; and what we see, compared with what we do not see, will be as the raindrop to the firmament. Our conception of him can never *correspond with the reality,* so as to be without omission, disproportion, or aberration; but can only *represent the reality,* and *stand for God* within our souls, till nobler thoughts arise and reveal themselves as his interpreters. And this is precisely what we mean by a symbolical idea. The devotee who prostrates himself before a black stone—the Egyptian who in his prayers was haunted by the ideal form of the graceful ibis or the monstrous sphinx—the theist who bends beneath the starry porch that midnight opens to the temple of the universe—the Christian who sees in heaven a spirit akin to that which divinely lived in Galilee, and with glorious pity died on Calvary—all alike assume a representation of him whose immeasurable nature they can neither compass nor escape. And the only question is, whether the conception they portray upon the wall of their ideal temple is an abominable idol, or a true and sanctifying mediatorial thought."

IV

In their endeavor thus to think of God in terms of personality, some are perplexed because in their imagination a person is inseparable from flesh. "I think of God as a personal being," writes a college student. "A personal being would have a form that you could see or touch." But this would be true only if the grossest materialism were accepted, and the spiritual life declared to be the product of brain as digestive fluids are of salivary glands. On any other basis, personality is not indissolubly bound to body nor by it necessarily delimited. A man cannot hear without his ear, but he is not his ear; he cannot hear without the auditory nerve, but he is not the auditory nerve; he cannot hear without the temporal lobe of the brain, but he is not the brain or any portion of it. These may be the instruments which he uses; he is free when they are well, hampered when they are broken, and at last he is separable from them all. John Quincy Adams at the age of eighty met a friend upon a Boston street. "Good morning," said the friend, "and how is John Quincy Adams today?" "Thank you," was the ex-president's reply, "John Quincy Adams himself is well, quite well, I thank you. But the house in which he lives at present is becoming dilapidated. It is tottering upon its foundations. Time and the seasons have nearly destroyed it. Its roof is pretty well worn out. Its walls are much shattered and it trembles with every wind. The old tenement is becoming almost uninhabitable and I think John Quincy Adams will have to move out of it soon. But he himself is quite well, quite well." Such a conception of man as *being* a permanent personality and *having* a temporary body is essential to any worthy meaning when we use personal terms about God.

With such an elevated thought, however, of what personality does mean, it soon is evident that no other reality with which we deal is so worthy to be the symbol of an Eternal Spirit. Is one perplexed that God, who is invisible, should be pictured in the similitude of human persons? But *we* are invisible. The outward husks and fleshy garment of our friends we indeed have seen, but upon the friend himself—consciousness, love, purpose, ideal, and character—no eye has looked. No mirror ever has been strong enough to show us to ourselves. In every homely conversation this ineffable miracle is wrought: out of the unseen where I dwell, I signal by word and gesture to you back in the unseen where you dwell. We are inhabitants now of the intangible and unseen world; we are as invisible as God.

Indeed, personality is essentially the most unlimited reality with which we deal; in comparison a solar system is a little thing. Consider *memory,* by which we can retrace our youthful days, build our shanties once again at brooksides, replay our games, and recapitulate the struggles and the joys of the first days at school. Nothing in all the universe can remember except persons. Were we not so familiar with this element in human greatness, we would more often pause to exclaim, as did Augustine, fifteen centuries ago, "Great is the power of memory. Amazement overcomes me when I think of it. And yet men go abroad to gaze upon the mountains, the broad rivers, the wide ocean, the courses of the stars, and pass themselves, the crowning wonder, by!" Consider *imagination,* by which sitting still in body we can project ourselves around the world, can walk down Princes Street in Edinburgh, or stand in mingled awe and condemnation before the tomb of Napoleon in Paris, or rise uncovered before the majesty of the Matterhorn. Nothing in all the universe can do that except persons. Were full power to act wherever we can *think* added to our gifts, we should come so near to incipient omnipresence as to be in dread of our responsibility. Consider *love,* by which we live not so much where our bodies are as where our friends and family may be. Love expands the individual until his real life is independent of geography. Says one lover to another:

> "The widest land
> Doom takes to part us, leaves thy heart in mine
> With pulses that beat double."

Many a mother in America has *lived* in the trenches of France; *many* a man has found that what might happen to him where his body was could not be compared with what might happen to him where his friendships were; and as we grow in love and loyalty we find ourselves scattered all over creation. How far such an expansion of life may go our Lord revealed when he said, "Inasmuch as ye did it unto me" (Matt. 25:40). Nothing in heaven above or on the earth beneath can so extend itself in love save persons.

Finally, consider *creative power* by which human beings project themselves into the future, and, with masterful ideals in mind, lay hold on circumstance and bend it to their will. As if he shared creative power with the Eternal, an engineer summons nature's forces to his bidding and lays his will upon them, until where nothing was a structure stands that mankind may use for centuries. Nothing in all the universe can so create except persons. In that essentially creative act where deathless ideas and harmonies are given being by poets and musicians, so that something out of nothing is brought to pass by personality, man faces a mystery as abysmal as God's making of the world. *Paradise Lost* is wonderful; but not half as wonderful as the creative personality itself who years before projected it. "An inward prompting," Milton says, "which now grew daily upon me, that by labor and intense study, joined with the strong propensity of nature, I might perhaps leave something so written to after times as they should not willingly let it die." Nothing can so create save personality.

Personality is not so limited that we should be ashamed to think of God in terms of it. Rather, of all realities with which we deal, personality alone, invisible, reaching back in memory, reaching out in imagination, expanding itself in love, and laying hold upon the future with creative power, is a worthy symbol of the Eternal Spirit.

Even when the meaning of personality has been so enlarged and elevated, we should not leave our statement of belief in God as though our experience of personality were a mold into which our thought of him is poured and so delimited. We are not presumptuous Lilliputians, running out with verbal stakes and threads, to pin down the tall, majestic Gulliver of the Eternal and dance in theological exultation round our capture. We know better than that. We understand how insufficient is every human name for God. We know that when we have said our best—"How unsearchable are his judgments and his ways past tracing out!" (Rom. 11:33).

Nothing more has marred the Christian message and

discredited the Christian faith than the unwise presumption that has forced its definitions into the secrets of the Infinite. "It is enough to say," exclaims Leslie Stephen, "that they defined the nature of God Almighty with an accuracy from which modest naturalists would shrink in describing the genesis of a black beetle." The antidote to such vain pride of theology is found in the wholesome modesty of the Bible. There man inquires, "Canst thou by searching find out God? Canst thou find out the Almighty unto perfection? It is high as heaven; what canst thou do? Deeper than Sheol; what canst thou know?" (Job 11:7). There God replies: "As the heavens are higher than the earth, so are my ways higher than your ways and my thoughts than your thoughts" (Isa. 55:9). Scripture bears abundant testimony to the symbolic nature of our human terms for God. "Like as a father pitieth his children, so Jehovah pitieth them that fear him" (Ps. 103:13). "As one whom his mother comforteth, so will I comfort you" (Isa. 66:13). "I will betroth thee unto me" (Hos. 2:20). "Return, . . . saith Jehovah, for I am a husband unto you" (Jer. 3:14). "The Lord spake unto Moses . . . as a man speaketh unto his friend" (Exod. 33:11). Father, Mother, Bridegroom, Husband, Friend— these are symbols of God. Men, endeavoring to frame some worthy thought of the Eternal, lift up their best in phrases such as these, and in them enshrine their noblest concepts of the divine. They have no better, truer thing to say of God, no wiser way in which to say it. But when they think of the Eternal as he must be, and of their human words, infinitesimal in comparison, they know that all their best names for God are like small measures of water dipped from an immeasurable sea. For all that, so much of God as they can grasp and understand is the most important truth that mankind knows. Let even a teacup of water be taken to a laboratory and it will tell the truth about the sea; *that one teacup will reveal the quality of the whole ocean.* Yet it will not reveal all the truth about the ocean. When one considers the reach of the sea over the rim of the world; thinks of the depths that no eye can pierce, the distances that no mind can imagine; remembers the currents that sweep through the sea, the tides that rise there, and the storms that beat it to its nether wells, he dare not try to put *these* into a teacup. So God sweeps out beyond the reach of human symbols. At once so true and so inadequate are all our words for him.

So we might speak to one who incredulously looks upon our faith, but for one who wholeheartedly approaches God as Christianity suggests, no negative and cautionary word is adequate. The Christian method of conceiving God brings the most exhilarating thought of him that man has ever had. It says in brief: take your *best* and think of God as most truly symbolized in that. As to what our best is, not even the agnostics doubt. The physical universe belittles us on one side only; it makes a pygmy of the body. In our spirits we still tower above the physical; we are greater than the world we know. Our supreme good, the divinest reality with which we deal, is personality. Then lift that up, says Christianity; it is your best, and you dare not think of God in terms of less; you have Christ's example in arguing from the human best to the divine: "If ye, being evil, know how to give good gifts unto your children, *how much more . . .* your Father" (Matt. 7:11).

The Christian faith asserts that when a man thus thinks of God in terms of the best he knows he is on the road toward truth. How many billion spiritual miles he may have to travel to the end, no man can tell. Only he will never need to stop, retrace his steps, and start upon a lower path than personality, a road that lies beneath righteousness and love. The road leads on and up beyond our imagination, but it is the same road and not another. *God is personality plus, or else he alone is completely personal and we are but in embryo.*

If God so is personal, then all the deep meanings of religious life and faith that the saints, our spiritual sires, have known are open to us modern men and women. Forms of thought indeed have changed, but if God is thus our Father and our Friend, the essentials of Christian experience are waiting for us all. Life then is not purposeless; all creation is bound into spiritual unity by personal Will; and in sacrificial labor we are serving one who is able to guard that which we "have committed unto him against that day" (II Tim. 1:12). Old hymns of confidence in time of trial, we too can sing:

"Still will we trust, though earth seem dark and dreary,
  And the heart faint beneath His chastening rod;
Though steep and hard our pathway, worn and weary,
  Still will we trust in God."

And we can pray, not indeed with clamorous beggary as though the grace of God were a wayside stall where every greedy hand can pluck what passing whim may wish, but we can commune with God as the real saints have always prayed with humility and gratitude and confident desire for good. Most of all, that priceless privilege is open to us which is the center and sun of Christian thought and life. For if among all realities in our experience, we have dared take the best, personality, as a symbol in terms of which to think of God, how should we not, among all personalities, take the best we know as the highroad of approach to him. Therefore our real symbol of God shall be no man among us, frail and sinful, but our Lord himself "fairest among ten thousand"—"the one altogether beautiful." We shall think of God in terms of him. We shall see "the light of the knowledge of the glory of God in the face of Jesus Christ" (II Cor. 4:6).

CHAPTER IV

Belief and Trust

DAILY READINGS

We have tried to explain our faith in the personal God, and to see the transfiguring influence of that faith on life. But is belief in God always such a blessing as we have pictured? Rather faith, like every other experience of man, has its caricatures and burlesques. Many men are prevented from appreciation of faith in God, with its inestimable blessings, because they have so continually seen faith's perversions. The fact is that belief in God may be an utterly negligible matter in a man's experience or may even become a positively pernicious influence. Let us, in the daily readings, consider some of the *familiar travesties on faith*.

Fourth Week, First Day

Praise ye Jehovah.
Praise Jehovah, O my soul.
While I live will I praise Jehovah:
I will sing praises unto my God while I have any being.
Put not your trust in princes,
Nor in the son of man, in whom there is no help.
His breath goeth forth, he returneth to his earth;
In that very day his thoughts perish.
Happy is he that hath the God of Jacob for his help,
Whose hope is in Jehovah his God.

—Ps. 146:1-5.

No one can mistake the note of reality in this psalmist's experience of God. But every one of us knows people who, if asked whether they believed in God, would readily assent, yet to whom faith makes no such difference in life as this psalm expresses. Their faith is nothing but an opinion about God, lightly held, a formal consent that what church or family tradition says must be correct. They have what Luther used to call "the charcoal burner's faith." A man of that occupation when asked what he believed, said, "What Holy Church believes"; but, questioned further, he could not tell what it was that Holy Church did believe. So formal, vitally unpossessed, and practically unreal is much of our religious opinion that passes for faith. Dean Swift was a churchman of high rank, and yet his biographer is compelled to say of him: "He clung to the doctrines of his church, not because he could give abstract reasons for his belief, but simply because the church happened to be his." Vital religious faith is a very different thing from such dry conventionality. A man may assent to the contents of a college catalogue and yet never have experience of college life; he may agree that a menu is dietetically correct and yet never grow strong from the food; and he may believe in every creed in Christendom and not know what faith in God really means. Opinions about God are a roadway to God, but the end of the journey is a personal fellowship that transfigures life; and to seize opinions as though they were the object of faith is, to use Tagore's figure, "like a man who tries to reach his destination by firmly clutching the dust of the road."

O Thou great Father of us all, we rejoice that at last we know Thee. All our soul within us is glad because we need no longer cringe before Thee as slaves of holy fear, seeking to appease Thine anger by sacrifice and self-inflicted pain, but may come like little children, trustful and happy, to the God of love. Thou art the only true Father, and all the tender beauty of our human loves is the reflected radiance of Thy lovingkindness, like the moonlight from the sunlight, and testifies to the eternal passion that kindled it.

Grant us growth of spiritual vision, that with the passing years we may enter into the fulness of this our faith. Since Thou art our Father, may we not hide our sins from Thee, but overcome them by the stern comfort of Thy presence. By this knowledge uphold us in our sorrows and make us patient even amid the unsolved mysteries of the years. Reveal to us the larger goodness and love that speak through the unbending laws of Thy world. Through this faith make us the willing equals of all Thy other children.

As Thou art ever pouring out Thy life in sacrificial father-love, may we accept the eternal law of the cross and give ourselves to Thee and to all men. We praise Thee for Jesus Christ, whose life has revealed to us this faith and law, and we rejoice that he has become the first-born among many brethren. Grant that in us, too, the faith in Thy fatherhood may shine through all our life with such persuasive beauty that some who still creep in the dusk of fear may stand erect as free sons of God, and that others who now through unbelief are living as orphans in an empty world may stretch out their hands to the great Father of their spirits and find Thee near. Amen.—Walter Rauschenbusch.

Fourth Week, Second Day

Faith is travestied in many lives not so much by the substitution of opinion for experience, as by making religion consist in certain devout practices, such as church-going. Ceremonialism, instead of being an aid in making God real, takes the place of fellowship with God. How scathing were the attacks of the prophets on this distortion of religion!

Hear the word of Jehovah, ye rulers of Sodom; give ear unto the law of our God, ye people of Gomorrah. What unto me is the multitude of your sacrifices? saith Jehovah: I have had enough of the burnt-offerings of rams, and the fat of fed beasts; and I delight not in the blood of bullocks, or of lambs, or of he-goats. When ye come to appear before me, who hath required this at your hand, to trample my courts? Bring no more vain oblations; incense is an abomination unto me; new moon and sabbath, the calling of assemblies—I cannot away with iniquity and the solemn meeting. Your new moons and your appointed feasts my soul hateth; they are a trouble unto me; I am weary of bearing them. And when ye spread forth your hands, I will hide mine eyes from you; yea, when ye make many prayers, I will not hear: your hands are full of blood. Wash you, make you clean; put away the evil of your doings from before mine eyes; cease to do evil; learn to do well; seek justice, relieve the oppressed, judge the fatherless, plead for the widow.—Isa. 1:10-17.

Many young people, watching conventional observances in religious worship and perceiving no real life active there, come to the conclusion that religious faith is a decent and negligible formality. So William Scott Palmer, tracing his progress from agnosticism to Christianity, describes the religion of his boyhood: "Religion as a personal matter, religion as a life, did not exist for me or for my family. The borderland of my native village went to church at eleven o'clock on fine Sundays, and I went in and with it. There were unlucky Sundays when the Litany was said, and the service prolonged by its unmeaning length; the lucky Sundays were wet ones that cleared up later. . . . I did not know that there was any vital meaning in religion." And even Sir Wilfred Grenfell, whose work in Labrador is one of this generation's outstanding triumphs of Christian faith, says of his young manhood: "The ordinary exponents of the Christian faith had never succeeded in interesting me in any way, or even in making me believe that they were more than professionally concerned themselves. Religion appeared to be a profession, exceedingly conventional, and most unattractive in my estimation—the very last I should have thought of selecting." No travesty on faith is more deadly in its effects than this substitution of conventional observance for life.

O Jesus, we thy ministers bow before Thee to confess the common sins of our calling. Thou knowest all things; Thou knowest that we love Thee and that our hearts' desire is to serve Thee in faithfulness; and yet, like Peter, we have so often failed Thee in the hour of Thy need. If ever we have loved our own leadership and power when we sought to lead our people to Thee, we pray Thee to forgive. If we have been engrossed in narrow duties and little questions, when the vast needs of humanity called aloud for prophetic vision and apostolic sympathy, we pray Thee to forgive. If in our loyalty to the Church of the past we have distrusted Thy living voice and have suffered Thee to pass from our door unheard, we pray Thee to forgive. If ever we have been more concerned for the strong and the rich than for the shepherdless throngs of the people for whom Thy soul grieved, we pray Thee to forgive.

O Master, amidst our failures we cast ourselves upon Thee in humility and contrition. We need new light and a new message. We need the ancient spirit of prophecy and the leaping fire and joy of a new conviction, and Thou alone canst give it. Inspire the ministry of Thy Church with dauntless courage to face the vast needs of the future. Free us from all entanglements that have hushed our voice and bound our action. Grant us grace to look upon the veiled sins of the rich and the coarse vices of the poor through Thine eyes. Give us Thine inflexible sternness against sin, and Thine inexhaustible compassion for the frailty and tragedy of those who do the sin. Make us faithful shepherds of Thy flock, true seers of God, and true followers of Jesus. Amen.—Walter Rauschenbusch.

Fourth Week, Third Day

And he spake also this parable unto certain who trusted in themselves that they were righteous, and set all others at nought: Two men went up into the temple to pray; the one a Pharisee, and the other a publican. The Pharisee stood and prayed thus with himself, God, I thank thee, that I am not as the rest of men, extortioners, unjust, adulterers, or even as this publican. I fast twice in the week; I give tithes of all that I get. But the publican, standing afar off, would not lift up so much as his eyes unto heaven, but smote his breast, saying, God, be thou merciful to me a sinner. I say unto you, This man went down to his house justified rather than the other: for every one that exalteth himself shall be humbled; but he that humbleth himself shall be exalted.—Luke 18:9-14.

The men against whom the Master directed this parable were bigots. Self-opinionated, self-conceited, dogmatic, and contemptuous—they wore all the attributes of bigotry. *And bigotry is a very familiar perversion of faith.* Vital fellowship with God ought to make men gracious, magnanimous, generous; it ought to make life with God seem so incomparably important that when anyone has that, his opinions about God will be tolerantly regarded, however mistaken they may appear to be. Dr. Pritchett, when President of the Massachusetts Institute of Technology, passed through a classroom where a young instructor was conducting a chemical experiment. "The reaction itself," says Dr. Pritchett, "was going on in a retort on the table, while on a blackboard was written the conventional formula, which in the science of chemistry is used to describe the reaction. It so happened that the instructor had made a mistake in writing the formula; instead of CO_2 he had written CO_3. But this made not the slightest difference in the reaction which was going on in the flask." So, a man may live his life with an admirably Christian spirit, although he describes it with a mistaken formula. His error is theoretical, not vital. But a bigot is so sure that he alone knows the true formula, that a man without that formula is altogether wrong, and that he must either set him right or condemn him utterly, that he grows bitter, hard, unlovely. His opinions may be right, but his spirit is wrong. The faith that should make his life radiant is perverted to make it narrow, harsh, contemptuous. He renders hateful the very faith he seeks to commend and ruins the reputation of the God whom he is zealous to exalt. So the Pharisee of the parable missed all the beauty of the publican's life because he thought the publican's formula was wrong. No one can estimate the irreparable damage which zealous bigots have done to true faith.

O Thou who art of purer eyes than to behold iniquity, canst Thou bear to look on us conscious of our great transgression? Yet hide not Thy face from us, for in Thy light alone shall we see light.

Forgive us for the sins which crowd into the mind as we realize Thy presence; our ungovernable tempers, our shuffling insincerities, the craven fear of our hearts, the pettiness of our spirits, the foul lusts and fatal leanings of our souls. Not for pardon only, but for cleansing, Lord, we pray.

Forgive us, we beseech Thee, our unconscious sins; things which must be awful to Thy sight, of which we yet know nothing. Forgive by giving us in fuller measure the awakening of Thy presence, that we may know ourselves, and lose all love of sin in the knowledge of what Thou art.

Forgive us for the things for which we can never forgive ourselves; those sad turned pages of our life which some chance wind of memory blows back again with shame; for the moment of cruel passion, the hour beyond recall, the word that went forth to poison and defame, the carelessness that lost our opportunity, the unheeded fading of bright ideals.

Forgive us for the things that others can never forgive; the idle tale, the cruel wrong, the uncharitable condemnation, the unfair judgment, the careless criticism, the irresponsible conduct.

Forgive us for the sins of our holy things; that we have turned the sacred page without a sigh, read the confessions of holy men and women and never joined therein, lived in Thy light and never prayed to be forgiven or rendered Thee thanksgiving; professed to believe in Thee and love Thee, yet dared to injure and hate.

Naught save being born again, nothing but a miracle of grace, can ever be to us forgiveness. Cleanse our hearts, renew our minds, and take not Thy Holy Spirit from us. Amen. —W. E. Orchard.

Fourth Week, Fourth Day

Of all perversions of faith none is more fatal than the substitution of opinions about God for integrity of character and usefulness of life. With what scathing vehemence does James, as Dr. Moffatt renders him, attack this travesty on faith.

"My brothers, what is the use of anyone declaring he has faith, if he has no deeds to show? Can his faith save him? Suppose some brother or sister is ill-clad and short of daily food; if any of you says to them, 'Depart in peace! Get warm, get food,' without supplying their bodily needs, what use is that? So faith, unless it has deeds, is dead in itself. Someone will object, 'And you claim to have faith!' Yes, and I claim to have deeds as well; you show me your faith without any

deeds, and I will show you by my deeds what faith is! You
believe in one God? Well and good. So do the devils, and they
shudder. But will you understand, you senseless fellow, that
faith without deeds is dead? When our father Abraham
offered his son Isaac on the altar, was he not justified by what
he did?"—James 2:14-21.

An American businessman not long dead, who hated any
word from the pulpit about social righteousness, used to
complain: "Preachers are talking so everlastingly about this
earth. I've done my best to get them to stick to the Gospel,
and not allow 'worldliness' to get into the teachings of the
Church; but the good old preachers have gone to glory."
Yet this pious zealot helped wreck the finances of a great
railroad system, and with part of the proceeds built a
theological seminary. *There was no vital, intelligent
connection between his faith in God and his ideals of
character and service.* One verse should be made to flame in
Christian pulpits: "If any provideth not for his own, and
specially his own household, he hath denied the faith and is
worse than an unbeliever" (I Tim. 5:8). Domestic fidelity is
here only typical of all basic moral obligations. What this
verse says in principle is clear: theoretical unbelief is not the
worst sin in God's sight; any man who fails in the
fundamental duties of rectitude and service has thereby
denied the faith and is worse than an atheist.

*O thou holy One and just! if alone the pure in heart can see
thee, truly we must stand afar off, and not so much as lift up
our eyes unto heaven. Were it not that thou hast help and pity
for the contrite spirit, we could only cry, "Depart from us, we
are sinful men, O Lord!" For idle words, for proud thoughts
and unloving deeds; for wasted moments and reluctant
duties, and too eager rest; for the wandering desire, the vain
fancy, the scornful doubt, the untrustful care; for impatient
murmurs, and unruly passions, and the hardness of a
worldly heart; thou, Lord, canst call us unto judgment, and
we have naught to answer thee. But, O thou Judge of men,
thou art witness that we do not love our guilty ways; make
our conscience true and tender that we may duly hate them,
and refuse them any peace as enemies to thee. Stir up within
us a great and effectual repentance that we may redeem the*

time which we have lost, and in the hours that remain do the work of many days. Thou knowest all our secret snares; drive from us every root of bitterness: with thy severity pluck out, O Lord, the thorns of sin from our entangled souls, and bind them as a crown of contrition around our bleeding brows; and having made our peace with thee may we henceforth watch and pray that we enter not again into temptation, but bear our cross with patience to the close. Amen.—James Martineau.

Fourth Week, Fifth Day

Some of the most lamentable perversions of religious faith arise from inadequate ideas of God. Consider, for example, the way Manasseh thought that the Divine ought to be worshiped.

For he built again the high places which Hezekiah his father had destroyed; and he reared up altars for Baal, and made an Asherah, as did Ahab king of Israel, and worshipped all the host of heaven, and served them. And he built altars in the house of Jehovah, whereof Jehovah said, In Jerusalem will I put my name. And he built altars for all the host of heaven in the two courts of the house of Jehovah. And he made his son to pass through the fire, and practised augury, and used enchantments, and dealt with them that had familiar spirits, and with wizards: he wrought much evil in the sight of Jehovah, to provoke him to anger.—II Kings 21:3-6.

Then compare the thought of the Master on the same subject.

But the hour cometh, and now is, when the true worshippers shall worship the Father in spirit and truth: for such doth the Father seek to be his worshippers. God is a Spirit: and they that worship him must worship in spirit and truth.—John 4:23-24.

There is no reason to suppose that Manasseh was insincere; he is one of an innumerable company in whom the religious motive has been harnassed to warped and ignorant ideas of God. Religious faith, like any other tremendous power, is terrific in evil consequences when it goes wrong. Men, under its subtle and prevailing influence, have waged bloody wars, worshiped with licentious rituals, carried on pitiless persecutions, and in bigotry, cruelty, and deceit have grown worse than they would have been with no religion whatsoever. And men, in its inspiring light, have launched missionary movements, founded great philanthropies, built schools, hospitals, orphanages, and in sacrifice, courageous service, and hope of human brotherhood have made man's history glorious. Religion needs intelligence to save it from becoming a ruinous curse; like all power of the first magnitude it is a disaster if ignorantly used. Since religious faith will always be a major human motive, under what obligations are we to save it from perversion and to keep it clean and right!

Almighty God, our heavenly Father, we are most unworthy to be called Thy children; for when light and darkness have been set before us, we have often chosen darkness rather than light. Conscious that within us are the elements of a nobler and a meaner life, we have yet given way to the meaner appetites, and have not obeyed the inspiration Thou hast kindled within us. We entreat Thee now of Thy grace to call us back from the ways of temptation and sin into that higher life which Thou dost breathe upon us, and which is manifested in Jesus Christ our Lord. Give us the self-knowledge, the humility, the repentance, the aspiration which draw us to the Cross of Christ, that worshiping there in lowliness, we may see the weakness of falsehood and the strength of truth, the exceeding sinfulness of selfishness, and the beauty of love and sacrifice.

O Thou whose secret is with them that fear Thee, inspire us with that loyalty of soul, that willingness to do Thy will to which all things are clear. Darkness, we know, cometh upon the proud and disobedient; confusion is ever attendant upon self-will; while to the humble, the earnest, and the pure-minded, the way of duty and spiritual health is made clear. O Spirit of the Eternal, subdue within us all pride, all vain-glory, all self-seeking, and bring every thought and every desire into obedience to the law of Christ our Lord.

Almighty Father, to Thee would we consecrate these earthly days from infancy to age. Thee would we remember in childhood and youth. Thee would we serve in all the relations and activities of middle age. Thee would we teach our children to love and serve. Be Thou our stay and hope when health and strength shall fail. And when we are summoned hence, do Thou, O Life of our life, illumine the mystery of the invisible world with Thy presence and love. We ask these blessings in the spirit of Jesus Christ our Lord. Amen.—John Hunter.

Fourth Week, Sixth Day

The perversions of religious faith, working pitiable instead of benevolent consequences, are often seen on mission fields. Consider Paul's address in Athens:

And Paul stood in the midst of the Areopagus, and said, Ye men of Athens, in all things I perceive that ye are very religious. For as I passed along, and observed the objects of your worship, I found also an altar with this inscription, TO AN UNKNOWN GOD. What therefore ye worship in ignorance, this I set forth unto you. The God that made the world and all things therein, he, being Lord of heaven and earth, dwelleth not in temples made with hands; neither is he served by men's hands, as though he needed anything, seeing he himself giveth to all life, and breath, and all things; and he made of one every nation of men to dwell on all the face of the earth, having determined their appointed seasons, and the bounds of their habitation; that they should seek God, if haply they might feel after him and find him, though he is not far from each one of us: for in him we live, and move, and have our being; as certain even of your own poets have said,
For we are also his offspring.
—Acts 17:22-28.

Paul did not need to plead for religion with the Athenians; they were already "very religious." Only religion was not doing for them what it ought; it was a power used "in ignorance"; and Paul, valuing all that was good there, quoting their own poets with appreciation, neverthe-less longed to take their strong religious motives and so clarify and direct them that faith might mean unqualified benediction. Is not this always the right missionary method? The people of India are intensely religious; no tribe in Africa lacks its gods; and everywhere the faith-motive is immensely powerful. But often it makes mothers drown their babies in sacred rivers, it consecrates caste systems as holy things, it centers man's adoration around unworthy objects, its powers, gone wrong, are a curse and not a blessing. If in Jesus Christ religious faith has come to us, through no merit of our own, as an unspeakable benediction, ought we not, humbly, without dogmatism or intolerance, and yet with passionate earnestness, to share our best with all the world? Religious faith may either depress or lift a people's life; it is forever doing one or the other in every nation under heaven; and *there is no hope for the world until this master-motive is lifting everywhere.*

Almighty God, our Father in heaven, who hast so greatly loved the world that Thou hast given Thine only-begotten Son, the Redeemer, communicate Thy love to the hearts of all believers, and revive Thy Church to preach the Gospel to every creature.

O Thou who rulest by Thy providence over land and sea, defend and guide and bless the messengers of Christ; in danger be their shield, in darkness be their hope; enrich their word and work with wisdom, joy, and power, and let them gather souls for Thee in far fields white unto the harvest.

O Thou who by Thy Holy Spirit workest wonders in secret, open the eyes that dimly look for light to see the day-star in Christ; open the minds that seek the unknown God to know their Heavenly Father in Christ; open the hearts that hunger for righteousness to find eternal peace in Christ. Deliver the poor prisoners of ignorance and captives of idolatry, break down the bars of error, and dispel the shadows of the ancient night; lift up the gates and let the King of glory and the Prince of Peace come in.

Thy kingdom, O Christ, is an everlasting kingdom! Strengthen Thy servants to pray and labor and wait for its appearing; forgive our little faith and the weakness of our endeavor; hasten the day when all nations shall be at peace in

Thee, and every land and every heart throughout the world shall bless the name of the Lord Jesus, to the glory of God the Father. Amen.—Henry van Dyke.

Fourth Week, Seventh Day

The sad perversions of religious faith are not a matter for foreign missions only. At home, too, we find people who seem to be rather worse than better because they are religious. Just as power in any other form may be abused, so may religious faith. Some in the name of religion become censorious and intolerant, some superstitious, some slaves to morbid fears; and ignorance, self-conceit, pride, and worldly ambition when driven and enforced by a religious motive are infinitely worse than they would have been without it. Toward this fact two attitudes are possible. One is to throw over religion on account of its abuses; which is as reasonable as to deny all the blessings of electricity because in ignorant hands it is a dangerous power. The other is to take religious faith more seriously than ever, to see how great a force for weal or woe it always is in human life, and to strive in ourselves and in others for a high, intelligent, and worthy understanding and use of it. For religion can mean what Amiel said of it: "There is but one thing needful—to possess God. Religion is not a method: it is a life—a higher and supernatural life, mystical in its root and practical in its fruits; a communion with God, a calm and deep enthusiasm, a love which radiates, a force which acts, a happiness which overflows." From our study of the perversions and travesties of faith, we turn therefore in the weekly comment to consider faith's vital meaning. So Paul, writing to the Galatians, rejoices in religion as a gloriously transforming power in life.

But I say, Walk by the Spirit, and ye shall not fulfil the lust of the flesh. For the flesh lusteth against the Spirit, and the Spirit against the flesh; for these are contrary the one to the other; that ye may not do the things that ye would. But if ye are led by the Spirit, ye are not under the law. Now the works of the flesh are manifest, which are these: fornication, uncleanness, lasciviousness, idolatry, sorcery, enmities, strife, jealousies, wraths, factions, divisions, parties, envyings, drunkenness, revelings, and such like; of which I forewarn you even as I did forewarn you, that they who practise such things shall not inherit the kingdom of God. But the fruit of the Spirit is love, joy, peace, long-suffering, kindness, goodness, faithfulness, meekness, self-control; against such there is no law. And they that are of Christ Jesus have crucified the flesh with the passions and the lusts thereof.—Gal. 5:16-23.

Thou, O God, has exalted us so that no longer we walk with prone head among the animals that perish. Thou has ordained us as Thine own children, and has planted within us that spiritual life which ever seeks, as the flame, to rise upward and mingle with Thee. Every exaltation, every pure sentiment, all urgency of true affection, and all yearning after things higher and nobler, are testimonies of the divinity that is in us. These are the threads by which Thou art drawing us away from sense, away from the earth, away from things coarse and unspiritual, and toward the ineffable. We rejoice that we have in us the witness of the Spirit, the indwelling of God. For, although we are temples defiled, though we are unworthy of such a Guest, and though we perpetually grieve Thee, and drive Thee from us, so that Thou canst not do the mighty work that Thou wouldst within us, yet we rejoice to believe that Thou dost linger near us. Even upon the outside, Thou standest knocking at the door until Thy locks are wet with the night dews, and dost persuade us with the everlasting importunity of love, and draw us upward, whether with or without our own knowledge. Thou art evermore striving to imbue us with Thyself, and to give us that divine nature which shall triumph over time and sense and matter; and we pray that we may have an enlightened understanding of this Thy work in us and upon us, and work together with Thee. Amen.—Henry Ward Beecher.

COMMENT FOR THE WEEK

I

One might be tempted by the last chapter to suppose that, if he could accept the proposition that God is personal, he would be well upon his way toward Christianity. But in theory at least Plato accepted this proposition four hundred years before Christ, when he said: "God is never in any way unrighteous—He is perfect righteousness; and he of us who is most righteous is most like Him." He, too, used personality as a symbol of God. When, however, one compares Plato with Jesus, how incalculably greater is the religious meaning of our Lord! There is something more in the Master's experience and thought than the belief that God is personal. Evidently our quest must be followed further than the last chapter carried us.

In Scripture two kinds of faith in the personal God are clearly indicated. On the one side stand verses such as this: "Thou believest that God is one; thou doest well; the demons also believe and shudder" (James 2:19). On the other, one finds through both the Testaments witness and appeal for a kind of faith that plainly differs from the first: "O my God, in thee have I trusted" (Ps. 25:2). It is not difficult to guess the terms in which many would describe this difference. In the first, so the familiar explanation runs, we are dealing with the *mind's* faith in God; the man's intellect assents to the belief that God is and that He is one. In the second we are dealing with the *heart's* faith in God; the whole man is here involved in an adoring trust that finds in reliance upon God life's stimulus and joy.

This distinction between the faith of the intellect and of the heart is valid, but it does not go to the pith of the truth. When a professor in the classroom, discussing conflicting theories of life's origin, concludes that theism is the reasonable interpretation of the universe, the listener understands that the lecturer believes in God's existence. But if the professor could be followed home and overheard in a private prayer, like Fénelon's: "Lord, I know not what I ought to ask of Thee; Thou only knowest what I need; Thou lovest me better than I know how to love myself. O Father! give to Thy child that which he himself knows not how to ask," something incalculably more than the classroom talk disclosed would be revealed about the meaning of the teacher's faith. And as the classroom lecture and the private prayer stand so contrasted, the gist of the difference is plain. In the one, faith was directed toward a *theory;* in the other faith laid hold upon a *Person.* That the intellect was more involved in the first and the emotions in the second is incidental to the main matter, that *two differing objects were in view*. Toward these two objects we continually are exercising faith—*ideas and people, propositions and persons*.

Now faith in a proposition we conveniently may call belief; and faith in a person, trust. We believe that gravitation and the conservation of energy universally apply, that democracy will prove better than absolutism, and that prison systems can be radically reformed; these and innumerable other propositions that cannot be demonstrated we confidently believe. But in quite another way we daily are exercising faith; *we have faith in our friends*. How profound a change comes over the quality and value of faith when it thus finds its objective in a person! Our beliefs in propositions are of basic import and without them we could not well exist, but it is by trust in persons that we live indeed. Belief in monogamy, for all its importance, is a cold abstraction, and few could be found to die for it. Men do not lay down their lives for abstract theories, any more than they would suffer martyrdom, as Chesterton remarked, for the Meridian of Greenwich. But when monogamy is translated from theory into personal experience, when belief in the idea becomes trust in a life-long comrade of whom one may sing:

> "What I do
> And what I dream include thee, as the wine
> Must taste of its own grapes,"

faith has taken a form for which men do live and die in glad surrender. Although the same word, faith, be applied to both, trust in persons reaches deeper than belief in propositions and supplies a warmth and power that belief cannot attain.

In religion these two aspects of faith continually are found and both are indispensable. Trust in a person, for example, presupposes belief in his existence and fidelity. "He that cometh to God must believe that he is, and that he is a rewarder of them that seek after him" (Heb. 11:6). Trust cannot exist without belief, but when one seeks the inner glory of the religious life that has overflowed in prayer and hymn, supplied motive for service and power for character, he finds it not in belief, but in the vital relationships involved in trusting a Person. Men often have discussed their particular beliefs with cool deliberation, have stated them in formal creeds, have changed them with access of new knowledge and experience. But *trust,* the inner reliance of the soul on God and glad self-surrender to his will, has persisted through many changes, clothing itself with beliefs like garments and casting them aside when old. Trust has made rituals and churches and unmade them when they were ineffectual, it has been the life behind the theory, the experience behind the explanation; and its proper voice has been not creed and controversy, but psalm and song and sacrifice. Men have felt in describing this inward friendship that their best words were but the "vocal gestures of the dumb," able to indicate but unable to express their thoughts. *For while belief is theology, trust is religion.*

II

This central position of trust in the Christian life is evident when one considers that in its presence or absence lies the chief point of difference between a religious and an irreligious man. The peculiarity of religion is not that it has beliefs; everybody has them. As we have seen, Huxley, who called himself an agnostic, said that he thoroughly believed the universe to be rational, than which only a few greater ventures of faith can be imagined. A man may not want to have beliefs. He may say that knowledge is wool, warm to clothe oneself withall, that belief is cotton, and that he will not mingle them. But for all that he still does have beliefs and he cannot help it.

When, therefore, a Christian and an atheist converse they can match belief with belief. "I believe," says one, "in God the Father"; and "I believe," says the other, "in the eternal physical universe, without spiritual origin or moral purpose." Says the Christian, "I believe in the immortality of persons," and the atheist replies, "I believe that the spirit dies with the body as sound ceases when the bell's swinging iron grows still." Says the Christian, "I believe in the ultimate triumph of righteousness"; and the atheist replies, "I believe that all man's aspiration after good is but the endless sailing of a ship that never shall arrive." So the two may play battledore and shuttlecock, but if, so having paired beliefs, they part with no more said, they have missed the real point of their difference. The irreligious man can match the Christian's belief with his own, but one thing he cannot match—the Christian's trust. *He has nothing that remotely corresponds with that.*

The Christian always has this case to plead with an unbelieving man: Do not suppose that the difference between us is exhausted in a conflict of contrasting propositions. Great indeed is the divergence there! But the issue of all such difference lies in another realm. When you face life's abysmal mysteries that your eyes can no more pierce than mine, you have no one to trust. When misfortunes fall that send men to their graves, as Sydney Smith said, with souls scarred like a soldier's body, you have no one to trust. When you face the last mystery of all and whether going say farewell to those who stay, or staying bid farewell to those who go, you have no one to trust. You can match my belief with your belief, but for one thing you have no counterpart. "Jehovah is my shepherd, I shall not want" (Ps. 23:1). You cannot match that! "My heart hath trusted in him, and I am helped" (Ps. 28:7). You cannot match that! "Shall not the Judge of all the earth do right?" (Gen. 18:25); "We have our hope set on the living God" (I Tim. 4:10); "Father, into thy hands I commend my spirit" (Luke 23:46). That trust you cannot match!

III

In the light of this distinction between belief and trust some mistaken types of faith can be easily described. There, for example, is the *faith of formal creedalism.* We cannot have trust without some belief, but we may unhappily have belief without any trust. Now a man who believes the doctrines that underlie the Christian life but who does not vitally trust the Person whom those doctrines present, has missed the heart out of faith's meaning. He is like one who cherishes a letter of introduction to a great personality, but has never used it; he has the formal credentials, but not the transforming experience. It follows that we cannot estimate a man merely by knowing his beliefs. I believe in all the Christian truths, says one; and the curious question rises, how did these beliefs of his come into his possession? They may have been handed to him by his forbears like a set of family jewels, a static and external heritage, which now he keeps in some ecclesiastical safe-deposit vault and on state days, at Christmas or at Easter, goes to see. Still he may claim that they are his beliefs; he may even quarrel about their genuineness, not because he ever uses them but because they are his. He may repeat the creed with the same unquestioning assent that he gives to the conventional cut of his clothes. His beliefs are not the natural utterance and explanation of his inner life with God and man, but are put on as they were handed to him, like the fashions of his coats. So easy is it to be formally orthodox!

Over against such conventional believers one thinks of other folk whom he has known. They have no such stereotyped, clear-cut beliefs. They are very puzzled about life. It seems to them abysmally mysterious. And when they speak they talk with a modesty the formal creedalist has never felt: My beliefs are most uncertain. Confused by many voices shouting conflicting opinions about truths which I once accepted without thinking, I cannot easily define my thoughts. But I do trust God. That assent of the mind which I cannot give to propositions, I can give to him. Life is full of mystery, but I do not really think that the mystery is darkness at its heart. My faith has yet its standing ground in this, that the world's activities are not like the convulsions of an epileptic, unconscious and purposeless. There is a Mind behind the universe, and a good purpose in it.

> "Yet in the maddening maze of things,
>   And tossed by storm and flood,
> To one fixed trust my spirit clings;
>   I know that God is good."

Say as one may that such an attitude is far from adequate, yet as compared with the merely formal acceptance of inherited opinions how incomparably superior its religious value is!

The people of placid, stiff beliefs are not the successors of the real saints. When one reads George Matheson's books of devotion, for example, or sings his hymn "O Love, that wilt not let me go," or learns of his great work in his church in Edinburgh, one might suppose that he never had a doubt. Yet listen to his own confession: "At one time with a great thrill of horror, I found myself an absolute atheist. After being ordained at Innellan, I believed nothing; neither God nor immortality. I tendered my resignation to the Presbytery, but to their honor they would not accept it, even though a Highland Presbytery. They said I was a young man and would change. I have changed." One need only read such books of his as *Can the Old Faith Live with the New?* to see through what a searching discipline of strenuous thought he passed in the regaining of his faith. But if one would know what held his religious life secure while he was working out his beliefs from confusion to clarity, one must turn to Matheson's poem:

> "Couldst thou love *Me*
> When creeds are breaking—
> Old landmarks shaking
> With wind and sea?
> Couldst thou refrain the earth from quaking
> And rest thy heart on *Me?*"

Many a man has been held fast by his trust in God while in perplexity he thought out his beliefs about God.

Indeed, within the Scripture, whatever word is used to describe the attitude of faith, this vital personal alliance with God is everywhere intended. For convenience we have called faith in propositions belief, but that does not mean that when the Scriptures use "believe" they are urging the acceptance of propositions. Not often in the Bible are we invited merely to agree with an opinion; we are everywhere called to trust a Person. "Trust in the Lord" in the Old Testament, "Believe in the Lord Jesus Christ" in the New, are neither of them the proclamation of a theory, but the exaltation of a personality. Wherever in Scripture doctrines are insisted on—the unity of God, the deathlessness of the spirit, the divinity of Christ—they are never doctrines for their own sakes; *they are either commendatory truths about a Friend, that we may not fail to trust him, or they are ideas about life that have come to men because they did trust him. Trust in a Person is either the source or the goal of every Christian doctrine.* The Gospel at its center is not a series of propositions, but a concrete, personal relationship opened between the soul and the Divine, out of which new powers, joys, possibilities flow gloriously into human life. When out of this experience of divine fellowship Paul, for example, speaks of faith he means by it the alliance that binds him to his friend. He fairly sings of the peace that comes from such believing (Rom. 15:13), of the love that is its motive power and chief expression (Gal. 5:6), and of "the sacrifice and service" which are its issue (Phil. 2:17). He enthusiastically commends to everyone this divine alliance through which moral defeat is changed to victory in the "righteousness which is of God by faith" (Phil. 3:9); and his prose slips over into poetry when he describes his new transfigured life as "access by faith into that grace wherein we stand" (Rom. 5:2). Plainly he is not talking here about a set of propositions; he is rejoicing in a transforming personal relationship. Some faith is nothing but an inherited set of opinions and it gives a cold light like an incandescent bulb; some faith, like sunshine, is brighter for seeing than any incandescence can ever be, but warm too, so that under its persuasive touch new worlds of life spring into being. The faith of the New Testament and of the real saints is not the cold brilliance of a creed in whose presence one can freeze even while he sees; it is the warm, life-giving sunshine of a trust in God that makes all gracious things grow, and puts peace and joy, hope and love into life. Belief in propositions is there, but the crown and glory of it are trust in a Person.

IV

In the light of this distinction between belief and trust, the inadequacy of another type of faith can easily be understood. Many would protest that they have not accepted their beliefs as an external heritage from the past, but rather have thought them through, and hold them now as *reasonable theories to explain the facts of the spiritual life.* They would say that as a geologist observes the rocks and constructs an hypothesis to account for their origin and nature, so the mind, observing man's contacts with invisible powers, constructs religious beliefs as explanations of experience. They would insist that their theology is not merely traditional, but in large degree is independently appropriated and original. They hold it as an hypothesis to make intelligible man's experiences of the spiritual world.

There is significant truth in this view of faith. Man's ideals, his loves, hopes, aspirations, his unescapable sense of moral obligation, his consciousness of Someone other than himself, are facts, as solidly present in experience as stars and mountains. To explain these facts by theology is as rational as to explain the stars by astronomy. Every believer in religious truth should welcome this confirming word from Dr. Pritchett, written when he was President of the Massachusetts Institute of Technology: "Science is grounded in faith just as is religion, and scientific truth, like religious truth, consists of hypotheses, never wholly verified, that fit the facts more or less closely."

But when one turns from such a statement to inquire what faith has actually meant to religious men, he does not find that their experience could easily be defined as belief in an hypothesis. The prophets, standing their ground through national disaster, undiscourageable in their conviction of God's good purpose for His people, would have been surprised to hear their faith so described. When the Sons of Thunder were swept out into a new life by the influence of Jesus, or the seer of Patmos was ravished with visions of eternal victory, or Paul was made conqueror in a fight for character that had been his despair, they would hardly have spoken of their experiences as belief in an hypothesis. Real religion has always meant something more vital than holding a theory about life. When Robert Louis Stevenson says of his transformation of character, "I came about like a well-handled ship. There stood at the wheel that unknown steersman whom we call God"; when Tolstoi cries: "To know God and to live are one and the same thing"; when Professor William James, of Harvard, writes of his consciousness of God, "It is most indefinite to be sure and rather faint, and yet I know that if it should cease, there would be a great hush, a great void in my life"; one sees what conversion of character, what increase of life's value, what spiritual reenforcement religion has meant even to such unconventional believers. When they speak of it, they are evidently thinking of a vital power and not a theory.

The most obscure Christian to whom religion has become a necessity in living, knows how far short the plummet of hypothetical belief comes from reaching bottom. In sin, burdened by a sense of guilt that he could not shake off and unable to forgive himself, he has cried to be forgiven, and the Gospel that has been his hope was no injunction to hold hard by his hypothesis! In sorrow, when the blows have fallen that either hallow or embitter life, he has sought for necessary fortitude, and the Gospel which established him certainly was not, Cast thy care on thine hypothesis! And when, more than conqueror, he faces death, his confidence and hope will rest on no such prayer as this, O Hypothesis, guide me! The word of religion is of another sort, "Though I walk through the valley of the shadow of death, I will fear no evil, for *Thou* art with me." Not belief in propositions, but trust in a Person has been the heart of the Gospel, and to make any hypothesis, however true, do duty as religion is to give the soul a stone when it asks for bread.

The futility of seeking contentment in faith as an hypothesis alone is especially manifest in our time. This is an age of swiftly changing ideas in every realm. As in science, so in religion, today one theory holds the field to be displaced tomorrow by another. A man in theology, as much as in politics or psychology, goes to bed supposing he has settled his opinions, and wakes up to find a new array of evidence that disturbs his confidence. When, therefore, religious faith has meant no more to its possessor than theory, there is no security or rest. Each day the winds of opinion shift and veer, and minds at the beginning obstinate in their beliefs, at last, dismayed by the reiterated uncertainties of thought, give up their faith.

Where, then, have the men of faith found the immovable center of their confidence? Paul revealed the secret. On the side of his particular opinions he frankly confessed his limited and uncertain knowledge. "Now we know in fragments," he wrote, "now we see through a glass darkly."

"How unsearchable are his judgments and his ways past tracing out!" But on the side of his trust he is adamant: "I know *him* whom I have believed." The certainty of his life was his relationship with a person, and his beliefs were the best he yet had thought in the explication and establishment of that trust.

The great believers of the Church continually have exhibited this dual aspect of their faith. Even St. Augustine, facing the profound mysteries involved in his trinitarian belief, complains that human speech is pitiably futile in trying to explain what "Three persons" means, and that if he uses the familiar phrase, he does so not because he likes it, but because he may not be silent and knows no better thing to say. But when Augustine prays to God whose nature is so unfathomable that no man can see it fully or express it adequately, he reveals no such uncertain thought: "Grant me, even me, my dearest Lord, to know Thee and love Thee and rejoice in Thee. . . . Let the love of Thee grow every day more and more here, that it may be perfect hereafter; that my joy may be great in itself and full in Thee. I know, O God, that thou art a God of truth; O make good Thy gracious promises to me!" So children do not fully understand an earthly father and often hold conceptions grotesquely insufficient to do justice to his life and work. But they may have for him well-founded trust. Even in the years of infancy an ennobling personal relationship begins, despite the inadequacy of their beliefs, and that trust yearly deepens while mental concepts shift and change with access of new knowledge. *The abiding core of a child's life with his father is not belief but trust.*

Such has always been the secret of faith's stability in men who have entered into personal fellowship with God. Even of the first disciples it has been said—"They would have had difficulty sometimes to tell you *what* they believed, but they could always have told you in *whom* they believed."

V

The truth of which we have been speaking has pertinent bearing on the main object of our studies. We shall be considering the difficulties which Christians have with their beliefs, and the arguments which may clarify and establish our minds' confidence in God. But many problems in the realm of intellectual belief cannot be solved by any arguments which the mind devises. The trouble often lies not in our theories about the religious life, but in our religious life itself. *The deeper difficulty is not that our thinking is unreasonable, but that our experience is unreal.*

To a man who never had seen the stars or felt the wonder of their distances, astronomy would be a lifeless topic and his endeavors to think about it a blundering and futile operation. Our theories about anything depend for their interest and worth upon the vividness with which we experience the thing itself and care to understand its meaning. This is true about matters like the stars; how much more true about the intimate affairs of man's own life! Democracy vs. autocracy is a crucial problem. But plenty of men are so careless about human weal, think so little of their country and the world as objects of solicitude and devotion, that to discuss in their presence democratic and autocratic theories of state is a waste of time. The trouble is not with their minds; they may be very clever and acute. The trouble is with their lives. They need to experience patriotism as a vital motive; they need to care immensely what happens to mankind. Only then will the problems of government grow vivid, and the need of a solution become so critical that thinking will be urgent and productive. We never think well about anything for which we do not care.

Plenty of people today discuss theology as an academic pastime. It is a speculative game at which they play, as they do at golf, for its fun and lure. They do not really care about God; they feel no crucial need of him. Of little use is all their ingenuity in argument, clever and astute though it may be. Blind men might so discuss the color sceme of an Italian landscape and deaf men debate the harmonies of Handel's oratorios. What is lacking is experience. For our theories are only the explanations of experience, and an emptier game cannot be played than debating explanations of experiences which we have not had.

Everyone in difficulty with his faith should give due weight to this important truth. Our intellectual troubles are not all caused by the bankruptcy of our spiritual lives, but many of them are. Men live with drained and unreplenished spirits, from which communion with God and service of high causes have been crowded out. God grows unreal. The self-evidencing experiences that maintain vital confidence in the spiritual life grow dim and unimperative. Men pass years without habitually thinking as though God really were, without making any great decisions as though God's will were King, without engaging in any sacrificial work that makes the thought of God a need and a delight, without the companionship of great ideas or the sustenance of prayer. Then, when experience is denuded of any sense of God's reality, some intellectual doubt is suggested by books or friends, or fearful trouble shatters happiness. What recourse is there in such a case? The arguments of faith have no experience to get their grip upon; they can appeal to no solid and sustained fact of living. Religious confidence goes to pieces and men tell their friends that modern philosophy has been too much for faith. But the underlying difficulty was not philosophical; it was vital. The insolvency of "belief" was due to the bankruptcy of "trust." Personal fellowship with God failed first; the theory about him lapsed afterward.

Throughout our endeavor to deal with intellectual perplexity, this fundamental truth should not be forgotten. *The peril of religion is that vital experience shall be resolved into a formula of explanation, and that men, grasping the formula, shall suppose themselves thereby to possess the experience.* If one inquires what air is, the answer will probably be a formula stating that oxygen and nitrogen mixed in proportions of twenty-one to seventy-nine make air. But air in experience is not a formula. Air is the elixir we breathe and live thereby. Air is the magician who takes the words that our lips frame and bears them from friend to friend in daily converse. Air is the messenger who carries music to our ears and fragrance to our nostrils; it is the whisperer among the trees in June, and in March the wild dancer who shakes the bare branches for his castanets. Air is the giant who piles the surf against the rocky shore, and the nurse who fans the faces of the sick. One cannot put that into a formula. No more can God be put into a theology, however true. They who define him best may understand him least. God is the Unseen Friend, the Spiritual Presence, who calls us in ideals, warns us in remorse, renews us with his pardon, and comforts us with power. God is the Spirit of Righteousness in human life, whose victories we see in every moral gain, and allied with whom we have solid hopes of moral victory. God is the One who holds indeed the far stars in his hand, and yet in fellowship with whom each humblest son of man may find strength to do and to endure with constancy and fortitude and deathless hope. And when one lives close to him, so that the inner doors swing easily on quiet hinges to let him in, he is the One who illumines life with a radiance that human wills alone cannot attain. That is God—"Blessed is the man that taketh refuge in him" (Ps. 34:8).

CHAPTER V

Faith's Intellectual Difficulties

DAILY READINGS

Most people will readily grant that such a sense of personal fellowship with God as last week's study presented is obviously desirable. Every one who has experienced such filial life with God will bear witness to its incomparable blessing. Said Tennyson, "I should be sorely afraid to live my life without God's presence, but to feel he is by my side just now as much as you are, that is the very joy of my heart." But many who would admit the desirability of the experience are troubled about the reasonableness of the beliefs that underlie it. They want intellectual assurance about their faith. Let us in the daily readings present certain considerations which a mind so perplexed should take into account.

Fifth Week, First Day

We should let no one deny our right to bring religious belief to the test of reasonableness. Glanvill was right when in the seventeenth century he said, "There is not anything I know which hath done more mischief to Religion than the disparaging of Reason." In the New Testament Paul says:

Prove all things; hold fast that which is good.—I Thess. 5:21.

Peter says:

Yea, and for this very cause adding on your part all diligence, in your faith supply virtue; and in your virtue knowledge.—II Pet. 1:5.

This might be paraphrased to read, Faith should be *worked out* into character and *thought through* into knowledge. As for Jesus:

One of the scribes came, and heard them questioning together, and knowing that he had answered them well, asked him, What commandment is the first of all? Jesus answered, The first is, Hear, O Israel; The Lord our God, the Lord is one: and thou shalt love the Lord thy God with all thy heart, and with all thy soul, and with all thy mind, and with all thy strength.—Mark 12:28-30.

In many a life which has neglected these admonitions Lowell's words have proved true: "Nothing that keeps thought out is safe from thought." In our resolute endeavor to think through the mystery of life, however, and to find a reasonable basis for faith, we need to remember that *the very desire to know is indication of the reality which we seek.* The dim intuition that the world with all its diverse powers was in some sense a unity, preceded by ages the statement of nature's uniformity which modern science knows; and man's tireless desire to reach a reasonable statement of the unity was an intimation in advance that unity was there. So men do not believe in God because they have proved him; they rather strive endlessly to prove him because they cannot help being sure that he must be there. This in itself is an intimation about reality which no thoughtful man will lightly set aside. Tennyson rightly describes the reason for man's quest after proof about God:

"If e'er when faith had fallen asleep,
    I heard a voice 'believe no more'
    And heard an ever-breaking shore
That tumbled in the Godless deep;

A warmth within the breast would melt
    The freezing reason's colder part,
    And like a man in wrath the heart
Stood up and answer'd 'I have felt.' "

Eternal Father, Quest of ages, long sought, oft doubled or forsook; can it be that Thou art known to us, the Law within our minds, the Life of every breath we draw, the Love that yearneth in our hearts? Art Thou the Spirit who oft hast striven with us, and when we greatly feared, lest yielding to His strong embrace we should become more than we dared to be?

An impulse toward forgiveness has sometimes stirred within us, we have felt moved to show mercy, the sacrificial life has touched our aspiration; but we were unprepared to pay the price. Was this Thyself, and have we turned from Thee? Something like this we must have done, so barren, joyless and so dead has life become. Canst Thou not visit us again?

We hush our thoughts to silence, we school our spirits in sincerity, and here we wait. O may we not feel once more the light upon our straining eyes, the tides of life rise again within our waiting hearts?

We never looked to meet Thee in the stress of thought, the toil of life, or in the call of duty; we only knew that somehow life had lost for us all meaning, dignity, and beauty. How then shall we turn back again and see with eyes that fear has filmed? How can we be born again, now grown so old in fatal habit?

If we could see this life of ours lived out in Thee, its common days exalted, its circumstances made a throne, its bitterness, disappointment, and failure all redeemed, then our hearts might stir again, and these trembling hands lay hold on life for evermore. Amen.—W. E. Orchard.

Fifth Week, Second Day

Not only is man's tireless quest for assurance about God an intimation that God must be here to be sought after; but *the spiritual nature of man which insists on the quest is itself a revelation that God actually is here.* Some men say that our spiritual life is the result of evolution, and they suppose that by this magic word they have explained it. But what comes out of a process of growth was somehow latent in the Original Beginning from which the growth started. Palm trees do not grow from acorns; only oaks evolve from acorns and for the sufficient reason that oaks are somehow *involved in acorns* to start with. So a universe with spiritual life in it naturally presupposes an Original with spiritual life in It. Whatever evolves must first of all have been involved. The very fact that the seeker after God has a spiritual life, which is restless and unsatisfied without faith in the Eternal Spirit, is one of the clearest indications that, whatever else may be said about the source of life, it must be spiritual. The Nile for ages was a mystery; it flowed through Egypt—a blessed necessity to the land, enriching the soil, and sustaining the people—but nobody knew its source. Long before Victoria Nyanza was discovered, however, thinkers were sure that a great lake must be the explanation of the stream; and when at last they found the sources of the Nile, the lake was even greater than anyone had dreamed. So is man's spirit a revelation of a spiritual origin even before that origin is clearly known. As the Bible puts it:

Now he that wrought us for this very thing is God, who gave unto us the earnest of the Spirit.—II Cor. 5:5.

O God! mysterious and Infinite, Thou art the first and Thou the last: as our weeks pass away and our age rises or declines, we still return to Thee who ever art the same. We seek Thee as the sole abiding light amid the shadows of perishable things. O Thou most ancient God! to whom the heavens are but of yesterday, and the life of worlds but as the shooting star, there is no number of Thy days and mercies; and what can we do, O Lord, but throw ourselves on Thee who failest not, and from whom our pathway is not hid? With solemn and open heart we would meet Thee here. Cover not Thyself with a cloud, most High, but may our prayer pass through.

O Thou our constant Witness and our awful Judge! When we remember our thoughtless lives, our low desires, our impatient temper, our ungoverned wills, we know that Thou has left us without excuse. For Thou hast not made us blind, O Lord, as the creatures that have no sin; nor hast Thou spared the light of holy guidance. Thy still small voice of warning whispers through our deepest conscience; and Thine open Word hath dwelt among us, full of grace and truth, and called us to the feet of Christ to choose the better part. We are not our own, and are ashamed to have lived unto ourselves. Thou hast formed us for Thy service, and we must hide our face that we have shrunk from the glorious hardships of our task, and slumbered on our holy watch. Our daily work has not been wrought in Thy sight; and we have not made the outgoings of the morning and the evening to praise Thee. The trials of our patience we have received as earthly pains of nature, not as the heavenly discipline of faith; and the fulness of Thy bounties has come to us as dead comfort, not as the quickening touch of Thy everlasting love. O our true and only God! we have lived in a bondage of the world that bringeth no content; and the passions we serve are as strange idols that cannot deliver. Awake, awake, O Arm of the Lord! and burst our bonds in sunder; and help the spirit that struggles within us to turn unto Thee with a pure heart, and serve Thee in newness of spirit. Amen.—James Martineau.

Fifth Week, Third Day

Many stumble at the very beginning of their quest for God, because they are sure that finite mind can never know the Infinite. The Bible itself asserts that God is in one sense unknowable.

Touching the Almighty, we cannot find him out.—Job 37:23.

Man cannot find out the work that God hath done from the beginning even to the end.—Eccles. 3:11.

O the depth of the riches both of the wisdom and the knowledge of God! how unsearchable are his judgments, and his ways past tracing out! For who hath known the mind of the Lord? or who hath been his counsellor?—Rom. 11:33-34.

But in the same sense in which God is unknowable, all the most important realities with which we deal are also beyond our comprehension. We do not know what electricity is, what matter is, what life is. Ether is utterly beyond the reach of our definitions, and an English scientist calls it "unknown, impalpable, the necessary condition of scientific thought." As for the constituent elements of the material world, we are told that atoms are so infinitesimally minute as to be indivisible, and yet that an "electron ranges about in the atom as a mouse might in a cathedral." The plain fact is that in any realm, human knowledge soon runs off into an unknown region where it deals with invisible realities, which it cannot define, but on which life is based. While therefore we do not know what electricity, ether, electrons, and life itself *are*, we do know them well *in their relationship with our needs*. So we may know God. Deep beyond deep in him will be past our fathoming, but what God means in his relationships with our lives we may know gloriously.

O Thou who transcendest all thought of Thee as the heavens are higher than the earth; we acknowledge that we cannot search Thee out to perfection, but we thank Thee that Thou, the Invisible, comest to us in the things that are seen; that Thy exceeding glory is shadowed in the flower that blooms for a day, in the light that fades; that Thine infinite love has been incarnate in lowly human life; and that Thy presence surrounds all our ignorance, Thy holiness our sin, Thy peace our unrest.

Give us that lowly heart which is the only temple that can contain the infinite. Save us from the presumption that prides itself on a knowledge which is not ours, and from the hypocrisy and carelessness which professes an ignorance which Thy manifestation has made for ever impossible. Save us from calling ourselves by a name that Thou alone canst wear, and from despising the image of Thyself Thou hast formed us to bear, and grant that knowledge of Thee revealed in Jesus Christ which is our eternal life. Amen.— W. E. Orchard.

Fifth Week, Fourth Day

The assurance of God may come in part from looking outward at his creation. This universe seems superficially to be material, but really it is *saturated with the presence of mind*. So a city's streets, buildings, bridges, subways, and railroads might appear to careless thought grossly material; but the fact is that in their origin they all are *mental*. They are not simply iron and steel and stone; they are thought, plan, purpose materialized and made visible. The basic fact about them is that mind shaped them and permeates every use to which they are put. The most important and decisive force in their origination was not anything that can be seen, but the invisible thought that dreamed them and molded them. So when one looks at creation he finds something more than matter; he finds order, law, uniformity; his mind is at home in tracing regularities, discovering laws, and perceiving purposes. Creation is not grossly material; it is saturated with the evidence of mind. Lord Kelvin, the chemist, walking in the country with Liebig, his fellow-scientist, asked his companion if he believed that the grass and flowers grew by mere chemical forces; and Liebig answered, "No, more than I could believe that the books of botany describing them could grow by mere chemical forces."

Lift up your eyes on high, and see who hath created thee, that bringeth out their host by number; he calleth them all by name; by the greatness of his might, and for that he is strong in power, not one is lacking.

Why sayest thou, O Jacob, and speakest, O Israel, My way is hid from Jehovah, and the justice to me is passed away from my God? Hast thou not known? hast thou not heard? The everlasting God, Jehovah, the Creator of the ends of the earth, fainteth not, neither is weary; there is no searching of his understanding. He giveth power to the faint; and to him that hath no might he increaseth strength. Even the youths shall faint and be weary, and the young men shall utterly fall: but they that wait for Jehovah shall renew their strength; they shall mount up with wings as eagles; they shall run, and not be weary; they shall walk, and not faint.—Isa. 40:26-31.

O Thou Infinite Perfection, who art the soul of all things that are . . . we thank Thee for the world of matter whereon we live, wherewith our hands are occupied, and whereby our bodies are builded up and filled with food and furnished with all things needful to enjoy. We thank Thee for the calmness of Night, which folds Thy children in her arms, and rockest them into peaceful sleep, and when we wake we thank Thee

127

that we are still with Thee. We bless Thee for the heavens over our head, arched with loveliness, and starred with beauty, speaking in the poetry of nature the psalm of life which the spheres chant before Thee to every listening soul.

We thank Thee for this greater and nobler world of spirit wherein we live, whereof we are, whereby we are strengthened, upheld, and blessed. We thank Thee for the wondrous powers which Thou hast given to man, that Thou hast created him for so great an estate, that thou hast enriched him with such noble faculties of mind and conscience and heart and soul, capable of such continual increase of growth and income of inspiration from Thyself. We thank Thee for the wise mind, for the conscience, for the loving heart, and the soul which knows Thee as Thou art, and enters into communion with Thy spirit, rejoicing in its blessing from day to day. Amen.—Theodore Parker.

Fifth Week, Fifth Day

The vital assurance of faith always comes, not so much from observing the outer world, as from appreciating the meaning of man's inner life. Man knows that he is something more than a physical machine. Theorists may say that our minds are only a series of molecular changes in the brain; but man turns to ask: *Who is it that is watching these molecular changes? The very fact that we can discuss them, is proof that we are something more than they are and of another order.* Leslie Stephen was an agnostic, but at the thought of man as merely a physical machine he grew impatient. "I knock down a man and an image," he said, "both fall down because both are material. But when the man gets up and knocks me down, the result is not explicable by any merely mechanical action." Man denies his own inward consciousness of self when he refuses to acknowledge the mental and spiritual part of him as the thing he really is. Man may have a body, but he surely is a soul. And when man lets this highest part of him speak its own characteristic word, he always hears a message like this: I am spirit; to grow into great character is the one worthy end of my existence; but how came I to be spirit with spiritual purpose unless my Creator is of like quality? and how can I believe that my existence and my purpose are not a cruel joke unless I am begotten by a Spiritual Life that will sustain my strength and crown my effort? To believe that man's soul is a foundling, laid on the doorstep of a merely physical universe, crying in vain for any father who begot him or any mother who conceived him, is to make our highest life a liar. Therefore man at his best has always believed in God.

For as many as are led by the Spirit of God, these are the sons of God. For ye received not the spirit of bondage again unto fear; but ye received the spirit of adoption, whereby we cry, Abba, Father. The Spirit himself beareth witness with our spirit, that we are children of God.—Rom. 8:14-16.

O Thou whom no name can tell, whom all our thoughts cannot fully comprehend, we rejoice in all Thy goodness. . . . We thank Thee for our body, this handful of dust so curiously and wonderfully framed together. We bless Thee for this sparkle of Thy fire that we call our soul, which enchants the dust into thoughtful human life, and blesses us with so rich a gift. We thank Thee for the varied powers Thou has given us here on earth. We bless Thee for the far reaching mind, which puts all things underneath our feet, rides on the winds and the waters, and tames the lightning into useful service. . . . We thank Thee for this conscience, whereby face to face we commune with Thine everlasting justice. We thank Thee for the strength of will which can overpower the weakness of mortal flesh, face danger and endure hardship, and in all things acquit us like men. . . .

We thank Thee for this religious sense, whereby we know Thee, and, amid a world of things that perish, lay fast hold on Thyself, who alone art steadfast, without beginning of days or end of years, forever and forever still the same. We thank Thee that amid all the darkness of time, amid joys that deceive us and pleasures that cheat, amid the transgressions we commit, we can still lift up our hands to Thee, and draw near Thee with our heart, and Thou blessest us still with more than a father's or a mother's never-ending love. Amen.— Theodore Parker.

Fifth Week, Sixth Day

One ground of assurance concerning faith is the way a sincere fellowship with God affects life. In a delicious passage of his autobiography, Benjamin Franklin says, "I was scarce fifteen, when, after doubting by turns of several points, as I found them disputed in the different books I read, I began to doubt of Revelation itself. Some books against Deism fell into my hands; they were said to be the substance of sermons preached at Boyle's Lectures. It happened that they wrought an effect on me quite contrary to what was intended by them; for the arguments of the Deists which were quoted to be refuted, appeared to me much stronger than the refutations; in short I soon became a thorough Deist. My arguments perverted some others, particularly Collins and Ralph; but, each of them having afterwards wrong'd me greatly without the least compunction, and recollecting Keith's conduct towards me (who was another free thinker), and my own towards Vernon and Miss Read, which at times gave me great trouble, I began to suspect that this doctrine, tho' it might be true, was not very useful." Many men, not yet able to see clearly the issue of conflicting arguments, are practically convinced in favor of faith by the relative effects on life of faith and unbelief. When one carries this thought out until he imagines a world where no one any more believes in God, he feels even more emphatically the negative results of unbelief. As Sir James Stephen said, "We cannot judge of the effects of Atheism from the conduct of persons who have been educated as believers in God, and in the midst of a nation which believes in God. If we should ever see a generation of men to whom the word God has no meaning at all, we should get a light on the subject which might be lurid enough." A practical working conviction is often gained in religion, as in every other realm, not by argument, but by acting on a principle until it verifies itself by its results, or, as in Benjamin Franklin's case, by trying a negation until one is driven from it by its consequences.

Beware of false prophets, who come to you in sheep's clothing, but inwardly are ravening wolves. By their fruits ye shall know them. Do men gather grapes of thorns, or figs

of thistles? Even so every good tree bringeth forth good fruit; but the corrupt tree bringeth forth evil fruit. A good tree cannot bring forth evil fruit, neither can a corrupt tree bring forth good fruit. Every tree that bringeth not forth good fruit is hewn down, and cast into the fire. Therefore by their fruits ye shall know them.—Matt. 7:15-20.

O God, who remainest the same though all else fades, who changest not with our changing moods, who leavest us not when we leave Thee; we thank Thee that when we lose faith in Thee, soon or late we come to faith in something that leads us back again with firmer trust and more sincerity. Even if we wander into the far country we take ourselves with us; ourselves who are set towards Thee as rivers to the sea. If we turn to foolishness, our hearts grow faint and weary, our path is set with thorns, the night overtakes us, and we find we have strayed from light and life.

Grant to us clearer vision of the light which knows no shade of turning, that we stray not in folly away; incline our hearts to love the truth alone, so that we miss Thee not at last; give us to realize of what spirit we are, so that we cleave ever to Thee, who alone can give us rest and joy. Amen.—W. E. Orchard.

Fifth Week, Seventh Day

When all is said and done in the matter of intellectual assurance, many are confused by the seeming lack of finality in the result. After all these ages of debate, they say, see all the innumerable opinions of jarring sects about religious truth! Evidently there is no satisfying conclusion obtainable at all! But look at the innumerable schools of medicine—shall one on their account decide that health is a fruitless study? Consider the infinite variety of taste in food—shall we say that therefore hunger and its satisfaction is a futile question to discuss? Rather, the very variety of the answers in man's quest reveals the importance of the quest itself. Of course proof of God lacks the finalty of a scientific demonstration, and this is true *because it moves in a realm so much more important than anything that science touches*. Exactness and finality are possible only in the least important realms. One can measure and analyze and describe to a minute nicety a table which a carpenter has made, but when one turns to the carpenter himself and endeavors to analyze his motives, weigh his thoughts, estimate his quality, and prove his purposes, one drops minute nicety at once. The carpenter is not to be put into a column of figures and added with mathematical precision as his table is. The farther up one moves in the scale the less precise and undeniable do his conclusions become. So science is exact just because it deals with measurable things; but religion, by as much as its realm is more important, can less easily pack its conclusions into neat parcels finally tied up and sealed. A man who will not believe anything which is not precisely demonstrable must eliminate from his life everything except what yardsticks can measure and scales can weigh. Let no man ever give up the fight for faith because he does not seem at once to be reaching an answer which he can neatly formulate. Let him remember Tolstoi, writing on his birthday: "I am twenty-four, and I have not done a thing yet. But I feel that not in vain have I been struggling for nearly eight years against doubt and temptation. For what am I destined? This only the future will disclose."

Hear, O Jehovah, when I cry with my voice:
Have mercy also upon me, and answer me.
When thou saidst, Seek ye my face; my heart said unto thee,
Thy face, Jehovah, will I seek.
Hide not thy face from me;
Put not thy servant away in anger:
Thou hast been my help;
Cast me not off, neither forsake me, O God of my salvation.
When my father and my mother forsake me,
Then Jehovah will take me up.
Teach me thy way, O Jehovah;
And lead me in a plain path,
Because of mine enemies.
Deliver me not over unto the will of mine adversaries:
For false witnesses are risen up against me,
And such as breathe out cruelty.
I had fainted, unless I had believed to see the goodness of Jehovah

In the land of the living.
Wait for Jehovah:
Be strong, and let thy heart take courage;
Yea, wait thou for Jehovah.

—Ps. 27:7-13.

Deliver us, our Father, from all those mists which do arise from the low places where we dwell, which rise up and hide the sun, and the stars even, and Thee. Deliver us from the narrowness and the poverty of our conceptions. Deliver us from the depotism of our senses. And grant unto us this morning, the effusion of Thy Spirit, which shall bring us into the realm of spiritual things, so that we may, by the use of all that which is divine in us, rise into the sphere of Thy thought, into the realm where Thou dwellest, and whither have trooped from the ages the spirits of just men now made perfect. Grant, we pray Thee, that we may not look with time-eyes upon eternal things, measuring and dwarfing with our imperfectness the fitness and beauty of things heavenly. So teach us to come into Thy presence and to rise by sympathy into Thy way of thinking and feeling, that so much as we can discern of the invisible may come to us aright. Amen.—Henry Ward Beecher.

COMMENT FOR THE WEEK

I

While it is true that in many cases the apparent unreasonableness of Christian faith springs from the underlying unreality of Christian life, this is not always a sufficient diagnosis of doubt. Horace G. Hutchinson, the English golfer, who spent much of his life in agnosticism and has now come over into Christian faith, thus interprets the spirit of his long unbelief: "All the while I had the keenest consciousness of the comfort that one would gain could he but believe in the truth of the Christian promises. Surely that must always be the agnostic's mood. . . . It is not that they wilfully reject the appeal to the heart; their will is eager to respond to it. But man has his gift of reason;

it cannot be that he is not intended to use it. Least of all can it be part of the great design that he should suspend its use in regard to the most important subject to which his thought can be directed."

Such sincere intellectual difficulties with faith must be met with intellectual arguments and not with moral accusations. Plenty of folk of elevated character and admirable lives grant, sometimes impatiently, that the Christian faith is beautiful—but is it so? Is not its solacing power a deceptive sleight of hand, by which our pleasing fancies and desires are made to look like truth? So a mirage is beautiful to weary travelers, but their temporary comfort rests on fallacy. McTaggart summed up one of the most widespread and masterful desires of this generation when he said, "What people want is a religion they can believe to be true."

As one sets himself to meet faith's intellectual difficulties, the attitude in which he is to approach the problem is all important. Samuel M. Crothers tells us that a young man once left with him a manuscript for criticism, and remarked in passing, "It is only a little bit of my work, and it will not take you long to look it over. In fact it is only the first chapter in which I explain the Universe." When one outgrows this cocksure presumption of youth and gains a graver and more seasoned mind, he leaves behind the attempt to pierce to creation's last secret. He sees that we can no more neatly and finally demonstrate God than we can demonstrate any of life's important faiths.

Moreover proof of God, as a theorem in philosophy, is not a deep human need. Men often have supposed that they had such demonstration, but human experience was little affected by the fact. The exhaustless source of mankind's desire for assurance about God is not theoretical curiosity but vital need, and until a man feels the need, sees how urgently man's highest life reaches out toward God, he never will make much of any arguments. Browning's bishop asks his friend:

> "Like you this Christianity or not?
> It may be false, but will you wish it true?
> Has it your vote to be so if it can?"

Until a man gives an affirmative answer to that inquiry, until he possesses a life that itself suggests God and wants him, he is not likely to arrive anywhere by argument alone.

This is not the case with Christianity only. We cannot prove with theoretical finality that monogamy is the form of family life to which the universe is best adapted. But mankind, trying many experiments with family life, has found in the monogamous family values unique and indispensable. It is because men feel the value of such a lovebond, that they begin to argue for it. And their argument, when one sees deeply into it, is framed after this fashion: We know the *worth* of this family-life of faithful lovers. We want monogamy and we propose to have it. We do not pretend that our faith in monogamy, as the form of marriage best fitted this universe, is capable of exact demonstration; but we do see arguments of great weight in favor of it and we do not see any convincing arguments against it. We are persuaded that our faith has reasonable right of way; and we propose to go on believing in monogamy and practicing it and combating its enemies, until we prove our case in the only way such cases ever can be finally proved, by the issue of the matter in the end.

So men come into the sort of personal and social life itself—its ideals of character, friendship, service, trust. If honesty allows, they propose to live that life. When a man has gone far enough in Christian experience, so that he comes up to his intellectual difficulties by such a road, he is likely to profit by a consideration of the reasons in favor of faith. He is in the attitude of saying: I have found great living in Christ. No argument for the Christian experience can be quite so convincing as the Christian experience itself. I am bound to have that life if I honestly can, and I will search to see whether there is any insuperable intellectual difficulty in the way of it.

II

One of the initial perplexities of faith concerns the sort of intellectual assurance which we have a right to expect. In a laboratory of physics, the investigator gathers facts, makes inductions as to their laws, and then verifies his findings. He uses a simplicity of procedure and gains a finality of result that makes all other knowledge seem relatively insecure. To be sure, the scientist may seek long for his truth and make many ineffectual guesses that prove false, but, in the end, he reaches a conclusion so demonstrable that every man of wit enough to investigate the subject must agree that it is so. How the Christian wishes for such certainty concerning God!

Before, however, any one surrenders confidence in God, because confessedly the affirmations of religious faith cannot be established by such methods as a physicist employs, there is ample reason for delay. We are certain that heat expands and cold contracts, and we can prove the fact and state its laws. But are we not also sure that it is wrong to lie and right to tell the truth? This conviction about truthfulness at least equals in theoretical certainty and in practical right to determine conduct, our confidence in heat's expanding power. This conviction about truthfulness does actually sway life more than does any single scientific truth that one can name. Let us then set ourselves to prove our moral confidence by such methods as the physical laboratory can supply—with yardsticks, and Troy weight scales, and test tubes, and meters! At once it is evident that if we are to hold only such truth as is amenable to the demonstration of a laboratory, we must bid farewell to every *moral conviction* that hitherto has influenced our lives. God, banished because the physicist cannot prove him, will have good company in exile!

Moreover, all our *esthetic convictions* will have to share that banishment. We know that some things are beautiful. The consensus of the race's judgment has not so much agreed to accept the new astronomy as it has agreed to think sunrise glorious and snow-capped mountains wonderful. Take from our lives our judgments on beauty, so that we may call no music marvelous, no poetry inspiring, no scenery sublime, and some of the most intimate and assured convictions we possess will have to go. A man who has seen the Matterhorn at dawn, when the first shaft of light reaches its rocky pinnacle and streams down in glory over the glaciers that cape its shoulders, will not disbelieve the splendor of the scene, though all the world beside unanimously should cry that it is not beautiful. But prove it by the methods of a laboratory? When the geologist has analyzed all the mountain's rocks, the chemist all its minerals; when the astronomer has traced the earth's orbit that brings on the dawn, and the physicist has counted and tabulated the rays of light that make the colors, our conviction of the scene's beauty will be as little explained or proved as is our confidence in God. It becomes clear that some convictions which we both do and must hold are not amenable to the sort of proof which a scientific laboratory furnishes.

Moreover, if we will have no truth beyond the reach of a physicist's demonstration, all our *convictions in the realm of personal relationship* will have to go. We *know* that friendship-love is the crown of every human fellowship. Father and son, mother and daughter, brother and sister, wife and husband—these relationships are in themselves bare branches wanting the foliage and fruit of friendship. Of no truth is man at his best more sure than he is that "Life is just our chance o' the price of learning love." But no laboratory ever can deal with such a truth, much less establish it. For this is the neglected insight, for the want of which our religious confidence is needlessly unstable: *Every realm of reality has its own appropriate kind of proof, and a method of proof available in one realm is seldom, if ever, usable in another.* That truthfulness is right is in a way provable, but methods proper to the moral realm must be allowed; that the Matterhorn is sublime is in a sense provable, but by methods which the esthetic realm permits; that love is the crown of life can be soundly established, but one must employ a method appropriate to personal relationships. If, obsessed by the procedure of a laboratory as the solitary path to knowledge, one will have no convictions which cannot meet its tests, then in good logic there must be a great emigration from his soul. All his convictions about morals and beauty, all his convictions about personal friendships and about God must leave together. He will have a depopulated spirit. No man could live on such terms for a single hour. The most essential and valuable equipment of our souls is in convictions which the demonstrations of a physicist can as little reach as an inchworm, clambering up the Himalayas, can measure the distance to the sun.

III

A man to whom the Christian life has come to be preeminently valuable, and who is asking whether it is intellectually justifiable, is set free, by such considerations as we just have noted, to seek assurance where religious assurance may properly be found. For one thing, he may find help by *trying out the creed of no-God.* Many a man is a wavering believer, makes little excursions into doubt and returns hesitant and unhappy, because he never has dared to see his doubts through to their logical conclusion and to face the world with God eliminated.

One may sense the general atmosphere of the world, under the no-God hypothesis, by saying, *In all this universe there is no mind essentially greater than mine.* The import of such a statement grows weightier the more one ponders it. All human minds are infinitesimal in knowledge; endless realities must lie beyond our reach; "our science is a drop, our ignorance a sea." Yet human knowledge is all that anywhere exists, if the no-God hypothesis is true. There is no knower who knows more, and the infinite reality beyond our grasp is not known by any mind at all. No one ever thought it or will think it through eternity. Then, let a man add, *In all this universe there is no goodness essentially greater than mine.* Human goodness is pitiably partial; it is but prophecy of what goodness ought to mean; "Man is a dwarf of himself," as Emerson said. But human goodness is all anywhere exists, if the no-God hypothesis is true. There never will be any better goodness anywhere, and when the earth comes to its end in a solar catastrophe, there will be no goodness left at all. Certainly the hypothesis of no-God raises more questions than it easily can quell.

Indeed the Christian, long accused by unbelieving friends of gross credulity because he holds his creed, may well leave his defense and "go over the top" in an offensive charge. If it is a question of holding creeds, unbelief is a creed as certainly as belief is; it says, I believe that there is no God or that God cannot be known. If it is a question of credulity, the Christian suspects that of all the different kinds of credulousness which the world has seen, nothing ever has surpassed the capacity of modern sceptics to accept impossible beliefs. He who says, "I believe that there is no

God, nor anything which that name might reasonably connote," is saying, "I believe that the fundamental reality everywhere is physical." Long ages ago atoms, electrons, "mobile cosmic ethers" began their mysterious organization, whose present issue is planetary orbits, rocks, organic life, and, highest point of all, the brain of man. Man's mind is but the moving shadow cast by the activity of brain. Man's character is the subtle fragrance of his nerves. Everywhere, if the no-God hypothesis be true, spirit is a *result,* physical energy the *cause.*

Some startling corollaries follow such a view. *No man can be blamed for anything.* Molecular action in the brain is responsible alike for saints and sinners, and we are as powerless to change our quality of character or action as a planet is to change its course. Judas and Jesus, Festus and Paul, the Belgian lads and the Prussian officers who mutilated them, the raper and the raped—why blame the one or praise the other when all characters alike are ground from a physical machine, whose action is predetermined by the push of universal energy behind? One man even says that to condemn an immoral deed is like Xerxes whipping the Hellespont—punishment visited on physical necessity which is not to blame.

The second corollary is not less startling: *every man thinks as he does because of molecular action in the brain.* A Christian believes in God because his molecules maneuver so, and his opponent is an atheist because his molecules maneuver otherwise, and all convictions of truth, however well debated and reasoned out, are fundamentally the work of atoms, not of mind. What we call intellect as little causes anything as steam from a kettle causes the boiling out of which it comes. Some brains boil socialism, some do not; some brains boil Episcopalianism and some Christian Science. A determinist and a believer in freewill differ as do oaks and elm trees, for physical reasons only, and folk are Catholic in southern Europe—so we are informed—because their skulls are narrow, and in northern Europe Protestants because their skulls are broad. Truth is a nickname for a neurosis. The standing marvel is that on some matters like the multiplication table our brains boil so unanimously.

A third corollary still remains: *we have no creative power of mind and will.* All that is and is to be was wound up in primeval matter, and now in our thoughts and actions is ticking like a clock. "All of our philosophy," says Huxley, "all our poetry, all our science, and all our art—Plato, Shakespeare, Newton, and Raphael—are potential in the fires of the sun." That is to say, Plato had nothing to do with *creating* his philosophy, nor Shakespeare with writing plays—they were empty megaphones and the real voice is the physical machine from which all things come. Professor Bowne of Boston University, after the publication of his "Metaphysics," received from a physicist a protest against his emphasis on the reality of mind. The professor of physics insisted that the only fundamental reality was physical and that mind is always a result of brain's activity and never a cause of anything. To this Professor Bowne replied that according to the writer's own theory, as he understood it, the letter of protest was the result of certain physical forces issuing in nervous excitations that made scratches on paper, and that the writer's mind had nothing effectual to do with its composition. This, said Professor Bowne, might be a plausible explanation of the letter, but he was unwilling to apply it to the universe. What wonder that the physicist acknowledged to a friend that the retort nettled him, for he did not see just how to answer it?

IV

One's discontent with this reduction of our lives to physical causation is increased when he studies the *mental process* by which men *reach it*. It is as if a man should perceive in the works of Shakespeare insight and beauty, pathos and laughter, despair and hope, and should set himself to explain all these as the function of the type. How plausibly he could do it! If one takes Shakespeare's sentences full of spiritual meaning he can readily resolve them into twenty-six constituent letters of the alphabet, and these into certain hooks and dashes, and these into arithmetical points diffused in space. Starting with such abstract points, let one suppose that some fortunate day they arranged themselves into hooks and dashes, and these into letters of the alphabet, and these by fortuitous concourse came together into sentences. Reading them we think we see deep spiritual meaning, but they are all the work of type; the fundamental reality is arithmetical points diffused in space. Such is the process by which a man reduces the mental and moral life of man back to its physical basis; then breaks up the physical basis into atoms; then, starting with these abstractions, builds up again the whole world which he just has analyzed, and thinks he has explained the infinitely significant spiritual life of man. Not for a long time will we accept such a method of explaining the works of Shakespeare! Nor can man contentedly be made to follow so inconsequential a process of thought as that by which the mind and character of Jesus are reduced to a maneuver of molecules.

The attractiveness of this explanation of the universe as a huge physical machine is easily understood. It presents a simple picture, readily grasped. It packs the whole explanation of the world into a neat parcel, portable by any mind. In the days of monarchy the government of the universe was pictured in terms of an absolute sovereign; in feudal times the divine economy was pictured as a gigantic feudalism; we always use a dominant factor in the life of man to help us picture the eternal. So in the age whose builder and maker is machinery we easily portray the universe as a huge machine. The process is simple and natural, but to suppose that it is adequate is preposterous. Lord Kelvin, the chemist knew thoroughly the mechanistic idea of the world. He felt the fascination of it, for he said at Johns Hopkins University, "I never satisfy myself until I make a mechanical model of a thing. If I can make a mechanical model I can understand it. As long as I cannot make a mechanical model all the way through, I cannot understand." But Lord Kelvin knew better than to suppose that this figure comprehended all of reality. "The atheistic idea," said he, "is so nonsensical, that I do not know how to put it into words."

The rejection of the no-God hypothesis does not necessarily imply that a man becomes fully Christian in his thought of deity. There are way-stations between no-God and Jesus' Father. *But it does mean that to him reality must be fundamentally spiritual, not physical.* What other hypothesis possibly can fit the facts? For consider the view of a growing universe which we see from the outlook that modern science furnishes. Out of a primeval chaos where physical forces snarled at each other in unrelieved antagonism, where no man had yet arisen to love truth and serve righteousness, something has brought us to a time, when for all our evil, there are mothers and music and the laughter of children at play, men who love honor and for service' sake lay down their lives, and homes in every obscure street where fortitude and sacrifice are splendidly exhibited. Out of a chaos, where a contemporary observer, could there have been one, would have seen no slightest promise of spirit, something has brought us to the Ten Commandments, and the Sermon on the Mount, to great character and growing achievements in social righteousness, to lofty thoughts of the Divine and hopes of life eternal. *Something has been at work here besides matter. No explanation of all this will do, without God.*

V

Another source of confirmation for the man who, valuing Christian experience, seeks assurance that it is intellectually justifiable, is to be found in the effect of Christian faith on life itself. The nautical tables can be proved by an astronomer in his observatory; but if they are given to a sailor and he beats about the seas with them in safety, finding that they make adventurous voyages practical, that also would be important witness to their truth. So the Christian ideas of life have not been kept by studious recluses to ponder over and weave philosophies about; they have been down in the market place, men have been practically trying them for generations, and *they make great living*.

The ultimate ground of practical assurance about anything is that we have tried it and that it works. A man may have experience that other persons exist, may draw the inference that friendly relations with them are not impossible, but only when he launches out and verifies his thought in an adventure will he really be convinced of friendship's glory. In no other way has final assurance about God come home to man. They who have lived as though

God *were* have been convinced that he *is;* they who have willed to do his will have known.

That religious faith does justify itself in life is a fact to which mankind's experience amply testifies. Men have come to God, not as chemists to bread curious to analyze it; they have come as hungry men, needing to eat if they would live. And they have found life glorified by faith in him. The difference between religion and irreligion here is plain. *How seldom one finds enthusiastic unbelievers!* When all that is fine spirited and resolute in agnostic literature is duly weighed and credited, the pessimistic undertone is always heard. Leslie Stephen thus summarizes life—"There is a deep sadness in the world. Turn and twist the thought as you may there is no escape. Optimism would be soothing if it were possible; in fact, it is impossible, and therefore a constant mockery." No gospel burns in the unbeliever's mind, urgent for utterance; he has no inspiring outlooks to offer, no glad tidings to declare. The more intelligent he is the more plainly he sees this. With Clifford he laments that "the spring sun shines out of an empty heaven to light up a soulless earth" and feels "with utter loneliness that the Great Companion is dead"; with Romanes he frankly states, "So far as the ruination of individual happiness is concerned, no one can have a more lively conception than myself of the possibly disastrous tendency of my work." An unbeliever whose admirable life raised the question as to the philosophy by which he guided it, gave this summary of his creed, "I am making the best of a bad mess." Unbelievers do not spontaneously utter in song the glory of a creed like this, and when they do write poetry, it is of a sort that music will not fit—

> "The world rolls round forever like a mill,
> It grinds out death and life and good and ill,
> It has no purpose, heart, or mind or will."

When from poetry one turns to philosophy, he can see good reasons why hymnals and unbelief should be uncongenial. There is little to make life worth while in a creed which holds as Haeckel does that morality in man, like the tail of a monkey or the shell of a tortoise, is purely a physiological effect, and that man himself is "an affair of chance; the

143

froth and fume at the wave-top of a sterile ocean of matter."
Shall the practical unserviceableness of such an idea for the
purpose of life, awaken no suspicion as to its truth?

Upon the other hand, suppose that by some strange
chance the principles of Jesus should over night take
possession of mankind. Even as it is, when one starts his
thought with the Stone Age, the progress of mankind has
obviously been immense. From universal cannibalism after
a battle, to massacre without cannibalism marked one great
advance; from massacre of all prisoners taken in war to
enslavement of them marked another; and when slavery
ceased being a philanthropic improvement, as it was at first,
and became a sin and shame, humanity took another long
step forward. With all our present barbarity, a far look
backwards shows a clear ascent. As for the influence of
Jesus, Lecky, the historian, tells us that "The simple record
of three short years of Christ's active life has done more to
regenerate and soften mankind than all the disquisitions of
philosophers and all the exhortations of moralists." What if
this process were brought to its fulfillment between sunset
and dawn, and the new day came with everyone sure of
God's fatherhood and life eternal, of the law of love and the
supremacy of character and with everyone living as though
these were true? Whatever intellectual perplexities of belief
a man may have, he knows that such a world would be
divinely great. No war, no evil lust, no covetous selfishness,
no drunkenness! Mankind, relieved of ancient burdens
which have ruined character and crushed endeavor,
confident of faiths that give life infinite horizons and
deathless hopes, in cooperative international fraternity
would be making the earth a decent home for God to rear
his children in. One finds it hard to believe that ideas which,
incarnate in life, would so redeem the world are false.

As to the effect of the Christian affirmations on
individual character, we do not need to picture an imagined
future. A Character has been here who has lived them out.
A jury of philosophers might analyze the wood-work and
the metals of an organ, and guess from form and material
what it is, but we still should need for our assurance a
musician. When he sweeps the keys in harmony we *know*
that it is an organ. So when the philosophers have debated
the pros and cons of argument concerning faith, Jesus *plays*

the Gospel. His life is the Christian affirmations done into character. When religious faith, at its best, is incarnate in a Man, this is the consequence. And multitudes of folk, living out the implications of the faith, have found the likeness of the Master growing in them. Weighty confirmation of the Gospel's *truth arrives when its meaning is translated into life; the world will not soon reject the New Testament in this edition—bound in a Man.*

*To one in perplexity about belief, this proper question therefore rises: What do we think about the Christlike character? Is it not life at its sublimest elevation? But to acknowledge that and yet to deny the central faiths by which such life is lived is to say that those ideas which, incarnate, make living great are false, and those ide*as which leave life meager of motive and bereft of hope are true. No one lives on such a basis in any other realm. We always mistrust the validity of any idea which works poorly or not at all. And so far from being a practical makeshift, this "negative pragmatism" is a true principle of knowledge. Says Professor Hocking, of Harvard, "If a theory has no consequence, or bad ones; if it makes no difference to men, or else undesirable differences; if it lowers the capacity of men to meet the stress of existence, or diminishes the worth to them of what existence they have; such a theory is somehow false, and we have no peace until it is remedied." The last word against irreligion is that it makes life unlivable; the last word for faith is that it makes life glorious.

VI

One who is facing intellectual difficulties in the way of faith may well consider that the very Christian life for whose possession he is seeking justification is itself an argument of the first importance. This life grew up in the universe; it is one expression of the universe; and it is hard to think that it does not reveal a nature kindred to itself in the source from which it came.

Mankind has always experienced a relationship with the Unseen which has seemed like communion of soul with Soul. When a psychologist like Professor James, of

Harvard, reduces to its most general terms this religious Fact which has been practically universal in the race, he puts it thus: "Man becomes conscious that this higher part (his spiritual life) is coterminous and continuous with a MORE of the same quality, which is operative in the universe outside of him, and which he can keep in working touch with, and in a fashion get on board of and save himself when all his lower being has gone to pieces in the wreck." No experience of man is more common in occurrence, more tremendous in result than this. From the mystics whose vivid sense of God canceled their consciousness that anything else was real, to plain folk who in the strength of the divine alliance have lived ordinary lives with extraordinary spirit, mankind as a whole has known that the best in man is in contact with a MORE.

One does not need to be of a mystical temperament, given to raptures, to know what this means. Let him consider his own experience of love and duty, how he is bound by them to his ideals and woven into a community of personal life not only with his friends but with all humanity, until this spiritual life of his becomes the most august and commanding power he knows. When in our bodies we so discern a physical nature, whose laws and necessities we did not create, and whose power binds us into a community of need and labor with our fellows, our conclusion is confident. This experience is the basis of our assurance that a *physical universe is really here*. When, likewise in our inner selves we find a spiritual life, which man did not create, in obedience to which alone is safety, and peace, and power, what shall we conclude? That there is a *spiritual universe* as plainly evidenced in man's soul as the physical universe is in the body! And when we note the attributes of this Spiritual Order, how it demands righteousness, rebukes sin, welcomes obedience and holds out ideals of endless possibility, it is plain that we are talking about something close of kin to God. As in summer we beat out through some familiar bay, naming the headlands as we sail, until if we go far enough, we cannot prevent our eyes from looking out across the unbounded sea, so if a man moves out through his own familiar spiritual life far enough, he comes to the Spiritual Order which is God. Man has not drifted into his religion by accident or fallen on it merely as superstition; he has moved out from his inner life to affirm a Spiritual Order as inevitably as he has moved out from his bodily experiences to affirm a physical universe.

When from this general experience we turn to the specific experiences of religion, which prayer and worship represent, the testimony of the race is confident. Men have not all these ages been lifting up their souls to an unreality from which no response has come. The artesian well of transforming influence in human souls has not flowed from Nowhere. Some, indeed, hearing confidence in God founded on the individual experiences of man, derisively cry "Nonsense!" But if one were to prove that the Sistine Madonna is beautiful, he would have to offer his experience in evidence. "I went to Dresden," he might say, "up into the room where the Madonna hangs . . . and is *is* beautiful. I saw it." Met with derision by a doubter, as though his experience were no proof at all, how shall he proceed? "I am not the only one," he might continue, "who has perceived its beauty. All these centuries the folk best qualified to judge have gone up into that room and have come down again, sure that Raphael's work is beautiful." Is anyone in a position to deride that? So through all ages men and women, from lowest savages to the race's spiritual kings and queens, have gone up to the Divine, and, at their best, from experiences of prayer, worship, forgiven sins, transfigured lives, have come down sure that Reality is there. *One may not call nonsense the most universal and influential experience of the human race!*

The force of this fact is more clearly seen when one considers that man has grown up in this universe, gradually developing his powers and functions as responses to his environment. If he has eyes, so the biologists assure us, it is because the light waves played upon the skin and eyes came out in answer; if he has ears it is because the air waves were there first and ears came out to hear. Man never yet, according to the evolutionist, has developed any power save as a reality called it into being. There would be no fins if there were no water, no wings if there were no air, no legs if there were no land. Always the developing organism has been trying to "catch up with its environment." Yet some would tell us that man's noblest power of all has developed in a vacuum. They would say that his capacity to deal with a

Spiritual World, to believe in God, and in prayer to experience fellowship with him, has all grown up with no Reality to call it into being. If so, it stands alone in man's experience, the only function of his life that grew without an originating Fact to call it forth. It does not seem reasonable to think that. The evidence of man's experience is overwhelmingly in favor of a Reality to which his spirit has been trying to answer. Said Max Müller, "To the philosopher the existence of God may seem to rest on a syllogism; in the eyes of the historian it rests on the whole evolution of human thought."

CHAPTER VI

Faith's Greatest Obstacle

DAILY READINGS

The speculative doubts leave many minds untouched, but one universal human experience sooner or later faces every serious life with questions about God's goodness. We all meet trouble, in ourselves or others, and oftentimes the wonder why in God's world such calamities should fall, such wretchedness should continually exist, plunges faith into perplexity. Few folk of mature years can fail to understand Edwin Booth when he wrote to a friend, "Life is a great big spelling book, and on every page we turn the words grow harder to understand the meaning of." Now, the basis of any intelligent explanation of faith's problem must rest in a *right practical altitude toward trouble*. To the consideration of that we turn in the daily readings.

Sixth Week, First Day

Beloved, think it not strange concerning the fiery trial among you, which cometh upon you to prove you, as though a strange thing happened unto you: but insomuch as ye are partakers of Christ's sufferings, rejoice; that at the revelation of his glory also ye may rejoice with exceeding joy. If ye are reproached for the name of Christ, blessed are ye; because the Spirit of glory and the Spirit of God resteth upon you. For let none of you suffer as a murderer, or a thief, or an evil-doer, or as a meddler in other men's matters: but if a man suffer as a Christian, let him not be ashamed; but let him glorify God in this name. . . . Wherefore let them also

**that suffer according to the will of God commit their souls in
well-doing unto a faithful Creator.—I Pet. 4:12-16, 19.**

Such an attitude toward trouble as Peter here recom-
mends is the most wholesome and hopeful possible to man.
And it is reasonable too, if only on the ground that trouble
develops in men the essential qualities of strong character.
Our highest admiration is always reserved for men who
master difficult crises. If the story of Joseph, begun beside
Bedouin camp fires centuries ago, can easily be naturalized
beside modern radiators; if Robinson Crusoe, translated
into every tongue is understood by all, the reason lies in the
depth of man's heart, where to make the most out of
untoward situations is a daily problem. Not every one can
grasp the argument or perceive the beauty of "Paradise
Lost" and "Paradise Regained," but one thing about them
every man appreciates—the blind Milton, sitting down to
write them:

> "I argue not
> Against Heaven's hand or will, nor bate a jot
> Of heart or hope; but still bear up and steer
> Right onward."

The full understanding of Ole Bull's playing on the violin
was necessarily restricted to the musical, but no restriction
bounds the admiration of men, learned or simple, when in a
Munich concert, his A string snaps and he finishes the
composition on three strings. That is the human problem in
epitome. Getting music out of life's remainders after the
break has come; winning the battle with what is left from a
defeat; going blind, like Milton, and writing sublimest
poetry, or deaf, like Beethoven, and composing superb
sonatas; being reared in an almshouse and buried from
Westminster Abbey, like Henry M. Stanley; or, like
Kavanagh, born without arms or legs and yet sitting at last
in the British Parliament—all such hardihood and undiscourageable pluck reach back in a man's bosom beyond the
strings that ease and luxury can touch, and strike there an
iron, reverberating chord. Nothing in human life is so
impressive as pluck, "fighting with the scabbard after the
sword is gone." And no one who deeply considers life can

fail to see that our best character comes when, as Peter says, we "suffer as a Christian."

O Lord, our God, let our devout approach to Thee be that of the heart, not of the lips. Let it be in obedience to Thy spiritual law, not to any outward ritual. Thou desirest not temples nor offerings, but the sacrifice of a lowly and grateful heart Thou will not despise. Merciful Father, to all Thy dispensations we would submit ourselves, not grudgingly, not merely of necessity, but because we believe in Thy wisdom, Thy universal rule, and Thy goodness. In bereavement and in sorrow, in death as in life, in joys and in happiness, we would see Thy hand. Teach us to see it; increase our faith where we cannot see; teach us also to love justice, and to do mercy, and to walk humbly with Thee our God. Make us at peace with all mankind, gentle to those who offend us, faithful in all duties, and sincere in sorrow when we fail in duty. Make us loving to one another, patient in distress, and ever thankful to Thy divine power, which keeps, and guides, and blesses us every day. Lord, accept our humble prayer, accomplish in us Thy holy will. Let Thy peace reign in our hearts, and enable us to walk with Thee in love; through Jesus Christ our Lord. Amen. Francis W. Newman, 1805.

Sixth Week, Second Day

Even unto this present hour we both hunger, and thirst, and are naked, and are buffeted, and have no certain dwelling-place; and we toil, working with our own hands: being reviled, we bless; being persecuted, we endure; being defamed, we entreat; we are made as the filth of the world, the offscouring of all things, even until now.—I Cor. 4:11-13.

If Paul could be questioned about the experience of trouble which these verses vividly express, would he not say that there had been qualities of character in him and resources in his relationship with God which he never would have known about had it not been for the test of adversity? Trouble not only develops but also *reveals* character; we do not know ourselves until we have been tried out in calamity. The simplest demand of adversity on every man is that he be "game." Henry Newbolt is not indulging in rhetoric when he tells a Soudan battle where a British square made up of Clifton graduates is hard beset by a charge of fierce enemies, and, in that crisis, makes the cry of a Clifton football captain, "Play us, boys, play the game!" rally the men and save the day. At school or in the Soudan the problem is the same; the sling with which David plays in his youth is his chief reliance when Goliath comes; a "game" spirit is essential to character from birth to death. We turn from the story of Nelson at Aboukir, nailing six flags to his mast so that if even five were shot away no one would dream that he had surrendered, to find that the spirit there exemplified is applicable to our most common day. The quality which made Nelson an Admiral of England, in spite of his lost arm, his lost eye, his small stature, and his feeble health is one of our elemental needs. And to a supreme degree this quality was in great Christians like Paul. Read his letter to the Philippians and see! Adversity brought his spirit to light, and made it an asset of the cause. In a real sense, trouble, however forbidding, was one of Paul's best friends, and there was a good reason why he should "rejoice in tribulations."

O Father of spirits! Thou lovest whom Thou chastenest! Correct us in our weakness as the children of men, that we may love Thee in our strength as the sons of God. May the same mind be in us which was also in Jesus Christ, that we may never shrink, when our hour comes, from drinking of the cup that he drank of. Wake in us a soul to obey Thee, not with the weariness of servile spirits, but with the alacrity of the holy angels. Fill us with a contempt of evil pleasures and unfaithful ease; sustain us in the strictness of a devout life. Daily may we crucify every selfish affection, and delight to bear one another's burdens, to uphold each other's faith and charity, being tender-hearted and forgiving as we hope to be forgiven. Hold us to the true humility of the soul that has not yet attained; and may we be modest in our desire, diligent in our trust, and content with the disposals of Thy Providence. O Lord of life and death! Thy counsels are secret; Thy wisdom is infinite: we know not what a day may bring forth.

*When our hour arrives, and the veil between the worlds
begins to be lifted before us, may we freely trust ourselves to
Thee, and say, "Father, into Thy hands I commend my
spirit." Amen.*—James Martineau.

Sixth Week, Third Day

If adversity, rightly used, so develops and reveals
character, we may expect to find trouble as a background to
the most admirable men of the race. We read the luminous
histories of Francis Parkman and do not perceive, behind
the printed page, the original manuscript, covered with a
screen of parallel wires, along which the blind author ran his
pencil that he might write legibly. We think of James Watt
as a genius at invention, and perhaps recall that Wordsworth said of him, "I look upon him, considering both the
magnitude and the universality of his genius, as perhaps the
most extraordinary man that this country ever produced."
But Watt himself we forget—sickly of body, starving on
eight shillings a week, and saying, "Of all things in life there
is nothing more foolish than inventing." Kant's philosophy
was a turning point in human thought, but lauding Kant,
how few recall his struggle with a broken body! Said he,
speaking of his incurable illness, "I have become master of
its influence in my thoughts and actions by turning my
attention away from this feeling altogether, just as if it did
not at all concern me." Wilberforce, the liberator of British
slaves, we know, and beside his grave in Westminster
Abbey we recall the superb title that he earned, "the
attorney general of the unprotected and of the friendless,"
but the Wilberforce who for twenty years was compelled to
use opium to keep himself alive, and had the resolution
never to increase the dose—who knows of him? One of the
chief rewards of reading biography is this introduction that
it gives to handicapped men; the knowledge it imparts of
the world's great saints and scripture makers, conquerors
and reformers, who, in the words of Thucydides, "dared
beyond their strength, hazarded against their judgment,
and in extremities were of excellent hope." And when one
turns to the supreme Character, could the dark background
be eliminated and still leave Him?

But now we see not yet all things subjected to him. But we behold him who hath been made a little lower than the angels, even Jesus, because of the suffering of death crowned with glory and honor, that by the grace of God he should taste of death for every man. For it became him, for whom are all things, and through whom are all things, in bringing many sons unto glory to make the author of their salvation perfect through sufferings.—Heb. 2:8-10.

O God, who art unsearchable in Thy judgments, and in Thy ways past finding out, we bow before the mystery of Thy Being, and confess that we know nothing, and can say nothing worthy of Thee. We cannot understand Thy dealings with us. We have faith, not sight; when we cannot see, we may only believe. Sometimes Thou seemest to have no mercy upon us. Thou dost pierce us through our most tender affections, quenching the light of our eyes in dreadful darkness. Death tears from us all that we love, and Thou art seemingly deaf to all our cries. Our earthly circumstances are reversed and bitter poverty is appointed us, yet Thou takest no heed, and bringest no comfort to the sorrow and the barrenness of our life. Still would we trust in Thee and cling to that deepest of our instincts which tells us that we come from Thee and return to Thee. Be with us, Father of Mercies, in love and pity and tenderness unspeakable. Lift our souls into thy perfect calm, where all our wills are in harmony with Thine. Amen.—Samuel McComb.

Sixth Week, Fourth Day

To one perplexed and disheartened by adversity, a theoretical explanation is generally not half as valuable as concrete instances of courage and fortitude, founded on faith. Whether we be theologians or scientists or as ignorant of both as Caliban, there is an immediate, personal call to arms in the brave fight of George Matheson, one of Scotland's great preachers for all his blindness, or in Louis Pasteur's indomitable will, making his discoveries despite the paralytic stroke that in his forty-sixth year crippled his strength. The qualities which we admire in them are a sort of apotheosis of the qualities which we need in ourselves.

For we all are handicapped, some by ill-starred heredity, by unhappy environment, or by the consequences of our own neglect and sin; some by poverty, some by broken bodies, or by dissevered family ties—and all of us by unfortunate dispositions. It does us good then to know that Phillips Brooks failed as a teacher. His biographer tells us that in the prime of life, when he was the prince of preachers, he came from President's Eliot's office, pale and trembling, because he had refused a professorship at Harvard. So Robertson, of Brighton, whose sermons began a new epoch in British Christianity, was prevented from being a soldier only by the feebleness of his body, and Sir Walter Scott, who wanted to be a poet, turned to novel writing, anonymously and tentatively trying a new role, because, as he frankly put it, "Because Byron beat me." He is an excellent cook who knows how to make a good dinner out of the leftovers, and hardly a more invigorating truth is taught by history than that most of the finest banquets spread for the delectation of the race have been prepared by men who made them out of the leavings of disappointed hopes.

Therefore let us also, seeing we are compassed about with so great a cloud of witnesses, lay aside every weight, and the sin which doth so easily beset us, and let us run with patience the race that is set before us, looking unto Jesus the author and perfecter of our faith, who for the joy that was set before him endured the cross, despising shame, and hath sat down at the right hand of the throne of God. For consider him that hath endured such gainsaying of sinners against himself, that ye wax not weary, fainting in your souls.—Heb. 12:1-3.

Our Father, we thank Thee that while we are sure of Thy protecting care, Thy casual providence, which foresees all things, we can bear the sorrows of this world, and do its duties, and endure its manifold and heavy cross. We thank Thee that when distress comes upon us, and our mortal schemes vanish into thin air, we know there is something solid which we can lay hold of, and not be frustrate in our hopes. Yea, we thank Thee that when death breaks asunder the slender thread of life whereon our family jewels are strung, and the precious stones of our affection fall from our arms or neck, we know Thou takest them and elsewhere givest them a heavenly setting, wherein they shine before the light of Thy presence as morning stars, brightening and brightening to more perfect glory, as they are transfigured by Thine own almighty power.

We thank Thee for all the truth which the stream of time has brought to us from many a land and every age. We thank Thee for the noble examples of human nature which Thou hast raised up, that in times of darkness there are wise men, in times of doubt there are firm men, and in every peril there stand up heroes of the soul to teach us feebler men our duty, and to lead all of Thy children to trust in Thee. Father, we thank Thee that the seed of righteousness is never lost, but through many a deluge is carried safe, to make the wilderness to bloom and blossom with beauty ever fragrant and ever new, and the desert bear corn for men and sustain the souls of the feeble when they faint. Amen.—Theodore Parker.

Sixth Week, Fifth Day

One distinguishing mark of the men who have won their victories with the remnants of their defeat is that they refuse to describe their unideal conditions in negative terms. If they cannot live in southern California where they would choose to live, but must abide in New England instead, they do not describe New England in terms of its deficiencies— no orange groves, no acres of calla lilies, no palm trees. There are compensations even in New England, if one will carefully take account of stock and see what positively is there! Or if a man would choose to live in Boston and must live in Labrador, the case of Grenfell suggests that a positive attitude toward his necessity will discover worth, and material for splendid triumphs even on that inhospitable coast. The mark of the handicapped men who have made the race's history glorious has always been their patriotism for the country where they had to live. They do not stop long to pity themselves, or to envy another's opportunity, or to blame circumstances for their defeat, or to dream of what might have been, or to bewail their disappointed hopes. If the soil of their condition will not grow one crop, they discover what it will grow. They have insight, as did Moses, to see holy ground where an ordinary man would have seen only sand and sagebrush and sheep.

No Moses was keeping the flock of Jethro his father-in-law, the priest of Midian: and he led the flock to the back of the wilderness, and came to the mountain of God, and Horeb. And the angel of Jehovah appeared unto him in a flame of fire out of the midst of a bush: and he looked, and, behold, the bush burned with fire, and the bush was not consumed. And Moses said, I will turn aside now, and see this great sight, why the bush is not burnt. And when Jehovah saw that he turned aside to see, God called unto him out of the midst of the bush, and said, Moses, Moses. And he said, Here am I. And he said, Draw not nigh hither: put off thy shoes from off thy feet, for the place whereon thou standest is holy ground.—Exod. 3:1-5.

Father of life, and God of the living, Fountain of our being and Light of all our day; we thank Thee for that knowledge of Thyself which lights our life with eternal splendor, for that giving of Thyself which has made us partakers of Thy divine nature. We bless Thee for everything around us which ministers Thee to our minds; for the greatness and glory of nature, for the history of our race, and the lives of noble men; for the thoughts of Thee expressed in human words, in the art of painters and musicians, in the work of builders and craftsmen. We bless Thee for the constant memories of what we are that rise within ourselves; for the pressure of duty, the hush of solemn thoughts, for moments of insight when the veil on the face of all things falls away, for hours of high resolve when life is quickened within, for seasons of communion when, earth and sense forgotten, heaven holds our silent spirits raptured and aflame.

We have learned to praise Thee for the darker days when we had to walk by faith, for weary hours that strengthened patience and endeavor, for moments of gloom and times of depression which taught us to trust, not to changing tides of feeling, but to Thee who changest not. And now since Christ has won his throne by His cross of shame, risen from His tomb to reign forever in the hearts of men, we know that nothing can ever separate us from Thee; that in all conflicts we may be more than conquerors; that all dark and hostile

*things shall be transformed and work for good to those who
know the secret of Thy love.*
Glory be to Thee, O Lord. Amen.—W. E. Orchard.

Sixth Week, Sixth Day

When folk have seen into human life deeply enough so
that they perceive how adversity can be used to high issues,
faith in God becomes not so much a speculative problem as
a practical need. They want to deal with trouble nobly.
They see that faith in God gives the outlook on life which
makes the hopeful facing of adverse situations reasonable
and which supplies power to make it possible. The result is
that the *great sufferers have been the great believers.* The
idea that fortunate circumstances make vital faith in God
probable is utterly unsupported by history. Hardly an
outstanding champion of faith who has left an indelible
impress on man's spiritual life can anywhere be found, who
has not won his faith and confirmed it in the face of trouble.
What is true of individuals is true of generations. The days
of Israel's triumphant faith did not come in Solomon's
reign, when wealth was plentiful and national ambitions ran
high. The great prophets and the great psalms stand out
against the dark background of the Exile and its
consequences.

**Awake, awake, put on strength, O arm of Jehovah;
awake, as in the days of old, the generations of ancient times.
Is it not thou that didst cut Rahab in pieces, that didst pierce
the monster? Is it not thou that driedst up the sea, the waters
of the great deep; that madest the depths of the sea a way for
the redeemed to pass over? And the ransomed of Jehovah
shall return, and come with singing unto Zion; and
everlasting joy shall be upon their heads: they shall obtain
gladness and joy; and sorrow and sighing shall flee away.
I, even I, am he that comforteth you: who art thou, that
thou art afraid of man that shall die, and of the son of man
that shall be made as grass; and hast forgotten Jehovah thy
Maker, that stretched forth the heavens, and laid the
foundations of the earth; and fearest continually all the day
because of the fury of the oppressor, when he maketh ready**

to destroy? and where is the fury of the oppressor? The captive exile shall speedily be loosed; and he shall not die and go down into the pit, neither shall his bread fail. For I am Jehovah thy God, who stirreth up the sea, so that the waves thereof roar: Jehovah of hosts is his name. And I have put my words in thy mouth, and have covered thee in the shadow of my hand, that I may plant the heavens, and lay the foundations of the earth, and say unto Zion, Thou art my people.—Isa. 51:9-16.

That is a voice out of the Exile. Such great believers, whose faith shone brightest when the night was darkest, have not pretended to know the explanation of suffering in God's world. But they have had insight to see a little and trust for the rest. Stevenson has expressed their faith: "If I from my spy-hole, looking with purblind eyes upon at least part of a fraction of the universe, yet perceive in my own destiny some broken evidences of a plan, and some signals of an overruling goodness; shall I then be so mad as to complain that all cannot be deciphered? Shall I not rather wonder, with infinite and grateful surprise, that in so vast a scheme I seem to have been able to read, however little, and that little was encouraging to faith?"

We thank Thee, O God, that Thou dost ride upon the cloud, and govern the storm. All that to us is dark is light to Thee. The night shineth as the day. All that which seems to us irregular and ungoverned, is held in thine hand, even as the steed by the rein. From age to age Thou dost control the long procession of events, discerning the end from the beginning; and all the wild mixture, all the confusion, all the sorrow and the suffering, is discerned of Thee. As is the palette to the color, as is violence to development in strength, as is the crushing of the grape to the wine, so in Thy sight all things are beneficent that to us are most confusing and seemingly conflicting and threatening. Sorrow and pain and disaster are woven in the loom of God; and in the end we, too, shall be permitted to discern the fair pattern, and understand how that which brought tears here shall bring righteousness there.

O, how good it is to trust Thee, and to believe that Thou art wise, and that Thou art full of compassion, as Thou carriest on thy great work of love and benevolence, sympathizing

*with all that suffer on the way, and gathering them at last with
an exceeding great salvation! We trust Thee, not because we
understand Thee, but because in many things Thou hast
taught us where we should have been afraid to trust. We have
crossed many a gulf and many a roaring stream upon the
bridge of faith, and have exulted to find ourselves safe
landed, and have learned to trust Thee, as a child a parent, as
a passenger the master of a ship, not because we know, but
because Thou knowest. Amen.*—Henry Ward Beecher.

Sixth Week, Seventh Day

**Every one therefore that heareth these words of mine, and
doeth them, shall be likened to a wise man, who built his
house upon the rock: and the rain descended, and the floods
came, and the winds blew, and beat upon that house; and it
fell not: for it was founded upon the rock. And every one that
heareth these words of mine, and doeth them not, shall be
likened unto a foolish man, who built his house upon the
sand; and the rain descended, and the floods came, and the
winds blew, and smote upon that house; and it fell: and great
was the fall thereof.—Matt. 7:24-27.**

An important fact is here asserted by the Master, which is
commonly obscured in the commentaries. He says that no
matter whether a man's life be built on sand or on rock, he
yet will experience the blasts of adversity; on both houses
alike "the rain descended, and the floods came, and the
winds blew." The Master repeatedly affirmed that trouble
comes without necessary reference to character, that while
we may always argue that sin causes suffering, we never can
confidently argue that suffering comes from sin (Luke 13:4;
John 9:1-3). Folks needlessly and unscripturally harass
their souls when they suppose that some special trouble
must have befallen them because of some special sin. The
Book of Job was written to disprove that, and as for the
Master, he distinctly says that the man of faith with his
house on a rock faces the same storm that wrecks the
faithless man. *The difference is not in the adversity, but in the
adversity's effect.* No more important question faces any
soul than this: seeing that trouble is an unevadable portion

of every life, good or bad, what am I to do with it? Says Oliver Wendell Holmes, "Did you ever happen to see that most soft-spoken and velvet-handed steam-engine at the Mint? The smooth piston slides backward and forward as a lady might slip her delicate finger in and out of a ring. The engine lays one of its fingers calmly, but firmly, upon a bit of metal; it is a coin now, and will remember that touch, and tell a new race about it, when the date upon it is crusted over with twenty centuries. So it is that a great silent-moving misery puts a new stamp on us in an hour or a moment—as sharp an impression as if it had taken half a lifetime to engrave it." The only flaw in that simile is that the coin cannot decide what impression shall be made. But we can. Rebellion, despair, bitterness, or triumphant faith—we can say which impression adversity shall leave upon us.

O God of our life, whom we dimly apprehend and never can comprehend, to whom nevertheless we justly ascribe all goodness as well as all greatness; as a father teaches his children, so teach us, Lord, truer thoughts of Thee. Teach us to aspire, so far as man may lawfully aspire, to a knowledge of Thee. Thou art not only a God to be honored in times of rest and ease, Thou art also the Refuge of the distressed, the Comforter of the afflicted, the Healer of the contrite, and the Support of the unstable. As we sympathize with those who are sore smitten by calamity, wounded by sudden accident, wrecked in the midst of security, so must we believe that Thy mighty all-embracing heart sympathizes. Pitier of the orphan, God of the widow, cause us to share Thy pity and become Thy messengers of tenderness in our small measure. Be Thou the Stay of all in life and death. Teach all to know and trust Thee, give us a portion here and everywhere with Thy saints; through Jesus Christ our Lord. Amen.—Francis W. Newman, 1805.

COMMENT FOR THE WEEK

I

Few who have sincerely tried to believe in God's goodness and who have lived long enough to face the harrowing facts of human wretchedness will doubt what obstacle most hampers faith. The major difficulty which perplexes many Christians, when they try to reconcile God's love with their experience, is not belief's irrationality but life's injustice. According to the Psalmist, "The fool hath said in his heart, 'There is no God' " (Ps. 14:1). But the fool is not the only one who has said that. He said it, jeering; he announced it in derision; he did not want God, and contemptuous denial was a joy. It was the temper of his negation that made him a fool. But many hearts, in tones far different from his, have said, "There is no God." Parents cry it brokenheartedly beside the graves of children; the diseased cry it, suffering from keener agony than they can bear; fathers cry it when their battle against poverty has failed and their children plead in vain for bread; and men who care about their kind say it as they watch the anguish with which war, drunkenness, lust, disease, and poverty afflict the race. No man of moral insight will call such folk fools. The wretchedness and squalor, the misery and sin which rest upon so much of humankind are a notorious difficulty in the way of faith.

In dealing with this problem two shortcuts are often tried, and by them some minds endeavor to evade the issue which faith ought to meet. Some *minimize the suffering* which creation cost and which man and animals are now enduring. We must grant that when we read the experience of animals in terms of man's own life, we always exaggerate their pain. Animals never suffer as we do; their misery is not compounded by our mental agonies for regret and fear; and even their physical wretchedness is as much lower in intensity as their nerves are less exquisitely tuned. Darwin, who surely did not underestimate the struggle for existence, said in a letter, "According to my judgment, happiness decidedly prevails. All sentient beings have been formed so as to enjoy, as a general rule, happiness." We must grant also that man's practical attitude toward life gives the lie to pessimism. Only the suicides are the logical pessimists, and all the rest of men, most with good heart and multitudes with jubilant enthusiasm, do actually cling to life. Indeed, all normal men discover, that, within limits, their very hardships are a condition of their happiness and do not so much abate their love of life as they add zest and tang. We must grant further that suffering should be measured not by quantity, but by intensity. One sensitive man enduring bereavement, poverty, or disease represents *all* the suffering that ever has been or ever can be felt. To speak of limitless suffering, therefore, is false. There is no more wretchedness anywhere nor in all the world together, than each one can know in his own person.

When all this, however, has been granted, the facts of the world's misery are staggering. Modern science has given terrific sweep and harrowing detail to Paul's assertion, "The whole creation groaneth and travaileth in pain together until now" (Rom. 8:22). Let one whose insight into misery's meanings is quickened by even a little imagination try to sum up the agony of drunkards' homes, of bereaved families, of hospitals, insane asylums, jails, and prisons, of war with its unmentionable horrors—its blinded, deafened, maddened, raped—and no small palliatives can solve his problem. Rather he understands the picture which James Russell Lowell said he saw years ago in Belgium: an angel holding back the Creator and saying, "If about to make such a world, stay thine hand."

Another shortcut by which some endeavor to simplify the problem and content their thought is *to lift responsibility for life's wretchedness from God's shoulders and to put it upon man's.* Were man's sin no factor in the world, some say, life's miseries would cease; all the anguish of our earthly lot stands not to God's responsibility but to man's shame. But the sufferings of God's creatures did not begin with man's arrival, and the pain of creation before man sinned is a longer story than earth's misery since. Let Romanes picture the scene: "Some hundred of millions of years ago, some millions of millions of animals must be supposed to have become sentient. Since that time till the present, there must have been millions and millions of generations of millions and millions of individuals. And throughout all this period of incalculable duration, this inconceivable host of sentient organizations have been in a state of unceasing battle, dread, ravin, pain. Looking to the outcome, we find that more than one-half of the species which have survived the ceaseless struggle are parasitic in their habits, lower and insentient forms of life, feasting on higher and sentient forms, we find teeth and talons whetted for slaughter, hooks and suckers molded for torture—everywhere a reign of terror, hunger, sickness, with oozing blood and quivering limbs, with gasping breath and eyes of innocence that dimly close in deaths of cruel torture." Is man responsible for that? For cold that freezes God's living creatures, for lightning that kills them, for volcanoes that burn them, for typhoons that crush them—is man responsible? By no such easy evasion may we escape the problem which faith must meet. "In sober truth," as John Stuart Mill exclaimed, "nearly all the things which men are hanged or imprisoned for doing to one another, are Nature's everyday performances." Who can avoid seeing the patent contrast between the Father of Jesus and the Creator of such a world? "The power that launches earthquakes and arms cuttlefish," said one perplexed believer, "has but a meager relationship to the power that blesses infants and forgive enemies."

II

Could we hold this problem at arm's length, discussing it in speculative moods when we grow curious about the makeup of the universe, our case would be more simple. But of all life's problems, this most certainly—sometimes creeping, sometimes crashing—invades our private lives. Every man has a date with adversity which he must keep and which adversity does not forget. One notes the evidence of this in every normally maturing life. As children we wanted happiness and were impatient, lacking it. Our cups of pleasure easily brimmed and overflowed. A Christmas tree or a birthday party—and our hearts were like sun-parlors on cloudless days with all the windows open to the light! But the time comes to all when happiness like this is not our problem; we recognize that it is gone; our Edens are behind us with flaming angels at the gate. We have had friends and lost them and something has gone from our hearts that does not return; we have won successes which we do not estimate as highly in possession as we did in dreams, and it may be have lost what little we achieved; we have sinned, and though forgiven, the scars are still upon us; we have been weathered by the rains and floods and winds. Happiness in the old fashion we no longer seek. We want peace, the power to possess our souls in patience and to do our work. We want joy, which is a profound and spiritually begotten grace as happiness is not. This maturity which so has faced the tragic aspects of our human life is not less desirable than childhood; it may be richer, fuller, steadier. We may think of it as Wordsworth did about the English landscape—that not for all the sunny skies of Italy would he give up the mists that spiritualize the English hills. But when trouble comes, life faces a new set of problems that childhood little knew. We have joined the human procession that moves out into the inevitable need of comfort and fortitude.

The decisive crisis in many lives concerns the attitude which this experience evokes. Some are led by it more deeply into the meanings of religion. The Bible grows in their apprehension with the enlarging of their life; new passages become radiant as, in a great landscape, hills and valleys lately unillumined catch the rays of the rising sun. At first the human friendliness of Jesus is most real, and the Bible's stories of adventure for God's cause; then knightly calls to character and service become luminous; but soon or late another kind of passage grows meaningful: "Now our Lord Jesus Christ himself, and God, our Father who loved us and gave us eternal comfort and good hope through grace, comfort your hearts and establish them" (II Thess. 2:16). Others, so far from being led by adversity into the deeper meanings of faith, renounce faith altogether, and fling themselves into open rebellion against life and any God who may be responsible for its tragedy. They may not dare to say what James Thomson did, but they think it—

"Who is most wretched in this dolorous place?
 I think myself; yet I would rather be
 My miserable self than He, than He
Who formed such creatures to his own disgrace.

The vilest thing must be less vile than Thou
 From whom it had its being, God and Lord!
 Creator of all woe and sin! abhorred,
Malignant and implacable! I vow

That not for all Thy power furled and unfurled,
 For all the temples to Thy glory built,
 Would I assume the ignominious guilt
Of having made such men in such a world!"

Many, however, are not by adversity made more sure of God, nor are they driven into rebellion against him. They are perplexed. It had been so much easier, in the sheltered and innocent idealism of their youth, to believe in God than it is now. As children they looked on life as they might have listened to Mozart's music, ravished with unqualified delight; but now they know that Mozart died in abject poverty, that the coffin which his wife could not buy was donated by charity, that as the hearse went to the grave the driver loudly damned the dead because no drink money had been given him, and that to this day no one knows where Mozart's body lies. Maturity has to deal with so much more tragic facts than youth can ever know. With all the philosophy that man's wit can supply, the wisest find themselves saying what Emerson did, two years after his son's death: "I have had no experience, no progress to put me into better intelligence with my calamity than when it was new." And in this inevitable wrestling with adversity, the cry of men is not simply for more courage. They might easily steady their hearts to endure and overcome, were only one question's answer clear—is there any *sense* in life's suffering? The one unsupportable thought is that all life's pain and hardship is meaningless and futile, that it has no worthy origin, serves no high purpose, that in misery we are the sport of forces that have no consciousness of what they do, no meaning in it and no care. Such folk want to believe in God, but—can they?

III

Two preliminary facts about Christianity's relationship with our problem may help to clarify our thought. The doubt sometimes obtrudes itself on minds perplexed about life's tragedies that the Christian's faith in a God of love is an idealistic dream. Such faiths as the Fatherhood of God have come to men, they think, in happy hours when calamity was absent or forgotten; they are the fruition of man's fortunate days. And born thus of a view of life from which the miseries of men had been shut out, this happy, ideal faith comes back to painful realities with a shock which it cannot sustain. But is Christian faith thus the child of man's happy days? Rather the very symbol of Christianity is the Cross. Our faith took its rise in one of history's most appalling tragedies, and the Gospel of a loving God, so far from being an ideal dream, conceived apart from life's forbidding facts, has all these centuries been intertwined with the public brutality of a crucifixion. Every emphasis of the Christian's faith has the mark of the Cross upon it. Jesus had said in words that God was love, but it was at Calvary that the words took fire: "God so loved the world that he gave his only begotten son" (John 3:16). Jesus had preached the divine forgiveness, but on Golgotha the message grew imperative: "God commendeth his own love toward us, in that, while we were yet sinners, Christ died for us" (Rom. 5:8). Jesus had put into parables the individual care of the Father for every child, but it was the Cross that drove the great faith home: Christ tasted "death for every man" (Heb. 2:9). Nothing in Christian faith has escaped the formative influence of the Tragedy. The last thing to be said about the Gospel is that it is a beautiful childlike dream which has not faced the facts of suffering. In the New Testament are all the miseries on which those who deny God's love count for support. We are at home there with suffering men: "They were stoned, they were sawn asunder, they were tempted, they were slain with the sword: they went about in sheepskins, in goatskins; being destitute, afflicted, ill-treated (of whom the world was not worthy), wandering in deserts and mountains and caves and the holes of the earth" (Heb. 11:37-38). The men with whom Christianity began were not strangers to such trouble, so that some modern need remind their innocent and dreaming faith that life is filled with mysterious adversity. *Christianity was suckled on adversity; it was cradled in pain. At the heart of its Book and its Gospel is a Good Man crowned with thorns, nailed to a cross, with a spear wound in his side.*

Nor have the great affirmations of faith in God's fatherhood ever been associated with men of ease in fortunate circumstance. The voice that cried "Father, into thy hands I commend my spirit" spoke in agonizing pain. And through history one finds those words best spoken with a cross for a background. Thomas á Becket said them, martyred in his own cathedral; John Huss said them, going to the stake at Constance; George Wishart said them, roasted at the foot of the sea-tower of St. Andrews. Christian faith is not a dream that came in hours when human trouble had been forgotten; it has furnished from the beginning an interpretation of human trouble and an attitude in meeting it that has made men "more than conquerors."

The second preliminary fact is this: *Christianity has never pretended to supply a theoretical explanation of why suffering had to be.* This seeming lack has excellent reason, for such an explanation, if it be complete, is essentially beyond the reach of any finite mind. The most comprehensive question ever asked, some philosopher has said, was put by a child. "Why was there ever anything at all?" No finite mind can answer that. And next in comprehensiveness, and in penetration to the very pith of creation's meaning, is this query, "Why, if something had to be, was it made as it is?" One must be God himself fully to answer that, or to comprehend the answer, could it be written down. To expect, therefore, from Christianity or from any other source a theoretical explanation that will plumb the depths of the mystery of suffering is to cry for the essentially impossible. So Carlyle says with typical vividness: "To the minnow every cranny and pebble, and quality and accident of its little native creek may have become familiar; but does the minnow understand the Ocean Tides and periodic Currents, the Trade-winds, and Monsoons, and Moon's Eclipses; by all which the condition of its little Creek is regulated, and may, from time to time (*un*miraculously enough), be quite overset and reversed? Such a minnow is Man; his Creek this Planet Earth; his Ocean the immeasurable All; his Monsoons and periodic Currents the mysterious Course of Providence through Aeons of Aeons."

So little is this inability of ours to know all that we wish about the world a cause for regret, that it ought to be an occasion of positive rejoicing. If *we* could understand the universe through and through, how small and meager the universe would have to be! The fact is that we cannot understand anything through and through. If one is disheartened because he cannot pierce to the heart of Providence and know all its secrets, let him try his hand upon a pebble and see how much better he will fare. What is a pebble? If one defines it roughly as granite he must ask what granite is; if that be defined in terms of chemical properties, he must ask what they are; if they be defined as ultimate forms of matter, he must inquire what matter is; and then he will be told that matter is a "mode of motion," or will be assured by a more candid scientist, like Professor Tait, that "we do not know and are probably incapable of discovering what matter *is*." No one ever solves the innermost problems of a stone, but what can be done with stones our engineering feats are evidence.

If, therefore, we recognize at the beginning that the question why suffering has to be is an ultimate problem, essentially insoluble by finite minds, we need not be dismayed. Two opposing mysteries are in the world—goodness and evil. If we *deny* God, then *goodness* is a mystery, for no one has ever yet suggested how spiritual life could rise out of an unspiritual source, how souls could come from dust. If we *affirm* God, then *evil* is a mystery, for why, we ask, should love create a world with so much pain and sin? Our task is not to solve insoluble problems; it is to balance these alternatives—no God and the mystery of man's spiritual life, against God and the mystery of evil. Such a comparison is not altogether beyond our powers, nor are weighty considerations lacking to affect our choice.

IV

For one thing, we may well inquire, when we complain of this world's misery, what sort of world we are seeking in its place. Are we asking for a perfectly happy world? But happiness, at its deepest and its best, is not the portion of a cushioned life which never struggled, overpassed obstacles, bore hardships, or adventured in sacrifice for costly aims. A heart of joy is never found in luxuriously coddled lives, but in men and women who achieve and dare, who have tried their powers against antagonisms, who have met even sickness and bereavement and have tempered their souls in fire. Joy is begotten not chiefly from the impression of happy circumstance, but from the expression of overcoming power. Were we set upon making a happy world, therefore, we could not leave struggle out nor make adversity impossible. The unhappiest world conceivable by man would be a world with nothing hard to do, no conflicts to wage for ends worth while; a world where courage was not needed and sacrifice was a superfluity. Beside such an inane lotos-land of tranquil ease this present world with all its suffering is a paradise. Men in fact find joy where in philosophy we might not look for it. Said MacMillan, after a terrific twelve-month with Peary on the Arctic continent: "This has been the greatest year of my life."

The impossibility of imagining a worth-while world from which adversity had all been banished is even more evident when one grows ill-content to think of happiness as the goal of life. That we should be merely happy is not an adequate end of the creative purpose for us, or of our purpose for ourselves. In our best hours we acknowledge this in the way we handle trouble. *However much in doubt a man may be about the theory of suffering, he knows infallibly how suffering practically should be meet.* To be rebellious, cursing fate and hating life; to pity oneself, nursing one's hurts in morbid self-commiseration—the ignobility of such dealing with calamity we indubitably know. Even where we fall feebly short of the ideal, we have no question what the ideal is. When in biography or among our friends we see folk face crushing trouble, not embittered by it, made cynical, or thrust into despair, but hallowed, sweetened, illumined, and empowered, we are aware that noble characters do not alone *bear* trouble; they *use* it. As men at first faced electricity in dread, conceiving toward it no attitude beyond building lightning-rods to ward away its stroke, but now with greater understanding harness it to do their will, so men, as they grow wise and strong, deal with their suffering. They make it the minister of character; they set it to build in them what nothing save adversity can ever build—patience, courage, sympathy, and power. They even choose it in vicarious sacrifice for the good of others, and by it save the world from evils that nothing save some one's suffering could cure. They act as though *character,* not happiness, were the end of life. and when they are at their best they do this not with stoic intrepidity, as though trouble's usefulness were but their fancy, but joyfully, as though a good purpose in the world included trouble, even though not intending it. So Robert Louis Stevenson, facing death, writes to a friend about an old woman whose ventriloquism had frightened the natives of Vailima, "All the old women in the world might talk with their mouths shut and not frighten you or me, but there are plenty of other things that frighten us badly. And if we only knew about them, perhaps we should find them no more worthy to be feared than an old woman talking with her mouth shut. And the names of some of these things are Death and Pain and Sorrow."

Whatever, then, may be our theoretical difficulty about suffering, this truth is clear: when we are at our best we practically deal with suffering as though moral quality were the goal of life. We *use* adversity, as though discipline were its purpose and good its end. It is worth noting that the only theory which fully fits this noblest attitude toward trouble is Christianity. Men may think God a devil, as James Thomson sang, and yet may be practically brave and cheerful, but their theory does not fit their life. Men may believe in no God and no purpose in the world, and yet may face adversity with courage and hope, but their spirit belies their philosophy. When men are at their best in hardship *they act as though the Christian faith in God were true, as though moral quality were the purpose of creation.*

If now, we really want a world in which character is the end and aim—and no other world is worth God's making—we obviously may not demand the abolition of adversity. If one imagines a life from its beginning lapped in ease and utterly ignorant what worlds like hardship, sorrow, and calamity imply, he must imagine a life lacking every virtue that makes human nature admirable. Character grows on struggle; without the overcoming of obstacles great quality in character is unthinkable. Whoever has handled well any calamitous event possesses resources, insights, wise attitudes, qualities of sympathy and power that by no other road could have come to him. For all our complaints against life's misery, therefore, and for all our inability to understand it in detail, who would not hesitate, foreseeing the consequence, to take adversity away from men? He who banishes hardship banishes hardihood; and out of the same door with Calamity walk Courage, Fortitude, Triumphant Faith, and Sacrificial Love. If we abolish the cross in the world, we make impossible the Christ in man. It becomes more clear the more one ponders it, that while this is often a hard world in which to be happy, to men of insight and faith it may be a great world in which to build character.

V

Before too confidently, however, we accept this conclusion, there is one objection to be heard. So far is the world from being absolved from cruelty, on the plea of moral purpose, one may say, that its *injustice is the very crux of its offense*. See how negligent of justice the process of creation is! Its volcanoes and typhoons slay good and bad alike, its plagues are utterly indifferent to character; and in the human world which it embosoms some drunken Caesar sits upon the throne while Christ hangs on the cross. Who for a single day can watch the gross inequities of life, where good men so often suffer and bad men go free, and still think that the world has moral purpose in it? The Bible itself is burdened with complaint against the seeming senselessness and injustice of God. Moses cries: "Lord, wherefore hast thou dealt ill with this people? neither hast thou delivered thy people at all" (Exod. 5:22-23); Elijah laments, "O Jehovah, my God, hast Thou also brought evil upon the widow, with whom I sojourn, by slaying her son?" (I Kings 17:20); Habakkuk complains, "Wherefore lookest thou upon them that deal treacherously, and holdest thy peace, when the wicked swalloweth up the man that is more righteous than he?" (Hab. 1:13); and Job protests, "Although thou knowest that I am not wicked, . . . yet thou dost destroy me" (Job 10:7-8). Man's loss of faith springs often from this utter disparity between desert and fortune. The time comes to almost every man when he looks on, indignant, desperate, at some gross horror uninterrupted, some innocent victim entreated cruelly. He understands Carlyle's impatient cry, "God sits in heaven and does nothing!"

Natural as is this attitude, and unjust as many of life's tragic troubles are, we should at least see this: *man must not demand that goodness straightway receive its pay and wrong its punishment.* He may not ask that every virtuous deed be at once rewarded by proportionate happiness and every sin be immediately punished by proportionate pain. That, some might suppose, would put justice into life. But whatever it might put into life, such an arrangement obviously would take out *character.* The men whose moral quality we most highly honor were not paid for their goodness on Saturday night and did not expect to be. They chose their course *for righteousness' sake alone,* although they knew what crowns of thorns, what scornful crowds about their cross might end the journey. They did not drive close bargains with their fate, demanding insurance against trouble as the price of goodness. They chose the honorable deed for honor's sake; they chose it the more scrupulously, the more pleasure was offered for dishonor; their tone in the face of threatened suffering was like Milne's, Scotland's last martyr: "I will not recant the truth, for I am corn and no chaff; and I will not be blown away with the wind nor burst with the flail, but I will abide both."

Every man is instinctively aware and by his admiration makes it known, that the kind of character which chooses right, willing to suffer for it, is man's noblest quality. The words in which such character has found utterance are man's spiritual battle cries. Esther, going before the King, saying, "If I perish, I perish" (Esther 4:16); the three Hebrews, facing the fiery furnace saying, "Our God whom we serve is able to deliver us from the burning fiery furnace; and he will deliver us out of thy hand, O king. But if *not,* be it known unto thee, O king, that we will not serve thy gods" (Dan. 3:17-18); Peter and the apostles, facing the angry Council, saying, "We must obey God rather than men" (Acts 5:29); Anaxarchus, the martyr, crying, "Beat on at the case of Anaxarchus; Anaxarchus himself you cannot touch"; Luther, defying the Emperor, "Here stand I; I can do no other"—most words of men are easily dispensable, but no words like these can man afford to spare. They are his best. *And this sort of goodness has been possible, because God had not made the world as our complaints sometimes would have it.* For such character, a system where goodness was paid cash in pleasant circumstance would have no such character to show. Right and wrong for their own sakes would be impossible; only prudence and imprudence for happiness' sake could there exist. Out of the same door with the seeming injustice of life goes the possibility of man's noblest quality—his goodness "in scorn of consequence." Many special calamities no one on earth can hope to understand. But when one has granted the fitness to grow character is the only worth test of creation, it evidently is not so simple as at first to improve the fundamental structure of the world.

VI

Indeed, when one in imagination assumes the task of omnipotence and endeavors to construct a universe that shall be fitted for the growth of character, he cannot long hesitate concerning certain elements which must be there. *A system of regular law* would have to be the basis of that world, for only in a law-abiding universe could obedience be taught. If the stars and planets behaved "like swarms of flies" and nothing could be relied upon to act twice in the same way, character and intelligence alike would be impossible. In this new world, remolded, "nearer to our heart's desire," *progress* also would be a necessity. A stagnant world cannot grow character. There must be real work to do, aims to achieve; there must be imperfections to overpass and wrongs to right. Only in a system where the present situation is a point of departure and a better situation is a possibility, where ideal and hope, courage and sacrifice are indispensable can character grow. In this improved world of our dreams, *free will* in some measure must be granted man. If character is to be real, man must not in his choice between right and wrong be as Spinoza pictured him, a stone hurled through the air, which thinks that it is flying; he must have some control of conduct, some genuine, though limited, power of choice. And in this universe which we are planning for character's sake, individuals could not stand separate and unrelated; *they must be woven into a community.* Love which is the crown of character, lacking this, would be impossible. What happens to one must happen to all; good and ill alike must be contagious in a society where we are "members one of another."

No one of these four elements could be omitted from a world whose test was its adaptability for character. Men with genuine power of choice, fused into a fellowship of social life, living in a law-abiding and progressive world— on no other terms imaginable to man could character be possible. *Yet these four things contain all the sources of our misery.* Physical law—what tragic issues its stern, unbending course brings with terrific incidence on man! Progress—how obviously it implies conditions imperfect, wrong, through which we have to struggle toward the best! Free will—what a nightmare of horror man's misuse of it has caused since sin began! Social fellowship—how surely the innocent must suffer with the guilty, how impossible for any man to bear the consequence of his own sin alone! We may not see why these general conditions should involve the particular calamities which we bewail, but even our finite minds can see thus far into the mystery of suffering: *all our trouble springs from four basic factors in the universe, without any one of which, great character would be impossible.*

While, therefore, if one *deny* God, the mystery of goodness lacks both sense and solution; one may *affirm* God and find the mystery of evil, mysterious still but suffused with light. God is working out a spiritual purpose here by means without which no spiritual purpose is conceivable. Fundamentally creation is good. We misuse it, we fail to understand its meaning and to appropriate its discipline, and impatient because the eternal purpose is not timed by our small clocks, we have to confess with Theodore Parker, "The trouble seems to be that God is not in a hurry and I am." In hours of insight, however, we perceive how little our complaints will stand the test of dispassionate thought. Our miseries are not God's inflictions on us as individuals, so that we may judge his character and his thought of us by this special favor or by that particular calamity. The most careless thinker feels the poor philosophy of Lord Londonderry's petulant entry in his journal: "Here I learned that Almighty God, for reasons best known to himself, had been pleased to burn down my house in the county of Durham." One must escape such narrow egoism if he is to understand the purposes of God; one must rise to look on a creation, with character at all costs for its aim, and countless aeons for its settling. In the making of this world God has *limited himself;* he cannot lightly do what he will. He has limited himself in creating a law-abiding system where his children must learn obedience without special exemptions; in ordaining a progressive system where what *is* is the frontier from which men seek what *ought to be;* in giving men the power to choose right, with its inevitable corollary, the power to choose wrong; in weaving men into a communal fellowship where none can escape the contagious life at all. What Martineau said of the first of these is true in spirit of them all: "The universality of law is God's eternal act of self-limitation or abstinence from the movements of free affection, for the sake of a constancy that shall never falter or deceive."

When once a man has risen to the vision of so splendid a purpose in so great a world he rejoices in the outlook. Granted that now he sees in a mirror darkly, that many a cruel event in human life perplexes still—he has seen enough to give solid standing to his faith. What if an insect, someone has suggested, were born just after a thunderstorm began and died just before it stopped—how dark would be its picture of creation! But we who span a longer period of time, are not so obsessed by thunderstorms, although we may not like them. They have their place and serve their purpose; we see them in a broader perspective than an insect knows and on sultry days we even crave their coming. A broken doll is to a child a cruel tragedy, but to the father watching the child's struggle to accept the accident, to make the best of it and to come off conqueror, the event is not utterly undesirable. He is not glad at the child's suffering, but with his horizons he sees in it factors which she does not see. So God's horizons infinitely overpass our narrow outlooks. There is something more than whimsy in the theologian's saying, which President King reports, that an insect crawling up a column of the Parthenon, with difficulty and pain negotiating passage about a pore in the stone, is as well qualified to judge of the architecture of the Parthenon, as we of the infinitude of God's plans. Seeing as much as we have seen of sense and purpose in the structure of creation, we have seen all that our finite minds with small horizons could have hoped. We have gained ample justification for the attitude toward suffering which Dolly Winthrop in *Silas Marner* has immortalized: "Eh, there's trouble i' this world, and there's things as we can niver make out the rights on. And all as we've got to do is to trusten, Master Marner—to do the right thing as far as we know and to trusten. For if us, as knows so little, can see a bit o' good and rights, we may be sure as there's a good and a rights bigger nor what we can know—I feel it i' my own inside as it must be so."

VII

We may not truthfully leave our subject in such a case that faith's concern with human misery will seem to lie merely in giving adversity an explanation. Faith is concerned not alone to *explain* misery but to *heal* it. For while it is impossible without hardship to develop character, there are woeful calamities on earth that do not help man's moral quality; they crush and mutilate it; they are barbarous intruders on the plan of God and they have no business in his world. Some ills are such that no theory can reconcile them with the love of God and no man ought to desire such reconciliation; in the love of God they ought to be abolished. Slavery must be a possibility in a world where man is free; but God's goodness was not chiefly vindicated by such a theory of explanation. It was chiefly vindicated by slavery's abolishment. The liquor traffic and war, needless poverty in a world so rich, avoidable diseases that science can overcome—how long a list of woes there is that faith should not so much explain as banish! When some ills like drunkenness and war and economic injustice are thrust against our faith, and men ask that the goodness of God be reconciled with these, faith's first answer should be not speculation but action. Such woes, so far from being capable of reconciliation with God's goodness, are irreconcilable with a decent world. God does not want to be reconciled with them; he hates them "with a perfect hatred." We may not make ourselves patient with them by any theory of their necessity. They are not necessary; they are perversions of man's life; and *the best defense of faith is their annihilation.*

Indeed, a man who, rebellious in complaint, has clamorously asked an explanation of life's ills as the price of faith in God, may well in shame consider God's real saints. When things were at their worst, when wrong was conqueror and evils that seemed blatantly to deny the love of God were in the saddle, these spiritual soldiers went out to fight. The winds of ill that blow out our flickering faith made their religion blaze—a pillar of fire in the night. The more evil they faced, the more religion they produced to answer it. They were the real believers, who "through faith subdued kingdoms, wrought righteousness, obtained promises." In comparison with such, it is obviously paltry business to drive a bargain with God that if all goes well we will believe in him, but if things look dark, then faith must go.

Many a man, therefore, who is no philosopher can be a great defender of the faith. He may not weave arguments to prove that such a world as this in its fundamental structure is fitted to a moral purpose. But he can join the battle to banish from the world those ills that have no business here and that God hates. He can help produce that final defense of the Christian faith—a world where it is easier to believe in God.

CHAPTER VII

Faith and Science

DAILY READINGS

The intellectual difficulties which trouble many folk involve the relations of faith with science, but often they do not so much concern the abstract theories of science as they do the particular attitudes of scientists. We are continually faced with quotations from scientific specialists, in which religion is denied or doubted or treated contemptuously, and even while the merits of the case may be beyond the ordinary man's power of argument, he nevertheless is shaken by the general opinion that what ministers say in the pulpit on Sunday is denied by what scientists say all the rest of the week. In the daily readings, therefore, we shall deal with the scientists themselves, as a problem which faith must meet.

Seventh Week, First Day

No one can hope to deal fairly with the scientists, in their relationship with faith, unless he begins with a warm appreciation of the splendid integrity and self-denial which the scientific search for truth has revealed.

Canst thou bind the cluster of the Pleiades,
Or loose the bands of Orion?
Canst thou lead forth the Mazzaroth in their season?
Or canst thou guide the Bear with her train?
Knowest thou the ordinances of the heavens?
Canst thou establish the dominion thereof in the earth?

Canst thou lift up thy voice to the clouds,
That abundance of waters may cover thee?
Canst thou send forth lightnings, that they may go,
And say unto thee, Here we are?
Who hath put wisdom in the inward parts?
Or who hath given understanding to the mind?
Who can number the clouds by wisdom?
Or who can pour out the bottles of heaven,
When the dust runneth into a mass,
And the clods cleave fast together?

—Job 38:31-38.

Such is man's ancient wonder before the physical universe; and in the endeavor to discover the truth about it science has developed saints and martyrs whose selfless and sacrificial spirit is unsurpassed even in the annals of the Church. Men have spent lives of obscure and unrewarded toil to get at a few new facts; they have suffered persecution, and, even after torture, have reaffirmed the truth of their discoveries, as did Galileo, when he insisted, "The earth does move." They have surrendered place and wealth, friends and life itself in their passion for the sheer truth, and when human service was at stake have inoculated themselves with deadly diseases that they might be the means of discovering the cure, or have sacrificed everything that men hold most dear to destroy an ancient, popular, and hurtful fallacy. The phrase "pride of science" is often used in depreciation of the scientists. There is some excuse for the phrase, but in general, when one finds pride, dogmatism, intolerance, they are the work of ignorance and not of science. The scientific spirit has been characteristically humble. Says Huxley: "Science seems to me to teach in the highest and strongest manner the great truth which is embodied in the Christian conception of entire surrender to the will of God. Sit down before the fact as a little child, be prepared to give up every preconceived notion, follow humbly wherever and to whatever end nature leads, or you shall learn nothing. . . . I have only begun to learn content and peace of mind since I have resolved at all risks to do this." The Christian, above all others, is bound to approach the study of the controversy between science and theology with a high estimate of the integrity and disinterested unselfishness of the scientists.

O God, we thank Thee for the world in which Thou hast placed us, for the universe whose vastness is revealed in the blue depths of the sky, whose immensities are lit by shining stars beyond the strength of mind to follow. We thank Thee for every sacrament of beauty; for the sweetness of flowers, the solemnity of the stars, the sound of streams and swelling seas; for far-stretching lands and mighty mountains which rest and satisfy the soul, the purity of dawn which calls to holy dedication, the peace of evening which speaks of everlasting rest. May we not fear to make this world for a little while our home, since it is Thy creation and we ourselves are part of it. Help us humbly to learn its laws and trust its mighty powers.

We thank Thee for the world within, deeper than we dare to look, higher than we care to climb; for the great kingdom of the mind and the silent spaces of the soul. Help us not to be afraid of ourselves, since we were made in Thy image, loved by Thee before the worlds began, and fashioned for Thy eternal habitation. May we be brave enough to bear the truth, strong enough to live in the light, glad to yield ourselves to Thee.

We thank Thee for that world brighter and better than all, opened for us in the broken heart of the Savior; for the universe of love and purity in Him, for the golden sunshine of His smile, the tender grace of His forgiveness, the red renewing ruin and crimson flood of His great sacrifice. May we not shrink from its searching and surpassing glory, nor, when this world fades away, fear to commit ourselves to that world which shall be our everlasting home. Amen.—W. E. Orchard.

Seventh Week, Second Day

The Christian's appreciation of scientists should not stop short of profound gratitude for their service to religion. If one reads Burns' "Tam o'Shanter," with its "ghaists," "warlocks and witches," and "ault Nick," and remembers that these demonic powers were veritable facts of terror once, he will see in what a world of superstitious fear mankind has lived. Bells were first put into church steeples, not to call folk to worship, but to scare the devils out of thunderclouds, and the old cathedral bells of Europe are inscribed with declarations of that purpose. The ancients hardly believed in God so vividly as they believed in malicious demons everywhere. Now the Gospel removed the *fear* of these from the first Christians; it made men aware of a conquering alliance with God, so that believers no longer shared the popular dread of unknown demons. But so long as thunderstorms, pestilences, droughts, and every sort of evil were supposed to be the work of devils, even the Gospel could not dispel the general dread. Only new knowledge could do that. While Christianity therefore at its best has removed the *fear* of evil spirits, science has removed the *fact* of them as an oppressive weight on life. Today we not only do not dread them, but we do not think of them at all, and we have science to thank for our freedom. By its clear facing of facts and tracing of laws, science has lifted from man's soul an intolerable burden of misbeliefs and has cleansed religion of an oppressive mass of credulity. *True religion never had a deadlier foe than superstition and superstition has no deadlier foe than science.* Little children, brought up in our homes to trust the love of the Father, with no dark background of malignant devils to harass and frighten them, owe their liberty to the Gospel of Jesus indeed, but as well as to the illumination of science that has banished the ancient dreads.

These things have I spoken unto you, while yet abiding with you. But the Comforter, even the Holy Spirit, whom the Father will send in my name, he shall teach you all things, and bring to your remembrance all that I said unto you. Peace I leave with you; my peace I give unto you: not as the world giveth, give I unto you. Let not your heart be troubled, neither let it be fearful.—John 14:25-27.

To God the Father, God the Son, God the Spirit, we pour forth most humble and hearty supplications, that He, remembering the calamities of mankind, and the pilgrimage of this our life in which we spend our days, would please to open to us new consolations out of the fountain of His goodness for the alleviating of our miseries. We humbly and earnestly ask that human things may not prejudice such as are Divine, so that from the opening of the gates of sense, and the kindling of a greater natural light, nothing of incredulity . . . may arise in our minds towards Divine mysteries; but rather, O Lord, that our minds being thoroughly cleansed and purged from fancy, and yet subject to the Divine will, there may be given unto faith the things that are faith's, so that we may continually attain to a deeper knowledge and love of Thee, Who art the Fountain of Light, and dwellest in the Light which no man can approach unto; through Jesus Christ our Lord. Amen.—Francis Bacon, 1561.

Seventh Week, Third Day

If one approach the scientists, as we have suggested, with appreciation of their devoted spirit and of their beneficent service, he is likely to be fair and Christian in his judgment. For one thing, he will readily understand why some of them are not religious men. The laws of psychology are not suspended when religion is concerned; there as elsewhere persistent attention is the price of a vivid sense of reality. When, therefore, a man habitually thinks intensely of nothing but biological tissue, or chemical reactions, or the diseases of a special organ, the results are not difficult to forecast. Darwin's famous confession that in his exacting concentration on biology he utterly lost his power to appreciate music or poetry is a case in point. Said Darwin, "My mind seems to have become a kind of machine for grinding general laws out of a large collection of facts." It is needless to say that such a mind is not likely to be more vividly aware of God than it is to feel music's beauty or poetry's truth. The plain fact is that if any man should persistently restrict himself to a physical science, should never hear a symphony or an oratorio, should shut out from his experience any dealing with music or enjoyment of it, he would in the end lose all musical capacity, and would become a man whose appreciation of music was nil and whose opinion on music was worthless. *Just such an atrophy of life is characteristic of intense specialists.* When one understands this he becomes capable of intelligent sympathy with scientists, even when he does not at all agree with their religious opinions. Jude gives us a remarkable injunction, plainly applicable here. "On some have mercy who are in doubt."

But ye, beloved, building up yourselves on your most holy faith, praying in the Holy Spirit, keep yourselves in the love of God, looking for the mercy of our Lord Jesus Christ unto eternal life. And on some have mercy, who are in doubt; and some save, snatching them out of the fire; and on some have mercy with fear; hating even the garment spotted by the flesh.

Now unto him that is able to guard you from stumbling, and to set you before the presence of his glory without blemish in exceeding joy, to the only God our Saviour, through Jesus Christ our Lord, be glory, majesty, dominion and power, before all time, and now, and for evermore. Amen.—Jude 20-25.

O God, who so fillest all things that they only thinly veil Thy presence; we adore Thee in the beauty of the world, in the goodness of human hearts and in Thy thought within the mind. We praise Thee for the channels through which Thy grace can come to us; sickness and health, joy and pain, freedom and necessity, sunshine and rain, life and death.

We thank Thee for all the gentle and healing ministries of life; the gladness of the morning, the freedom of the wind, the music of the rain, the joy of the sunshine, and the deep calm of the night; for trees, and flowers, the clouds, and skies; for the tender ministries of human love, the unselfishness of parents, the love that binds man and woman, the confidence of little children; for the patience of teachers and the encouragement of friends.

We bless Thee for the stirring ministry of the past, for the story of noble deeds, the memory of holy men, the printed book, the painter's art, the poet's craft; most of all for the ministry of the Son of Man, who taught us the eternal beauty of earthly things, who by His life sets us free from fear, and by His death won us from our sins to Thee; for His cradle, His cross, and His crown.

May His Spirit live within us, conquer all the selfishness of man, and take away the sin of the world. Amen.—W. E. Orchard.

Seventh Week, Fourth Day

The tendency of scientific specialization to shut out the appreciation of life's other values has one notable result: the opinions of scientific specialists in the physical realm on matters of religion are generally not of major importance. There is a popular fallacy that an expert in one realm must be listened to with reverence on all subjects. But the fact is that a great physicist is not by his scientific eminence thereby qualified to talk wisely on politics or literature or religion; rather, so far as *a priori* considerations are concerned, he is thereby disqualified. Mr. Edison cannot say anything on electricity that is insignificant; but when he gave an interview on immortality he revealed to everyone who knew the history of thought on that subject and the issues involved in it, that on matters outside his specialty he could say things very insignificant. The more one personally knows great specialists, the more he sees how human they are, how interest in one thing shuts out interest in others, how the subject on which the mind centers grows real and all else unreal, how very valuable their judgment is on their specialties, and how much less valuable even than ordinary men's is their judgment on anything beside. This truth does not concern religion only; it concerns any subject which calls into play appreciative faculties that their science does not use. For a man, therefore, to surrender religious faith because a specialist in another realm disowns it is absurd. If one wishes, outside of those whose vital interest in religion makes them specialists there, to get confirmation from another class of men, let him look not to physicists but to judges. They are accustomed to weigh evidence covering the general field of human life; and among the great judicial minds of this generation, as of all others, one finds an overwhelming preponderance of religious men.

But unto us God revealed them through the Spirit: for the Spirit searcheth all things, yea, the deep things of God. For who among men knoweth the things of a man, save the spirit

of the man, which is in him? even so the things of God none knoweth, save the Spirit of God. But we received, not the spirit of the world, but the spirit which is from God; that we might know the things that were freely given to us of God. which things also we speak, not in words which man's wisdom teacheth, but which the Spirit teacheth; combining spiritual things with spiritual word. Now the natural man receiveth not the things of the Spirit of God: for they are foolishness unto him; and he cannot know them, because they are spiritually judged.—I Cor. 2:10-14.

O Eternal and glorious Lord God, since Thy glory and honor is the great end of all Thy works, we desire that it may be the beginning and end of all our prayers and services. Let Thy great Name be glorious, and glorified, and sanctified throughout the world. Let the knowledge of Thee fill all the earth as the waters cover the sea. Let that be done in the world that may most advance Thy glory. Let all Thy works praise Thee. Let Thy wisdom, power, justice, goodness, mercy, and truth be evident unto all mankind, that they may observe, acknowledge, and admire it, and magnify the Name of Thee, the Eternal God. In all the dispensation of Thy Providence, enable us to see Thee, and to sanctify Thy Name in our hearts with thankfulness, in our lips with thanksgiving, in our lives with dutifulness and obedience. Enable us to live to the honor of that great Name of Thine by which we are called, and that, as we profess ourselves to be Thy children, so we may study and sincerely endeavor to be like Thee in all goodness and righteousness, that we may thereby bring glory to Thee our Father which art in heaven; that we and all mankind may have high and honorable thoughts concerning Thee, in some measure suitable to Thy glory, majesty, goodness, wisdom, bounty, and purity, and may in all our words and actions manifest these inward thoughts touching Thee with suitable and becoming words and actions; through Jesus Christ our Lord. Amen.—Lord Chief Justice Sir Matthew Hale, 1609.

Seventh Week, Fifth Day

So far in our thought we have tacitly consented to the popular supposition, that the scientists are at odds with religion. Many of them unquestionably are. But in view of the obsessing nature of scientific specialties, the wonder is not that some scientists are nonreligious; the wonder is that so many are profoundly men of faith in God. The idea that scientists as a whole are irreligious is untrue. Lists of testimonials from eminent specialists in favor of religion are not particularly useful, for, as we have said, the judgment of specialists outside their chosen realm is, at the most, no more valuable than that of ordinary men. But if anyone tries to rest his case against religion on the adverse opinions of great scientists, he easily can be driven from his position. Sir William Crookes, one of the world's greatest chemists, writes: "I cannot imagine the possibility of anyone with ordinary intelligence entertaining the least doubt as to the existence of a God—a Law-Giver and a Life-Giver." Lord Kelvin, called the "Napoleon of Science," said that he could think of nothing so absurd as atheism; Sir Oliver Lodge, perhaps the greatest living physicist and certainly an earnest believer, writes, "The tendency of science, whatever it is, is not in an irreligious direction at the present time"; Sir George Stokes, the great physicist (died 1903), affirmed his belief that disbelievers among men of science "form a very small minority"; and Sir James Geikie, Dean of the Faculty of Science at Edinburgh University, impatiently writes, "It is simply an impertinence to say that 'the leading scientists are irreligious or anti-Christian.' Such a statement could only be made by some scatter-brained chatterbox or zealous fanatic." The fact is that, in spite of the tendency of high specialization to crowd out religious interest and insight, our great scientists have never thrown the mass of their influence against religion, and today, in the opinion of one of their chief leaders, are growing to be increasingly men of religious spirit. Whatever argument is to be based on the testimony of the scientists is rather for religion than against it.

For this cause I also, having heard of the faith in the Lord Jesus which is among you, and the love which ye show toward all the saints, cease not to give thanks for you, making mention of you in my prayers; that the God of our Lord Jesus Christ, the Father of glory, may give unto you a spirit of wisdom and revelation in the knowledge of him;

having the eyes of your heart enlightened, that ye may know what is the hope of his calling, what the riches of the glory of his inheritance in the saints, and what the exceeding greatness of his power to us-ward who believe.—Eph. 1:15-19.

O Lord, who by Thy holy Apostle hast taught us to do all things in the name of the Lord Jesus and to Thy glory; give Thy blessing, we pray Thee, to this our work, that we may do it in faith, and heartily, as to the Lord, and not unto men. All our powers of body and mind are Thine, and we would fain devote them to Thy service. Sanctify them and the work in which we are engaged; let us not be slothful, but fervent in spirit, and do Thou, O Lord, so bless our efforts that they may bring forth in us the fruit of true wisdom. Strengthen the faculties of our minds, and dispose us to exert them for Thy glory and for the futherance of Thy Kingdom. Save us from all pride and vanity and reliance upon our own power or wisdom. Teach us to seek after truth, and enable us to gain it; while we know earthly things, may we know Thee, and be known by Thee through and in Thy Son Jesus Christ, that we may be Thine in body and spirit, in all our work and undertakings; through Jesus Christ. Amen.—Thomas Arnold, 1795.

Seventh Week, Sixth Day

Far more important than the opinions of individual scientists for religion or against it, is the fact that scientists are coming increasingly to recognize the limitations of their field. The field of science *is* limited; its domain is the system of facts and their laws, which make the immediate environment of man's life; but with the Origin of all life, with the character of the Power that sustains us and with the Destiny that lies ahead of us science does not, cannot deal. The most superficial observance shows how little any great soul lives within the confines of science's discoveries. Carlyle, after his great bereavement, writes to his friend Erskine:

" 'Our Father which art in heaven, hallowed be Thy name, Thy will be done'—what else can we say? The other night in my sleepless tossings about, which were growing more and more miserable, these words, that brief and grand Prayer, came strangely to my mind, with an altogether new emphasis; as if written and shining for me in mild pure splendor, on the black bosom of the Night there; when I, as it were, read them word by word—with a sudden check to my imperfect wanderings, with a sudden softness of composure which was much unexpected. Not for perhaps thirty or forty years had I once formally repeated that prayer—nay, I never felt before how intensely the voice of man's soul it is; the inmost aspiration of all that is high and pious in poor human nature." But supposing that the facts of science were all of reality and the laws of science all of truth, what sort of prayer could Carlyle have offered? Another has suggested the form which the Lord's Prayer would take in a world that lacked religious faith: "Our brethren who are upon the earth, hallowed be our name; our Kingdom come; our will be done on earth; for there is no heaven. We must get us this day our daily bread; we fear not temptation, for we deliver ourselves from evil; for ours is the Kingdom and ours is the power, and there is no glory and no forever. Amen." In such a barren prayer *the whole of man's life is not represented.*

Let no man deceive himself. If any man thinketh that he is wise among you in this world, let him become a fool, that he may become wise. For the wisdom of this world is foolishness with God. For it is written, He that taketh the wise in their craftiness: and again, The Lord knoweth the reasonings of the wise, that they are vain. Wherefore let no one glory in men. For all things are yours; whether Paul, or Apollos, or Cephas, or the world, or life, or death, or things present, or things to come; all are yours; and ye are Christ's; and Christ is God's.—I Cor. 3:18-23.

O Thou Infinite Spirit, who occupiest all space, who guidest all motion, thyself unchanged, and art the life of all that lives, we flee unto thee, in whom we also live and move and have our being, and would reverence Thee with what is highest and holiest in our soul. We know that Thou art not to be worshiped as though Thou needest aught, or askedst the psalm of praise from our lips; or our hearts poor prayer. O

Lord, the ground under our feet, and the seas which whelm it round, the air which holds them both, and the heavens sparkling with many a fire—these are a whisper of the psalm of praise which creation sends forth to Thee, and we know that Thou askest no homage of bended knee, nor heart bowed down, nor heart uplifted unto Thee. But in our feebleness and our darkness, dependent on Thee for all things, we lift up our eyes unto Thee; as a little child to the father and mother who guide him by their hands, so do our eyes look up Thy countenance, O Thou who art our Father and our Mother too, and bless thee for all thy gifts. We look to the infinity of Thy perfection with awe-touched heart, and we adore the sublimity which we cannot comprehend. We bow down before Thee, and would renew our sense of gratitude and quicken still more our certainty of trust, till we feel Thee a presence close to our heart, and are so strong in the heavenly confidence that nothing earthly can disturb us or make us fear. Amen.—Theodore Parker.

Seventh Week, Seventh Day

The difficulty which many Christians feel concerning science centers around their loyalty to the Bible. They still are under the domination of the thought that the Christian idea of the Bible is the same as the Mohammedan idea of the Koran or the Mormon idea of Joseph Smith's sacred plates. The Koran was all written in heaven, word for word, say orthodox Mohammedans, before ever it came to earth. As for the Mormon Bible, God buried the plates on which he wrote, said Smith, and then disclosed their hiding place, and his prophet translated them verbatim, so that the Mormon book is literally inerrant. But this is not the Christian idea of the Bible. Inspiration is never represented in Scripture as verbal dictation where human powers and limitations are suspended, so that like a phonographic plate the result is a mechanical reproduction of the words of God. Rather God spoke to men through their experience as they were able to understand him, and as a result the great Christian Book, like a true Christian man, represents alike the inbreathing of the Divine and the limitation of the human. So the Epistle to the Hebrews clearly states that

God did what he could in revealing partially to partial men what they could understand:

God, having of old time spoken unto the fathers in the prophets by divers portions and in divers manners, hath at the end of these days spoken unto us in his Son, whom he appointed heir of all things, through whom also he made the worlds.—Heb. 1:1-2.

Of all limitations that are entirely obvious in the ancient Hebrew-Christian world, the current view of the physical universe is the most unescapable. To suppose that God never can reveal to men anything about the world, transcending what the ancient Hebrews could understand, is to deny the principle which Jesus applied even to the more important realm of spiritual truth: "I have yet many things to say unto you, but ye cannot bear them now" (John 16:12).

O Thou who hast visited us with the Dayspring from on high, who hast made light to shine in the darkness, we praise Thy holy name and proclaim Thy wonderful goodness.

We bless Thee for the dawning of the light in far-off ages as soon as human eyes could bear its rays. We remember those who bore aloft the torch of truth when all was false and full of shame; those far-sighted souls who from the mountain tops of vision heralded the coming day; those who labored in the darkened valleys to lift men's eyes to the hills.

We thank Thee that in the fulness of the times Thou didst gather Thy light into life, so that even simple folk could see; for Jesus the Star of the morning and the Light of the world.

We commemorate His holy nativity, His lowly toil, His lonely way; the gracious words of His lips, the deep compassion of His heart, His friendship for the fallen, His love for the outcast; the crown of thorns, the cruel cross, the open shame. And we rejoice to know as He was here on earth, so Thou art eternally. Thou dost not abhor our flesh, nor shrink from our earthly toil. Thou rememberest our frailty, bearest with our sin, and tastest even our bitter cup of death.

And now we rejoice for the light that shines about our daily path from the cradle to the grave, and for the light that

*illumines its circuit beyond these spheres from our
conception in Thy mind to the day when we wake in Thy
image; for the breathing of Thy spirit into ours till we see
Thee face to face: in God, from God; to God at last.
Hallelujah. Amen.*—W. E. Orchard.

COMMENT FOR THE WEEK

I

The innermost questions which some minds raise about
religion cannot be answered without candid discussion of
the obvious contrasts between faith and science. The
conflict between science and theology is one of the saddest
stories ever written. It is a record of mutual misunderstnd-
ing, of bitterness, bigotry, and persecution, and to this day
one is likely to find the devotees of religion suspicious of
science and scientists impatient with the Church.

If we are to understand the reason for this controversy
between science and theology, we must take a far look back
into man's history. Stephen Leacock remarks that whenever a professor discusses anything, he has to retreat at least
2,000 years to get a running start. Our retreat must be
farther than that; it carries us to the earliest stage in which
we are able to describe the thoughts of men. *At the
beginning men attributed to superhuman spirits all activities
in the world which they themselves did not perform.* If the
wind blew, a spirit did it; if the sun rose, a spirit moved it; if
a storm came, a spirit drove it. Natural law was non-existent
to the primitive man; every movement in nature was the
direct result of somebody's active will. From the mysterious
whispering of a wind-swept field to the crashing thunder,
what man did not cause the gods did.

If, therefore, a primitive man were asked the cause of
rain, he had but one answer: a god made it rain. That was
his *scientific* answer, for no other explanation of rain could
he conceive. That was his *religious* answer, for he
worshiped the spirit on whom he must depend for showers.
This significant fact, therefore, stands clear: *To primitive
man a religious answer and a scientific answer were identical.*
Sunrise was explained, not by planetary movements which

were unknown, but by the direct activity of a god, and the Dawn then was worshiped in the same terms in which it was explained. The historic reason for the confusion between science and religion at once grows evident. *At the beginning they were fused and braided into one; the story of their relationship is the record of their gradual and difficult disentangling.*

Wherever peace has come between science and religion, one finds a realm where the boundaries between the two are acknowledged and respected. Ask *now* the question, What makes it rain? There is a scientific answer in terms of natural laws concerning atmospheric pressure and condensation. There is also a religious answer, since behind all laws and through them runs the will of God. These two replies are distinct, they move in different realms, and are held together without inconsistency. As Sabatier put it, "Since God is the final cause of all things, he is not the scientific explanation of any one thing." In how many realms where once confusion reigned between the believers in the gods and the seekers after natural laws, is peace now established! Rain and sunrise, the tides and the eclipses, the coming of the seasons and the growing of the crops—for all such events we have our scientific explanations, and at the same time through them all the man of religion feels the creative power of God. Peace reigns in these realms because here *no longer do we force religious answers on scientific questions or scientific answers on religious questions.* Evidently the old Deuteronomic law is the solution of the conflict between science and religion: "Cursed be he that removeth his neighbor's landmark" (Deut. 27:17).

II

Left thus in the negative, however, this might seem to mean that we are to divide our minds into air-tight compartments, and allow no influences from one to penetrate another. But science and religion do tremendously affect each other, and no honest dealing ever can endeavor to prevent their mutual reaction. Our position is not thus negative; it affirms a positive and most important truth. Life has many aspects; science, art, religion, approach it from different angles, with different interests and purposes; and while they do *influence* each other, they are not *identical* and each has solid standing in its own right. When science has grown domineering, as though her approach to reality were the only one and her conclusions all of truth, the poets have had as much distaste for her as have the theologians. Shelley, who called himself an atheist, had no interest in religion's conflict with the extreme claims of science; yet listen to his aroused and flaming language as he pleads the case for poetry against her: "Poetry is something divine. . . . It is the perfect and consummate surface and bloom of all things; it is as the odor and color of the rose to the texture of the elements which compose it, and the form and splendor of unfaded beauty to the secrets of anatomy and corruption. What were virtue, love, patriotism, friendship— what were the scenery of this beautiful universe which we inhabit; what were our consolations on this side of the grave—and what were our aspirations beyond it, if poetry did not ascend to bring light and fire from those eternal regions where the owl-winged faculty of calculation dare not even soar?" This involves no denial of science's absolute right to her own field—the "texture of the elements which compose" the rose, and the "secrets of anatomy." But it is a justified assertion that this field of science is not all of reality, and that what the "owl-winged faculty of calculation" can reach is not all of truth.

What is a sunset? Science sets forth the answer in tables where the light waves that compose the colors are counted and the planetary movements that bring on the dusk are all explained. Poetry answers in a way how different!

> "I've dreamed of sunsets when the sun, supine,
> Lay rocking on the ocean like a god,
> And threw his weary arms far up the sky,
> And with vermilion-tinted fingers,
> Toyed with the long tresses of the evening
> star."[1]

Is one of these answers more than the other? Rather it is absurd to compare their truth; they are not contradictory;

[1] J. G. Holland

they approach the same fact with diverse interests, and seek in it different aspects of reality. Each has its rights in its own field. And so far it is from being true that science has a clear case in favor of its own superior importance, that Höffding, the philosopher, remarks, "It well may be that poetry gives more perfect expression to the highest Reality than any scientific concept can ever do."

Any great fact is too manifold in its meanings to be exhausted by a single method of approach. If one would know the Bible thoroughly, he must understand the rules of grammar. Were one to make grammar his exclusive specialty, the Bible to him, so far as he held strictly to his science, would be nouns and verbs, adverbs, adjectives, and prepositions, and the law-abiding relationships between them. This mere grammarian would know by such a method one aspect of the Bible, but how little of the Book would that aspect be! No rules of grammar can interpret the thirteenth chapter of the First Corinthians or explain the story of the Cross. The facts and laws of the Book's language a grammarian could know, but the beauty and the soul of it, the innermost transforming truth of it, would be unperceived.

So life is too rich and various to be exhausted by any one approach. Science seeks facts and arranges them in systems of cause and effect. Poetry sees these bare facts adorned with beauty, she suffuses them with her preferences and her appreciations. Religion sees the whole gathered up into spiritual unity, filled with moral purpose and good will, and in this faith finds peace and power. There need be no conflict between these various approaches; they are complementary, not antagonistic; and no man sees all the truth by any one of them alone. So a chemist might come to a spring to analyze it; a painter to rejoice in its beauties and reproduce them on his canvas; and a man athirst might come to drink and live. Shall they quarrel because they do not all come alike? Let them rather see how partial is the experience of each without the others!

III

In the mutual trespassing which has caused our problem, religion has had her guilty share, and the reason is not difficult to find. God did not have to give a modern scientific education to his ancient Hebrew saints before he could begin to reveal to them something of his will and character. And they, writing their experience and thought of him, could not avoid—as no generation's writers can avoid—indicating the view of the physical world which they and their contemporaries held. It is easy, therefore, from scores of Scripture passages to reconstruct the early Hebrew world. Their earth was flat and was founded on an underlying sea. (Ps. 136:6; Ps. 24:1, 2; Gen. 7:11); it was stationary (Ps. 93:1; Ps. 104:5); the heavens, like an unturned bowl, "strong as a molten mirror" (Job 37:18; Gen. 1:6-8; Isa. 40:22; Ps. 104:2), rested on the earth beneath (Amos 9:6; Job 26:11); the sun, moon, and stars moved within this firmament, of special purpose to illumine man (Gen. 1:14-19); there was a sea above the sky, "the waters which were above the firmament" (Gen. 1:7; Ps. 148:4), and through the "windows of heaven" the rain came down (Gen. 7:11; Ps. 78:23); beneath the earth was mysterious Sheol where dwelt the shadowy dead (Isa. 14:9-11); and all this had been made in six days, a short and measurable time before (Gen. 1). This was the world of the Hebrews.

Because when the Hebrews wrote the Bible their thoughts of God, their deep experience of him, were interwoven with their early science, Christians, through the centuries, have thought that faith in God stood or fell with early Hebrew science and that the Hebrew view of the physical universe must last forever. In the seventeenth century, Dr. John Lightfoot, Vice-Chancellor of the University of Cambridge, said: "Heaven and earth, center and circumference, were created all together, in the same instant, and clouds full of water. . . . This work took place and man was created by the Trinity on October 23, 4004 B.C., at nine o'clock in the morning." Of what tragedy has this identification of science with religion been the cause!

When *astronomy* began to revolutionize man's idea of the solar universe, when for the first time in man's imagination the flat earth grew round and the stable earth began moving through space seventy-five times faster than a cannonball, Pope Paul V solemnly rendered a decree, that "the doctrine of the double motion of the earth about its axis and about the sun is false and entirely contrary to Holy

Scripture." When *geology* began to show from the rocks' unimpeachable testimony the long leisureliness of God, laying the foundations of the world, a Christian leader declared geology "not a subject of lawful inquiry," "a dark art," "dangerous and disreputable," "a forbidden province," "an awful evasion of the testimony of revelation." This tragic record of theology's vain conflict with science is the most pitiable part of the Church's story. How needless it was! For now when we face our universe of magnificent distances and regal laws has religion really suffered? Has a flat and stationary earth proved essential to Christianity, as Protestants and Catholics alike declared? Rather the psalmist could not guess the sweep of our meaning when now we say, "The heavens declare the glory of God and the firmament showeth his handiwork" (Ps. 19:1).

In the last generation the idea of *evolution* was the occasion of a struggle like that which attended the introduction of the new astronomy. How was the world made? asked the ancient Hebrew, and he answered, By the word of God at a stroke. That was his scientific answer, and his religious answer too. When, therefore, the evolving universe was disclosed by modern science, when men read in fossil and in living biological structure the undeniable evidence of a long history of gradually changing forms of life, until the world was seen *not made like a box but growing like a tree,* many men of religion thought the faith destroyed. They identified the Christian Gospel with early Hebrew science! Today, however, when the general idea of evolution is taken for granted as gravitation is, how false this identification obviously appears! Says Professor Bowne, "An Eastern king was seated in a garden, and one of his counselors was speaking of the wonderful works of God. 'Show me a sign,' said the king, 'and I will believe.' 'Here are four acorns,' said the counselor; 'will your Majesty plant them in the ground, and then stoop down and look into this clear pool of water?' The king did so. 'Now,' said the other, 'look up.' The king looked up and saw four oak trees where he had planted the acorns. 'Wonderful!' he exclaimed; 'this is indeed the work of God.' 'How long were you looking into the water?' asked the counselor. 'Only a second,' said the king. 'Eighty years have passed as a second,' said the other. The king looked at his garments;

they were threadbare. He looked at his reflection in the water; he had become an old man. 'There is no miracle here, then,' he said angrily. 'Yes,' said the other; 'it is God's work whether he do it in one second or in eighty years.' "

Such an attitude as this is now a commonplace with Christian folk. A vast and growing universe through which sweep the purposes of God is by far the most magnificent outlook for faith that man has ever had. The Gospel and Hebrew science are *not* identical; the Gospel is not indissolubly bound to any science ancient or modern; for science and religion have separable domains.

"A fire-mist and a planet,
    A crystal and a cell,
A jelly-fish and a saurian,
    And caves where cave men dwell.
Then a sense of Love and Duty
    And a face turned from the clod,
Some call it Evolution
    And others—call it God."

The same story of needless antagonism is now being written about religion and *natural law*. When science began plotting nature's laws, the control of the world seemed to be snatched from the hands of deity and given over to a system of impersonal rules. God, whose action had been defined in terms of miracle, was forced from one realm after another by the discovery of laws, until at last even comets were found to be not whimsical but as regular in their law-abiding courses as the planets, and God seemed to be escorted to the edge of the universe and bowed out. When Newton first formulated the law of gravitation, the artillery of many an earnest pulpit was let loose against him. One said that Newton took "from God that direct action on his works so constantly ascribed to him in Scripture and transferred it to material mechanism" and that he "substituted gravitation for Providence." But now, when science has so plainly won her case, in her own proper field; when we know to our glory and profit so many laws by which the world is governed, and use our knowledge as the most splendid engine of personal purpose and freedom which man ever had, we see how great our gain has been. *Nor is it more a practical than a religious gain.* God once was thought of chiefly in terms of miraculous action; he came into his world now and again, like the *deus-ex-machina* of a Greek tragedy, to solve a critical dilemma in the plot. Now all the laws we know and many more are his regular ways of action, and through them all continuously his purpose is being wrought. As Henry Drummond exclaimed, "If God appears periodically, he disappears periodically. If he comes upon the scene at special crises, he is absent from the scene in the intervals. Whether is all-God or occasional God the nobler theory?"

Nothing, therefore, can be more pathetic than the self-styled "defenders of the faith" who withstand the purpose of reverent students to give scientific answers to scientific questions. Such men are not really defending the faith. They are doing exactly what Father Inchofer did when he said, "The opinion that the earth moves is of all heresies the most abominable"; what Mr. Gosse did when he maintained, in explanation of geology's discoveries, that God by the use of stratified rock and fossils deliberately gave the earth the *appearance* of development through long ages, while really he made it in six days; what Mr. Southall did when, in the face of established anthropology, he claimed that the "Egyptians had no Stone Age and were born civilized"; what the Dean of Chichester did when he preached that "those who refuse to accept the history of the creation of our first parents according to its obvious literal intention, and are for substituting the modern dream of evolution in its place, cause the entire scheme of man's salvation to collapse." These were not defending the faith; they were making it ridiculous in the eyes of intelligent men and were embroiling religion in controversies where she did not belong and where, out of her proper realm she was foredoomed to defeat. *For scientific problems are not a matter for faith; they are a matter for investigation.* No one can settle by faith the movements of the planets, the method of the earth's formation, the age of mankind, the explanation of comets. These lie in science's realm, not in religion's, and religious faith demeans herself when she tries to settle them. Let science be the grammarian of the world to observe its parts of speech and their relations!

Religion deals with the soul of the world, its deepest source, its spiritual meaning, its divine purpose.

IV

Science, however, has not always been content with the grammarian's task. When we have frankly confessed religion's sins in trespassing on scientific territory, we must note that *science has her guilty share in the needless conflict.* Today one suspects that the Church's vain endeavor by ecclesiastical authority to force religious solutions on scientific problems is almost over. But the attempt of many scientists to claim the whole field of reality as theirs and to force their solutions on every sort of problem is not yet finished. This, too, is a vain endeavor. To suppose that the process of scientific observation and inference can exhaust the truth of life is like supposing that there is no more meaning in Westminster Abbey than is expressed in Baedeker.

Scientists, for example, sometimes claim domains which are not theirs by *spelling abstract nouns with capitals, by positing Law or Evolution as the makers and builders of the world.* But law never did anything; law is only man's statement of the way, according to his observation, in which things are done. To explain the universe as the creation of Law is on a par with explaining homes as the creation of Matrimony. Abstract nouns do not create anything and the capitalizing of a process never can explain it. So, too, Evolution does nothing to the world; it is the way in which whoever makes the world is making it. As well explain the difference between an acorn and an oak by saying that Growth did it, as to explain the progress of creation from stardust to civilization by changing e to E. Science may describe the process as evolutionary, but its source, its moving power, and its destiny are utterly beyond her ken.

For another thing, scientists often invade realms which are not theirs, by *stretching the working theories of some special science to the proportions of a complete philosophy of life.* A generation ago, when geology and biology were in their "green and salad days," the enthusiasm inspired by the splendid results of their hypotheses went to strange lengths. One professor of geology seriously explained the pyramids of Egypt to be the remains of volcanic eruption which had forced its way upwards by slow and stately motion. The hieroglyphs were crystalline formations and the shaft of the great pyramid was the airhold of a volcano. Scientists are human like all men; their specialties loom large; the ideas that work in their limited areas seem omnipotent. So a student of the influence of sunlight on life thinks reactions to the sun explain everything. "Heliotropism," he says, "doubtless wrote Hamlet." A specialist on the influence of geography on human nature interprets everything as the reaction of man to seas, mountains, plains, and deserts, and Lombroso even thinks the revolutionary temperament especially native to men who live on limestone formations! Specialists in economic history are sure that man is little more than an animated nucleus of hunger and that all life is explicable as a search for food. And psychologists, charmed by the neatness of description which casual connections introduce into our inner life, leap to the conclusion, which lies outside their realm, that personality is an illusion, freedom a myth, and our menal life the rattling of a casual chain forged and set in motion when the universe began. *All this is not science; it is making hypotheses from a limited field of facts masquerade as a total philosophy of life.*

The underlying reason why science, when she regards her province as covering everything, inevitably clashes with the interests of religion, is that *she starts her view of the world from the subhuman side.* The typical sciences are physics, chemistry, astronomy, geology, biology, and the view of the universe which they present is the basis on which all other sciences proceed. But this foundation is subhuman; the master ideas involved in it are all obtained with the life of man left out of account. Such an approach presents a world-machine, immense and regular, and when, later, psychology and sociology arise, how easy it is to call the human life which they study a by-product of the subhuman world, an exudation arising from the activities of matter.

Religion, on the contrary, *starts with human life.* Fall down in awe, Science cries, before this vast subhuman world! And the religious man answers: What world is this I am to bow before? Is it not the universe which my mind knows and whose laws my intellect has grasped? This universe, so far as it exists at all for me, is apprehended by my vision, penetrated by my thought, encompassed by my interpretations. *What is really great and wonderful here, is not the world which I understand, but the mind that understands it—not the subhuman but the human.* Man himself is the supreme Fact, and all the world that man could bow before, man's mind must first of all contain. The master truth is not that my mind exists within a physical universe, but that the physical universe is encompassed by my mind. Therefore, when I interpret life, I will start with man, and not with what lies below him.

Romanes, the English scientist, illustrates in his experience the difference which these two approaches make. When, returning from agnosticism to Christianity, he explained his lapse, he said, "I did not sufficiently appreciate the immense importance of *human* nature, as distinguished from physical nature, in any inquiry touching theism. . . . Human nature is the most important part of nature as a whole whereby to investigate the theory of theism. This I ought to have anticipated on merely *a priori* grounds, had I not been too much immersed in merely physical research." Of how many now does this same explanation hold! They segregate man from the rest of the universe, and endeavor an interpretation of the unhuman remainder. They forget that man is par and parcel of the universe, bone of its bone, as imperative an expression of its substantial nature as are rocks and stars, and that *any philosophy which interprets the world minus man has not interpreted the world.*

Here is the difference between a Haeckel and a Phillips Brooks. All the dominant ideas of the one are drawn from existence minus man; all the controlling convictions of the other are drawn from the heights and depths of man's own life. The first approach inevitably leads to irreligion, for Spirit cannot reveal itself except in spirit and until one has found God in man he will not find him in nature. The second as certainly leads to religion, for, as Augustine said, "If you dig deep enough in every man you find divinity." Over against the testimony of the subhuman that there is a mechanistic aspect to the world, stands the unalterable testimony of the human that there is as well an ideal, purposive, and spiritual aspect of the world. Surely the latter brings us nearer to the heart of truth. *We never understand anything except in terms of its highest expression and man is the summit of nature.*

Could religion find a voice, therefore, she would wish to speak not in terms of apology but of challenge, when science, assuming all of reality for its field, grows arrogant. Describe the aspect of the world that belongs to you, she would say, I have learned my lesson; your field is yours, and no interference at my hands shall trouble you again. But remember the limitations of your domain—to observe and describe phenomena and to plot their laws. That is an immense task and inexpressibly useful. But when you have completed it, the total result will be as unlike the real world as a medical manikin with his wire nerves and painted muscles is unlike a real man. The manikin is sufficiently correct; everything is truly pictured there—*except life.* So things are as science sees them, but things are more than science sees. Plot then the mechanistic aspect of the world, but do not suppose that you have caught all of truth in that wide-meshed net! When you have said your last word on facts observed and laws induced, man rises up to ask imperious questions with which you cannot deal, to present urgent problems for which no solution ever has been found save Augustine's, "I seek for God in order that my soul may *live.*"

V

Our thought so ended, however, would leave science and religion jealously guarding their boundaries, not cooperating as allies. *Such suspicious recognition of each other's realms does not exhaust the possibilities.* When once the separate functions each by the other have been granted, we are free to turn our thought to the inestimable service which each is rendering. Consider the usefulness of science to the ideal causes of which religion is the chief! Science has given us the *new universe,* not more marvelous in its vastness than in its unity. For the spectroscope has shown that everywhere through immeasurable space the same chemical properties and laws obtain; the telescope has revealed with what mathematical precision the orbits in the heavens are traced and how unwaveringly here or among the stars gravitation maintains its hold. Man never had so immense and various and yet so single and unified a world before. Polytheism once was possible, but science has banished it forever. Whatever may be the source of the universe, it is *one* Source, and whoever the creator, he is more glorious in man's imagination than he could ever have been before. Science also has put at the disposal of the ideal causes *such instruments as by themselves they would never have possessed.* We are hoping for a new world-brotherhood, and we pray for it in Christian churches as the Father's will. But the instruments by which the interracial fellowship must be maintained and without which it would be unthinkable are science's gift. Railroads, steamships, telegraphs, telephones, wireless—these are the shuttles by which the ideal faiths in man's fraternity may be woven into fact. When Christian physicians heal the sick or stamp out plagues that for ages have been man's curse and his despair, when social maladjustments are corrected by Christian philanthropy, and saner, happier ways of living are made possible; when comforts that once were luxuries are brought within the reach of all, and man's life is relieved of crushing handicaps; when old superstitions that had filled man's life with dread for ages are driven like fogs before science's illumination, and religious faith is freed of their incumbrance; when great causes of relief have at their disposal the unimaginable wealth which our modern economic system has created—can anyone do sufficient justice to man's debt to science? And once more science has done religion an inestimable service in establishing as a point of honor the ambition *to see straight and to report exactly.* The tireless patience, the inexorable honesty, the sacrificial heroism of scientists, pursuing truth, is a gift of incalculable magnitude. Huxley is typical of science at its best when he writes in his journal his ideal—"To smite all humbugs however big; to give a nobler tone to science; to set an example of abstinence from petty personal contro-versies and of toleration for everything but lying; to be indifferent as to whether the work is recognized as mine or not, so long as it is done." Countless obscurantisms and bigotries, shams and sophistries have been driven from the churches by this scientific spirit and more are yet to go. Science has shown intellectual dishonesty to be a sin of the first rank. Christianity never can be thankful enough for science; on our knees we should be grateful for her as one of God's most indispensable gifts. Nor should the fact that many a scientist whose contributions we rejoice in was not certain about God defer our gratitude. Cyrus, the Persian, is not the only one to whom the Eternal has said, "I will gird thee, though thou hast not known me" (Isa. 45:5).

When, however, science has done her necessary work, she needs her great ally, religion. Without the insight and hope which faith alone can bring, we learn a little about the world, our minds enclosed in boundaries beyond which is dark, unfathomable mystery. We rejoice in nature's beauty and in friendship, suffer much with broken bodies and more with broken family ties, until we die as we were born—the spawn of mindless, soulless powers that never purposed us and never cared. And the whole universe is purposeless, engaged with blind hands, that have no mind behind them, on tasks that mean nothing and are never done. Science and religion should not be antagonists; they are mutually indispensable allies in the understanding and mastery of life.

CHAPTER VIII

Faith and Moods

DAILY READINGS

The relationship of faith to feeling, rather than faith's relationship to mind, is with many people the more vital interest. The emotional results of faith are rightfully of intense concern to everyone, for our feelings put the sense of value into life. To see a sunset without being stirred by its beauty is to miss seeing the sunset; to have friends without feeling love for them is not to have friends; and to possess life without feeling it to be gloriously worth while is to miss living. Now, in this regard, the attitude of faith stands sharply opposed to its direct contrary—the attitude of fear. Faith and fear are the two emotional climates, in one or the other of which everyone tends habitually to live. To the compassion of these we set ourselves in the daily readings.

Eighth Week, First Day

Give ear to my prayer, O God;
And hide not thy self from my supplication.
Attend unto me, and answer me:
I am restless in my complaint, and moan,
Because of the voice of the enemy,
Because of the oppression of the wicked;
For they cast iniquity upon me,
And in anger they persecute me.
My heart is sore pained within me:
And the terrors of death are fallen upon me.
Fearfulness and trembling are come upon me,

And horror hath overwhelmed me.
And I said, Oh that I had wings like a dove!
Then would I fly away, and be at rest.
Lo, then would I wander far off,
I would lodge in the wilderness.

—Ps. 55:1-7.

How many people are slaves to the mood from which this psalmist suffered! "Fearfulness and trembling" are their habitual attitude toward life. They fear to die and just as much they fear to live; before every vexatious problem, before every opposing obstacle, even before the common tasks and responsibilities of daily living, they stand in dread; and every piece of work is done by them at least three times—in previous worry, in anxious performance, and in regretful retrospect. Such fear *imprisons* the soul. No two men really live in the same world; for while the outward geography may be identical, the real environment of each soul is created by our moods, tempers, and habits of thought. Fear builds a prison about the man, and bars him in with dreads, anxieties, and timid doubts. And the man will live forever in that prison unless faith sets him free. *Faith is the great liberator.* The psalmist who found himself a prisoner of "fearfulness and trembling" obtained his liberty and became a "soul in peace" (v. 18); and the secret of his freedom he revealed in the closing words of his psalm— "But I will trust in Thee." Faith of some sort is the only power that ever sets men free from the bondage of their timidities and dreads. If a man is the slave of fearfulness, there is no substance in his claim to be a man of faith; a man who has vital faith is not habitually fearful. And as Emerson said, "He has not learned the lesson of life who does not every day surmount a fear."

O God, we remember with sadness our want of faith in Thee. What might have been a garden we have turned into a desert by our sin and wilfulness. This beautiful life which Thou hast given us we have wasted in futile worries and vain regrets and empty fears. Instead of opening our eyes to the joy of life, the joy that shines in the leaf, the flower, the face of an innocent child, and rejoicing in it as in a sacrament, we have sunk back into the complainings of our narrow and blinded souls. O deliver us from the bondage of unchastened desires and unwholesome thoughts. Help us to conquer hopeless brooding and faithless reflection, and the impatience of irritable weakness. To this end, increase our faith, O Lord. Fill us with a completer trust in Thee, and the desire for a more wholehearted surrender to Thy will. Then every sorrow will become a joy. Then shall we say to the mountains that lie heavy on our souls, "Remove and be cast thence," and they shall remove, and nothing shall be impossible unto us. Then shall we renew our strength, and mount up with wings as eagles; we shall run and not be weary; we shall walk and not faint. We offer this prayer in the name of Jesus Christ our Lord. Amen.—Samuel McComb.

Eighth Week, Second Day

Not only is it true that fear imprisons while faith liberates; fear *paralyzes* and faith *empowers*. The only attitude in which a man has command of his faculties and is at his best, is the attitude of faith; while fear bewilders the mind and paralyzes the will. The physical effects of fear are deadly; it positively inhibits any useful thinking; and in the spiritual life its results are utterly demoralizing. Fear is the panic of a soul. Consider such an estate as the author of Deuteronomy presents:

And among these nations shalt thou find no ease, and there shall be no rest for the sole of thy foot: but Jehovah will give thee there a trembling heart, and failing of eyes, and pining of soul; and thy life shall hang in doubt before thee; and thou shalt fear night and day, and shalt have no assurance of thy life. In the morning thou shalt say, Would it were even! and at even thou shalt say, Would it were morning! for the fear of thy heart which thou shalt fear, and for the sight of thine eyes which thou shalt see.—Deut. 28:65-67.

Such a situation oppresses every vital power, and the conquest of such a situation must always be inward before it can be outward; *the man must pass from fear to faith.* Let even a little faith arise in him, and power begins to return. Men fear that they cannot overcome evil habits, that they cannot successfully meet difficult situations, that they cannot hold out in the Christian life, and that great causes cannot be fought through victory—and the weakness which appalls them is the creation of their own misgiving.

> "Our doubts are traitors,
> And make us lose the good we oft might win,
> By fearing to attempt."

But faith is tonic; the results which follow a change of heart from fear to faith are miraculous; spiritual dwarfs grow to giants and achieve successes that before would have been unbelievable. No verse in Scripture has behind it a greater mass of verifiable experience than: "This is the victory that hath overcome the world, even our faith" (I John 5:4).

Gracious Father, Thou has invited us, unworthy as we are, to pray for all sorts and conditions of men. . . . We pray for all who are in bondage to fear, unable to face the tasks of life or bear the thought of death with peace and dignity. Free them from the tyranny of these dark dreads. Let the inspiration of a great faith or hope seize their souls, and lift them above their fruitless worry and idle torments, into a region of joy and peace and blessedness. We pray for the victims of evil habits, the slaves of alcohol or morphine, or any other pretended redeemer of the soul from weariness and pain. Great is the power of these degrading temptations; but greater still is the saving energy of Thy Spirit. So let Thy Spirit enter the hearts of these unhappy children of Thine, that their will may be made strong to resist, and that the burning heat of high thoughts may consume the grosser desires of the flesh. We pray for souls bound beneath self-imposed burdens, vexed by miseries of their own making; for the children of melancholy, who have lost their way and grope without a light; for those who do their work with no enthusiasm, and, when night falls, can find no sleep though they search for it as for hidden treasure. Let Thy light pierce through their gloom and shine upon their path. . . .

Unite us to Jesus Christ, Thy perfect Son, in the bonds of a living trust, so that sustained by His example, and sanctified by His Spirit, we may grow more and more into the image of

His likeness. These, and all other blessings, we ask in His name and for His sake. Amen.—Samuel McComb.

Eighth Week, Third Day

There are many situations in life which naturally throw the pall of dread over man's soul. Life is seldom easy, it is often overwhelmingly difficult, and if a man has worry in his temperament, circumstances supply plenty of occasions on which to exercise it. The difference between men lies here: those in whom the fear-attitude is master hold the oppressive trouble so close to the eye that it hides everything else; those whom the faith-attitude dominates hold trouble off and see it in wide perspectives. A copper cent can hide the sun if we hold it close enough to the eye, and a transient difficulty can shut out from a fearful soul all life's large blessings and all the horizons of divine good will. Fear *disheartens* men by concentrating their attention on the unhappy aspects of life; *but faith is the great encourager.* Whittier lived in a generation full of turmoil and trouble, and his own life is a story of prolonged struggle against illness, disappointments, and poverty. But, listen:

> "Yet sometimes glimpses on my sight
> Through present wrong, the eternal right;
> And, step by step, since time began
> I see the steady gain of man."

That is the attitude of faith; it does not deny the evil, but it sees around it, refuses to be obsessed or scared by it, and takes heart from a large view when a small view would be appalling. And history always confirms the large view. Fear may be right for the moment, but in the long run it is a liar; only faith tells the truth.

**Be merciful unto me, O God; for man would swallow me up:
All the day long he fighting oppresseth me.
Mine enemies would swallow me up all the day long;
For they are many that fight proudly against me.
What time I am afraid,
I will put my trust in thee.**

—Ps. 56:1-3.

Almighty and every-living God, we draw near unto Thee, believing that Thou art, and that Thou wilt reward all those who diligently seek Thee. We are weak, mortal men, immersed in this world's affairs, buffeted by its sorrows, flung to and fro by its conflicts of right and wrong. We cry for some abiding stay, for some sure and steadfast anchorage. Reveal Thyself to us as the eternal God, as the unfathomable Love that encompasses every spirit Thou hast made, and bears it on, through the light and the darkness alike, to the goal of Thine own perfection. And yet, when Thou speakest to us, we are covered with confusion, for now we remember all the sadness and evil disorder of our lives. Thou hast visited our hearts with ideals fair and beautiful, but alas! we have grown weary in aspiration, and have declined into the sordid aims of our baser selves. Thou hast given us the love of parent and of friend, that we might thereby learn something of Thine own love; yet too often have we despised Thy gift and shut our hearts to all the wonder and the glory. We make confession before Thee of our sin and folly and ignorance. Again and again we have vowed ourselves to Thy service; again and again our languid wills have failed to do Thy Will. We have been seduced by the sweet poison of sin, and even against light and knowledge we have done that which Thou dost abhor, and which in our secret hearts we loathe. And now we almost fear to repent, lest Thou shouldst call us into judgment for a repentance that must needs be repented of. O mighty Saviour of men! be patient with us a little longer. Take us back to Thyself. Without Thee, we are undone; with Thee, we will take fresh heart of hope, and bind ourselves with a more effectual vow, and laying aside every weight and the sin which doth so easily beset us, we will follow Thee whithersoever Thou leadest. Amen.—Samuel McComb.

Eighth Week, Fourth Day

Fear depresses vitality and is a fruitful cause of nervous disorders, with all their disastrous reactions on man's health. Modern investigation has shown beyond any reasonable doubt that while illness comes often by way of the body; it comes also by way of the mind; our moods and tempers have a physical echo, and of all fatal mental states none is so ruinous as fear. It is not strange, therefore, that some people never are well. As Dr. McComb puts it, "Many play at living—they do not really live. They fear the responsibilities, the struggles, the adventures, not without risk, which life offers them. They fear illness. They fear poverty. They fear unhappiness. They fear danger. They fear the passion of sacrifice. They fear even the exaltation of a pure and noble love, until the settlements in money and social prestige have been duly certified. They fear to take a plunge into life's depths. They fear this world, and they fear still more the world beyond the grave." In such a mood no man can possibly be well. Faith, therefore, which drives out fear, has always been a minister of health. The Master's healings, which to the rationalism of a previous generation seemed incredible, in the light of the present knowledge seem inevitable. He had faith and he demanded faith, and wherever the faith-attitude can be set in motion against the fear-attitude and all its morbid brood, the consequences will be physical as well as moral. An outgrown custom of the early Church does not now seem so strange as it did a generation ago:

Is any among you suffering? let him pray. Is any cheerful? let him sing praise. Is any among you sick? let him call the elders of the church; and let them pray over him, anointing him with oil in the name of the Lord: and the prayer of faith shall save him that is sick, and the Lord shall raise him up; and if he have committed sins, it shall be forgiven him. Confess therefore your sins one to another, and pray one for another, that ye may be healed. The supplication of a righteous man availeth much in its working.—James 5:13-16.

Eternal God, who art above all change and darkness, whose will begat us, and whose all present love doth enfold and continually redeem us, Holy Guest who indwellest, and dost comfort us; we have gathered to worship Thee, and in communion with thee to find ourselves raised to the light of our life, and the Heaven of our desires.

Pour upon our consciousness the sense of Thy wonderful nearness to us. Reveal to our weakness and distress the power and the grace that are more than sufficient for us. May we see what we are, Thy Spirit-born children linked by nature, love, and choice to Thy mighty being; and may the vision make all fears to fade, and a Divine strength to pulse within.

Enable us to carry out from this place the peace and strength that here we gain, to take into our homes a kinder spirit, a new thoughtfulness; that we may brighten sadness, heal the sick, and make happiness to abound. May we take into our daily tasks and life of labor, a sense of righteousness that shall be as salt to every evil and corrupting influence.

Because we have walked here awhile with Thee, may we be able to walk more patiently with man. Send us forth with love to the fallen, hope for the despairing, strength to impart to the weak and wayward; and carry on through us the work Thou didst commence in Thy Son our Brother Man and Saviour God. Amen.—W. E. Orchard.

Eighth Week, Fifth Day

Fear makes impossible any satisfying joy in life. A man of faith may be deeply joyful even in disastrous circumstances, but a man of fear would be unhappy in heaven. Stevenson sings in "the saddest and the bravest song he ever wrote":

"God, if this were faith? . . .
To go on for ever and fail and go on again,
And be mauled to the earth and arise,
And contend for the shade of a word and a thing not seen
  with the eyes:
With half of a broken hope for a pillow at night
That somehow the right is the right,
And the smooth shall bloom from the rough:
Lord, if that were enough?"

Sad this song may be, but at the heart of it is yet a fierce joy because faith is there. But put a man of fear in luxury and remove from him every visible cause of disquiet and he will still be miserable. The more a man considers these two determinant moods in life, the more he sees that somehow the faith-attitude must be his, if life is to be worth living. Without it life dries up into a Sahara; with it, he comes into a company of the world's glad spirits, who one way or another have felt what the psalmist sings:

Jehovah is my light and my salvation;
Whom shall I fear?
Jehovah is the strength of my life;
Of whom shall I be afraid?
When evil-doers came upon me to eat up my flesh,
Even mine adversaries and my foes, they stumbled and fell.
Though a host should encamp against me,
My heart shall not fear:
Though war should rise against me,
Even then will I be confident.
One thing have I asked of Jehovah, that will I seek after:
That I may dwell in the house of Jehovah all the days of my
    life.
To behold the beauty of Jehovah,
And to inquire in his temple.
For in the day of trouble he will keep me secretly in his
    pavilion:
In the covert of his tabernacle will he hide me;
He will lift me up upon a rock.
And now shall my head be lifted up above mine enemies
    round about me;
And I will offer in his tabernacle sacrifices of joy;
I will sing, yea, I will sing praises unto Jehovah.

—Ps. 27:1-6.

Gracious Father! We confess the painful riddle of our being, that, while claiming kinship with Thee, we feel far from Thee. O, what means this strange bewilderment, this never-ending war between our worse and better thoughts? We are Thine by right, yet we have not given ourselves wholly to Thy care. Our hearts know no rest, save in thee, yet they have sought it in this world's vainglory, which passeth away. We seek to quench our thirst at the cisterns of this earth, but they are broken cisterns, that can hold no water. Lead us to Thy well of life that springeth up eternally. Give us to drink of that spiritual water, of which, if any man drink, he shall never thirst again. We lament our want and poverty before Thee. Open Thou our eyes to behold the unsearchable riches of Thy grace, and increase our faith that we may make them ours. Unite us to Thee in the bonds of will and love and purpose. Out of Thy fulness, which is in Christ, give to each one of us according to his need. Make us wise with His Wisdom; pure with His purity; strong with His strength; that we may rise into the power and glory of the life that is life indeed. Hear our heart's weak and wandering cries, and when Thou hearest, forgive and bless, for His sake. Amen.—Samuel McComb.

Eighth Week, Sixth Day

No man can serve two masters: for either he will hate the one, and love the other; or else he will hold to one, and despise the other. Ye cannot serve God and mammon. Therefore I say unto you, Be not anxious for your life, what ye shall put on. Is not the life more than the food, and the body than the raiment? Behold the birds of the heaven, that they sow not, neither do they reap, nor gather into barns; and your heavenly Father feedeth them. Are not ye of much more value than they? And which of you by being anxious can add one cubit unto the measure of his life? And why are ye anxious concerning raiment? Consider the lilies of the field, how they grow; they toil not, neither do they spin; yet I say unto you, that even Solomon in all his glory was not arrayed like one of these.

But if God doth so clothe the grass of the field, which to-day is, and to-morrow is cast into the oven, shall he not much more clothe you, O ye of little faith? Be not therefore anxious, saying, What shall we eat? or, What shall we drink? or, Wherewithal shall we be clothed? For after all these things do the Gentiles seek; for your heavenly Father knoweth that ye have need of all these things. But seek ye first his kingdom, and his righteousness; and all these things shall be added unto you.—Matt. 6:24-33.

The meaning of this passage hinges on the first "therefore." You cannot serve God and selfish gain at the same time, says Jesus; you should choose decisively to serve God; and *therefore* you must not be anxious about yourself. For *anxious fear so concentrates a man's thought on himself that he can serve no one else.* That this is the meaning of this familiar passage is clear also from its conclusion. The real reason for conquering anxious fear is that a man may give himself wholeheartedly to the service of the Kingdom. That fear does spoil usefulness is obvious; a man cannot be fearful for himself and considerate of his fellows. As Stevenson puts it in "Aes Triplex," "The man who has least fear for his own carcass has most time to consider others. That eminent chemist who took his walks abroad in tin shoes and subsisted wholly upon tepid milk had all his work cut out for him in considerate dealings with his own digestion. So soon as prudence has begun to grow up in the brain, like a dismal fungus, it finds its first expression in a paralysis of generous acts." The shame of our fearful living is that it circles about self, is narrowed down to mean solicitudes about our own comfort, and is utterly incapable of serving God or seeking first his Kingdom. Only faith puts folk at leisure from their small anxieties so that they can be servants of a worthy cause. Jesus, therefore, in this passage, is not giving us the impossible injunction not to think about tomorrow; he is stating a truth of experience, that anxious fear for oneself which so draws in the thought that God's great causes are forgotten is a deadly peril in man's life. By faith thrust out the mean and timid solicitudes, is his injunction, that life may be free to put first things first.

We come to Thee, our Father, that we may more deeply enter into Thy joy. Thou turnest darkness into day, and mourning into praise. Thou art our Fortress in temptation, our Shield in remorse, our Covert in calamity, our Star of Hope in every sorrow. O Lord, we would know Thy peace, deep, abiding, inexhaustible. When we seek Thy peace, our weariness is gone, the sense of our imperfection ceases to discourage us, and our tired souls forget their pain. When, strengthened and refreshed by Thy goodness, we return to the task of life, send us forth as servants of Jesus Christ in the service and redemption of the world. Send us to the hearts without love, to men and women burdened with heavy cares, to the miserable, the sad, the broken-hearted. Send us to the children whose heritage has been a curse, to the poor who doubt Thy Providence, to the sick who crave for healing and cannot find it, to the fallen for whom no man cares. May we be ministers of Thy mercy, messengers of Thy helpful pity, to all who need Thee. By our sympathy, our prayers, our kindness, our gifts, may we make a way for the inflow of Thy love into needy and loveless lives. And so may we have that love which alone is the fulfilling of Thy law. Hasten the time when all men shall love Thee and one another in Thee, when all the barriers that divide us shall be broken down, and every heart shall be filled with joy and every tongue with melody. These gracious gifts we ask, in Jesus' name. Amen.—Samuel McComb.

Eighth Week, Seventh Day

Fear does not reveal its disastrous consequences to the full until it colors one's thoughts about the source and destiny of life. Folk work joyfully at a picture puzzle so long as they believe that the puzzle can be put together, that it was meant, completed, to compose a picture, and that their labor is an effort made in reasonable hope. But if they begin to fear that they are being fooled, that the puzzle is a hoax and never can be pieced together anywhere by anyone, how swiftly that suspicion will benumb their work! So joyful living depends on man's conviction that this life is not a hapless accident, that a good purpose binds it all together, and that our labor for righteousness is not expended on a futile task without a worthy outcome. But fear blights all such hope; it whispers what one pessimist said aloud: "Life is not a tragedy but a farcical melodrama, which is the worst kind of play." That fear benumbs worthy living, kills hope, makes cynical disgust with life a reasonable attitude, and with its frost withers all man's finest aspirations. *Only faith in God can save men from such fear.* Fear or faith—there is no dilemma so full of consequence. Fear imprisons, faith liberates; fear paralyzes, faith empowers; fear disheartens, faith encourages; fear sickens, faith heals; fear makes useless, faith makes serviceable—and, most of all, fear puts hopelessness at the heart of life, while faith rejoices in its God.

O give thanks unto Jehovah; for he is good;
For his lovingkindness endureth for ever.

THE MEANING OF FAITH

Let Israel now say,
That his lovingkindness endureth for ever.
Let the house of Aaron now say,
That his lovingkindness endureth for ever.
Let them now that fear Jehovah say,
That his lovingkindness endureth for ever.
Out of my distress I called upon Jehovah:
Jehovah answered me and set me in a large place.
Jehovah is on my side; I will not fear:
What can man do unto me?

—Ps. 118:1-6.

O God, we invoke Thy blessing upon all who need Thee, and who are groping after Thee, if haply they may find Thee. Be gracious to those who bear the sins of others, who are vexed by the wrongdoing and selfishness of those near and dear to them, and reveal to them the glory of their fellowship with the sufferings of Christ. Brood in tenderness over the hearts of the anxious, the miserable, the victims of phantasmal fear and morbid imaginings. Redeem from slavery the men and women who have yielded to degrading habits. Put Thy Spirit within them, that they may rise up in shame and sorrow and make confession to Thee. "So brutish was I, and ignorant: I was as a beast before Thee." And then let them have the glad assurance that Thou art with them, the secret of all good, the promise and potency of better things. Console with Thy large consolation those who mourn for their loved dead, who count the empty places and long for the sound of a voice that is still. Inspire them with the firm conviction that the dead are safe in Thy keeping, nay, that they are not dead, but live unto Thee. Give to all sorrowing ones a garland for ashes, the oil of joy for mourning, and the garment of praise for the spirit of heaviness. Remember for good all who are perplexed with the mysteries of existence, and who grieve because the world is so sad and unintelligible. Teach them that Thy hand is on the helm of affairs, that Thou dost guide Thine own world, and canst change every dark cloud into bright sunshine. In this faith let them rest, and by this faith let them live. These blessings we ask in the name of our Lord and Saviour Jesus Christ. Amen.—Samuel McComb.

COMMENT FOR THE WEEK

I

Many people do not find their most perplexing difficulty either in the realm of trust or of belief, but in a problem which includes both. They are confused because neither their experience of God nor their intellectual conviction of the reasonableness of faith is dependable and steady. Faith comes and goes in them with fluctuating moods that bring an appalling sense of insecurity. Their religious life is not stable and consistent; it runs through variant degrees of confidence and doubt, and its whimsical ups and downs continually baffle them. To classify some folk as men of faith and some as men of doubt does not, in the light of this experience, quite tally with the facts. There are moods of faith and moods of doubt in all of us and rarely does either kind secure unanimous consent. Were we to decide for irreligion, a minority protest would be vigorously urged in the interests of faith, and when most assuredly we choose religion, the prayer, "Lord, I believe, help thou mine unbelief" (Mark 9:24) is still appropriate. We often seem to be exchanging, as Browning's bishop says:

"A life of doubt diversified by faith,
For one of faith diversified by doubt."

Some hope arises when we observe that this experience which so perplexes us is fully acknowledged in the Bible. The popular supposition is that when one opens the Scripture he finds himself in a world of constant and triumphant faith. No low moods and doubts can here obscure the trust of men; here God is always real, saints sing in prison or dying see their Lord enthroned in heaven. When one, however, really knows the Bible, it obviously is no serene record of untroubled faith. It is turbulent with moods and doubt.

Here, to be sure, is the fifteenth chapter of First Corinthians, on Immortality, but here too is another cry, burdened with all the doubt man ever felt about eternal life, "That which befalleth the sons of men befalleth beasts; even one thing befalleth them: as the one dieth, so dieth the other; yea, they have all one breath; and man hath no preeminence above the beasts" (Eccl. 3:19). The Scripture has many exultant passages on divine faithfulness, but Jeremiah's bitter prayer is not excluded: "Why is my pain perpetual, and my wound incurable, which refuseth to be healed? Wilt thou indeed be unto me as a deceitful brook, as waters that fail?" (Jer. 15:18). The confident texts on prayer are often quoted, but there are cries of another sort: Job's complaint, "Behold, I go forward, but he is not there; and backward, but I cannot perceive him" (Job 23:8); Habakkuk's bitterness, "O Jehovah, how long shall I cry, and thou wilt not hear? I cry unto thee of violence and thou wilt not save" (Hab. 1:2). The Bible is no book of tranquil faith. From the time when Gideon, in a mood like that of multitudes today, cried, "Oh, my Lord, if Jehovah is with us, why then is all this befallen us?" (Judg. 6:13) to the complaint of the slain saints in the Apocalypse, "How long, O Master, the holy and true, dost thou not judge and avenge our blood" (Rev. 6:10), the Bible is acquainted with doubt. It knows the searching, perplexing, terrifying questions that in all ages vex men's souls. If the psalmist, in an exultant mood, sang, "Jehovah is my shepherd," he also cried, "Jehovah, why casteth thou off my soul? Why hidest thou thy face from me?" (Ps. 88:14).

No aspect of the Scripture could bring it more warmly into touch with man's experience than this confession of fluctuating moods. At least in this the Bible is our book. Great heights are there, that we know something of. Psalmists sing in adoration, prophets are sure of God and of his coming victory; apostles pledge in sacrifice the certainty of their belief, and the Master on Transfiguration Mountain prays until his countenance is radiant. And depths are there, that modern men know well. Saints cry out against unanswered prayer and cannot understand how such an evil, wretched world is ruled by a good God; in their bitter griefs they complain that God has cast them off, and utterly forgotten and, dismayed, doubt even that a man's death differs from a dog's. This is our book. For the faith of many of us, however we insist that we are Christians, is not tranquil, steady, and serene. It is moody, occasional, spasmodic, with hours of great assurance, and other hours when confidence sags and trust is insecure.

Faith so generally is discussed as though it were a creed, accepted once for all and thereafter statically held, that the influence of our moods on faith is not often reckoned with. But the moods of faith are the very pith and marrow of our actual experience. When a Christian congregation recite together their creedal affirmation, "I believe in God," it *sounds* as though they all maintained a solid, constant faith. But when in imagination, one breaks up the congregation and interprets from his knowledge of men's lives what the faith of the individuals actually means, he sees that they believe in God not evenly and constantly, but more or less, sometimes very much, sometimes not confidently at all. Our faith in God is not a static matter such as the recitation of a creed suggests. Some things we do believe in steadily. That two plus two make four, that the summed angles of a triangle make two right angles—of such things we are unwaveringly sure. No moods can shake our confidence; no griefs confuse us, no moral failures quench our certainty. Though the heavens fall, two and two make four! But our faith in God belongs in another realm. It is a vital experience. It involves the whole man, with his chameleon moods, his glowing insights, his exalted hours, and his dejected days when life flows sluggishly and no great thing seems real.

This experience of variable moods in faith does not belong especially to feeble folk, whose ups and downs in their life with God would illustrate their whole irresolute and flimsy living. The great believers sometimes know best this tidal rise and fall of confidence. Elijah one day, with absolute belief in God, defied the hosts of Baal and the next, in desolate reaction, wanted to die. Luther put it with his rugged candor, "Sometimes I believe and sometimes I doubt." John Knox, at liberty to preach, "dings the pulpit into blads" in his confident utterance; but the same Knox recalled that, in the galleys, his soul knew "anger, wrath, and indignation which it conceived against God, calling all his promises in doubt." The Master himself was not a stranger to this experience. He believed in God with unwavering assurance, as one believes in the shining of the sun. But the fact that the sun perpetually shines did not imply that every day was a sunshiny day for him. The clouds came pouring up out of his dark horizons and hid the sun. "Now is my soul troubled; and what shall I say?" (John 12:27). And once the fog drove in, so dense and dark that one would think there never had been any sun at all. "My God, my God, why hast thou forsaken me?" (Matt. 27:46).

This experience of fluctuating moods is too familiar to be denied, too influential to be neglected. There can be no use in hiding it from candid thought behind the recitation of a creedal formula. There may be great use in searching out its meaning. For there are ways in which this common experience, at first vexatious and disquieting, may supply solid ground for Christian confidence.

III

In dealing with these variant moods of faith we are not left without an instrument. We have *the sense of value*. We discern not only the *existence* of things, but their *worth* as well. When, therefore, a man has recognized his moods as facts, he has not said all that he can say about them. Upon no objects of experience can the sense of value be used with so much certainty as upon our moods. *We know our best hours when they come.* The lapidary, with unerring skill, learns to distinguish a real diamond from a false, but his knowledge is external and contingent, compared with the inward and authoritative certainty with which we know our best hours from our worst. Our great moods carry with them the authentic marks of their superiority.

Experience readily confirms this truth. We all have, for example, *cynical and sordid moods*. At such times, only the appetites of physical life seem much to matter; only the things that minister to common comfort greatly count. When Sydney Smith, the English cleric, writes, "I feel an ungovernable interest in my horses, my pigs, and my plants, but I am forced and always was forced to task myself up to an interest in any higher objects," most of us can understand his mood. We grow obtuse at times to all that in our better moods had thrilled us most. Nature suffers in our eyes; great books seem dull; causes that once we served with zest lose interest, and personal relationships grow pale and tame. From such mere dullness we easily drift down to cynicism. Music once had stirred the depth, but now our spirits tally with the scoffer's jest, "What are you crying about with your Wagner and your Brahms? It is only horsehair scraping on catgut." Man's most holy things may lose their grandeur and become a butt of ridicule. When the mood of Aristophanes is on, we too may hoist serious Socrates among the clouds, and set him talking moonshine while the cynical look on and laugh. The spirit that "sits in the seat of the scornful" is an ancient malady.

But every man is thoroughly aware that these are not his best moods. From such depleted attitudes we come to worthier hours; *real life* arrives again. Nature and art become imperatively beautiful; moral causes seem worth sacrifice, and before man's highest life, revealed in character, ideal, and faith, we stand in reverence. These are our great hours, when spiritual values take the throne, when all else dons livery to serve them, and we find it easy to believe in God.

Again, we have *crushed and rebellious moods*. We may have been Christians for many years; yet when disaster, long delayed, at last descends, and our dreams are wrecked, we *do* rebel. Complaint rises hot within us. Joseph Parker, preacher at the City Temple, London, at the age of sixty-eight could write that he had never had a doubt. Neither the goodness of God nor the divinity of Christ, nor anything essential to his Christian faith had he ever questioned. But within a year an experience had fallen of which he wrote: "In that dark hour I became almost an atheist. For God had set his foot upon my prayers and treated my petitons with contempt. If I had seen a dog in such agony as mine, I would have pitied and helped the dumb beast; yet God spat upon me and cast me out as an offense—out into the waste wilderness and the night black and starless." No new philosophy had so shaken the faith of this long unquestioning believer. But his wife had died and he was in a brokenhearted mood that all his arguments, so often used on others, could not penetrate. He believed in God as one believes in the sun when he has lived six months in the polar night and has not seen it.

These heartbroken moods, however, are not our best. Out of rebellious grief we lift our eyes in time to see how other men have borne their sorrows off and built them into character. We see great lives shine out from suffering, like Rembrandt's radiant faces from dark backgrounds. We see that all the virtues which we most admire—constancy, patience, fortitude—are impossible without stern settings, and that in time of trouble they find their aptest opportunity, their noblest chance. We rise into a new mood, grow resolute not to be crushed, but, as though there were moral purpose in man's trials, to be hallowed, deepened, purified. The meaning of Samuel Rutherford's old saying dawns upon us, "When I am in the cellar of affliction, I reach out my hand for the king's wine." And folk, seeing us, it may be, take heart and are assured that God is real, since he can make a man bear off his trial like that and grow the finer for it. These are our great hours too, when the rains descend, and the winds blow, and the floods come, and beat upon our house, and it is founded on a rock!

Once more, we have hours of *discouragement about the world*. The more we have cared for moral causes and invested life in their advancement, the more we are desolate when they seem to fail. Some rising tide in which we trusted turns to ebb again, injustice wins its victories, the people listen to demagogues and not to statesmen, social causes essential to human weal are balked, wars come and undo the hopes of centuries. Who does not sometimes fall into the South of Despond? Cavour, disheartened about Italy, went to his room to kill himself. John Knox, dismayed about Scotland, in a pathetic prayer entitled, "John Knox with deliberate mind to his God," wrote, "Now, Lord put an end to my misery." We generally think of Luther in that intrepid hour when he faced Charles V at Worms; but he had times as well when he was sick with disappointment. "Old, decrepit, lazy, worn out, cold, and now one-eyed," so runs a letter, "I write, my Jacob, I who hoped there might at length be granted to me, already dead, a well-earned rest." During the Great War, this mood of discouragement has grown familiar. Many can understand what Robert Louis Stevenson meant when he wrote, of the Franco-Prussian war, "In that year, cannon were roaring for days together on French battlefields, and I would sit in my isle (I call it mine after the use of lovers) and think upon the war, and the pain of men's wounds, and the weariness of their marching. . . . It was something so distressing, so instant, that I lay in the heather on the top of the island, with my face hid, kicking my heels for agony."

But these dismayed hours are not our best. As Bunyan put it, even Giant Despair has fainting fits on sunshiny days. In moods of clearer insight we perceive out of how many Egypts, through how many round-about wilderness journeys, God has led his people to how many Promised Lands. The Exodus was not a failure, although the Hebrews, disheartened, thought it was and even Moses had his dubious hours; the mission of Israel did not come to an ignoble end in the Exile, although multitudes gave up their faith because of it and only prophets dared believe the hopeful truth. The crucifixion did not mean the Gospel's end, as the disciples thought, nor did Paul, imprisoned, lose his ministry. *Nothing in history is more assured than this, that only men of faith have known the truth.* And in hours of vision when this fact shines clear we rise to be our better selves again. What a clear ascent the race has made when wide horizons are taken into view! What endless possibilities must lie ahead! What ample reasons we possess to thrust despair aside, and to go out to play our part in the forward movement of the plan of God!

"Dreamer of dreams? we take the taunt with gladness,
　Knowing that God beyond the years you see,
Has wrought the dreams that count with you for madness
　Into the texture of the world to be."

These are our better hours.

IV

Such sordid, cynical, crushed, rebellious, and discouraged moods we suffer, but we have hours of insight, too, when we are at our best. And as we face this ebb and flow of confidence, which at the first vexatiously perplexed our faith, an arresting truth is clear. The creed of irreligion, to which men are tempted to resign their minds, is simply the *intellectual formulation of what is implied in our less noble hours.* Take what man's cynical, sordid, crushed, rebellious, and discouraged moods imply, and set it in a formal statement of life's meaning, and the result is the creed of irreligion. But take man's best hours, when the highest seems the realest, when even sorrows cannot crush his soul, and when the world is still the battlefield of God for men, and formulate what these hours imply, and the result is the central affirmations of religious faith. Even Renan is sure that "man is most religious in his best moments." Of this high interpretation our variant moods are susceptible, that *we know our best hours when they come, and the faith implied in them is essential Christianity.* As Browning sings it:

> "Faith is my waking life:
> One sleeps, indeed, and dreams at intervals,
> We know, but waking's the main point with
> us."

This fact which we so have come upon is a powerful consideration in favor of religion's truth. *Are we to trust for our guidance the testimony of our worse or better hours?* We have low moods; so, too we have cellars in our houses. But we do not *live* there; we live upstairs! It is not unnatural to have irreligious moods. There may be hours when the eternal Energy from which this universe has come seems to be playing solitaire for fun. It shuffles the stars and planets to see what may chance from their combinations, and careless of the consequence, from everlasting to everlasting it shuffles and plays, and shuffles and plays again. But these are not our best hours. We may have moods when the universe seems to us, as Carlyle's figure pictures it, "as if the heavens and the earth were but boundless jaws of a devouring monster, wherein, I, palpitating, lay waiting to be devoured," but we are inwardly ashamed of times like that. Man comes to this brutal universe of irreligion by way of his ignoble moods. When he lifts up his soul in his great hours of love, of insight, and of devotion, life never looks to him as irreligion pictures it; it never has so looked to him and it never will!

In his best hours man always suspects that the Eternal must be akin to what is best in us, that our ideals are born from above, have there their source and destiny, that the

Eternal Purpose reigns and yet shall justify the struggle of the ages, and that in anyone who is the best we know, we see most clearly what the Eternal is and means. That goodness is deeper than evil, that spirit is more than flesh, that life is lord of death, that love is the source of all—such convictions come naturally to us when we are at our best. When one examines such affirmations, he perceives that Christianity in its essential faiths is the expression of our finest hours. This is the source whence Christianity has come; it is man's best become articulate. Some used to say that Christian faith had been foisted on mankind by priests. Christian faith has no more artificially been foisted upon human life than the full blown rose is foisted on the bud. Christianity springs up out of man's best life; it is the utterance of his transcendent moods; *it is man believing in the validity of his own noblest days.*

Christianity, therefore, at its heart can never fail. Its theologies may come and go, its institutions rise and fall, its rituals have their dawn, their zenith, and their decline, but one persistent force goes on and will go on. *The Gospel is saying to man what man at his best is saying to himself.* Christ has a tremendous ally in human life—our noblest hours. They are all upon his side, What he says, they rise to cry "Amen" to. When we are most truly ourselves we are nearest to him. Antagonistic philosophies, therefore, may spring up to assail the Gospel's influence, and seem to triumph, and fall at last and be forgotten. Still Christ will go on speaking. Nothing can tear him from his spiritual influence over men. *In every generation he has man's noblest hours for his ally.*

V

In the fact to which our study of man's variant moods has brought us we have not only a confirming consideration in favor of religion's truth, but an *explanation of some people's unbelief.* They live habitually in their low moods; they inhabit spiritual cellars. We are accustomed to say that some friend would be saved from his ignoble attitudes by a vital religious faith; but it is also true that this persistent clinging to ignoble attitudes may be the factor that makes religious faith impossible. According to Dickens' *Tale of Two Cities* a prisoner in the Bastille, who had lived in a cell and cobbled shoes for many years, became so enamored of the narrow walls, the darkness, the task's monotony, that, when liberated, he built a cell at the center of his English home, and on days when the skies were clear and birds were singing, the tap of his cobbler's hammer in the dark could still be heard. So men, by an habitual residence in imprisoning moods, render themselves incapable of loving the wide horizons, the great faiths and hopes of religion. They do not merely make excursions of transient emotion into morose hours and, like men that find that the road is running into malarial swamps, turn swiftly to the hills. They dwell in their moroseness; they choose it, and often obstinately resist deliverance.

The common moods that thus incapacitate the soul for faith are easily seen in any man's experience. There are *sullen* tempers when we are churlish and want so to be. There are *stupid* tempers, when our soul is too negligent to care, too dull to ask for what only aspiring minds can crave or find. There are *bored* moods when we feel about all life what Malachi's people felt about worship, "behold, what a weariness is it!" (Mal. 1:13); *rebellious* moods when, like Jonah, deprived of a comfort he desired, we cry, "I do well to be angry, even unto death" (Jon. 4:9); *suspicious* moods, when we mistrust everyone, and even of some righteous Job hear Satan's insinuating sneer, "Does Job fear God for nought?" (Job 1:9). No man is altogether strange to *frivolous* hours, when those thoughts are lost which must be handled seriously if at all, and *willful* hours, when some private desire assumes the center of the stage and angrily resents another voice than his. To say that one who habitually harbors such moods cannot know God is only a portion of the truth; such a man cannot know anything worth knowing. He can know neither fine friends nor great books; he cannot appreciate beautiful music or sublime scenery; he is lost to the deepest loves of family and to every noble enthusiasm for human help. Athwart the knowledge of these most gracious and necessary things stand our obtuse, ignoble moods. The sullen, stupid, bored, rebellious, suspicious, frivolous, or willful tempers, made into spiritual residence, are the most deadly prison of the soul.

Of course one who dwells there has no confidence in God. Lord Shaftesbury, the English philanthropist, made too sweeping a statement about this, but one can see the basis for his judgment: "Nothing beside ill-humor, either natural or forced, can bring a man to think seriously that the world is governed by any devilish or malicious power. I very much question whether anything beside ill-humor can be the cause of atheism." At least one may be sure that where ill-humor habitually reigns, vital faith in God is made impossible.

After full acknowledgment, therefore, of the momentous intellectual problems of belief, we must add that there is a *moral qualification for faith in God.* So great a matter is not achieved by any sort of person, with any kind of habitual moods and tempers. There are views which cellar windows do not afford; one must have balconies to see them. When Jesus said that the pure in heart are blessed because they see God, he was not thinking merely, perhaps not chiefly, of sexual impurity as hindering vision. He was pleading for a heart cleansed of all such perverse, morose, and wayward moods as shut the blinds on the soul's windows. He knew that men could not easily escape the sense of God's reality if they kept their vision clear. On elevated days we naturally think of Spirit as real, and see ourselves as expressions of spiritual purpose, our lives as servants of a spiritual cause. When one habitually dwells in these finer moods, he cannot tolerate a world where his best is a transient accident. *He must have God, for faith in God is the supreme assertion of the reality and eternity of man's best.* Any man who habitually lives in his finest moods will not easily escape the penetrating sense of God's reality.

VI

The certainty with which we tend to be most deeply religious in our best hours is clear when we consider that a man does practically believe in the things which count of highest worth. Lotze, the philosopher, even says that "Faith *is* the feeling that is appreciative of value." It is conceivable that one might be so constituted that without any sense of value he could study facts, as a deaf man might observe a symphony. The sound-waves such a man could mechanically measure; he could analyze the motions of the players and note the reactions of the crowd, but he would hear no music. He would not suffuse the whole performance with his musical appreciations; he would neither like it nor condemn. Man might be so constituted as to face facts without feeling, but he is not. Facts never stand in our experience thus barren and unappreciated—mere neutral *things* that mean nothing and have no value. The botanist in us may analyze the flowers, but the poet in us estimates them. The penologist in us may take the Bertillon measurements of a boy, but the father in us best can tell how much, in spite of all his sin, that boy is worth. This power to estimate life's *values* in the fountain from which spring our music, painting, and literature, our ideals and loves and purposes, our morals and religion. Without it no man can live in the real world at all.

If we would know, therefore, in what, at our highest altitudes, we tend to believe, we should ask *what it is that we value most, when we rise toward our best.* In our lowest hours what sordid, mercenary beastly things men may prize each heart knows well. But ever as we approach our best the things that are worth most to us become elevated and refined. Our better moods open our eyes to a world where character is of more worth than all the rest beside, and through which moral purpose runs, to be served with sacrifice. We become aware of spiritual values in behalf of which at need physical existence must be willingly laid down; and words like honor, love fidelity, and service in our hours of insight have halos over them that poorer moods cannot discern. Man at his best, that is to say, *believes in* an invisible world of spiritual values, and he furnishes the final proof of his faith's reality by sacrificing to it all lesser things. The good, the true, the beautiful command him in his finer hours, and at their beck and call he lays down wealth and ease and earthly hopes to be their servant. Men really *do believe in* the things for which they sacrifice and die.

In no more searching way can a man's faith be described than *in terms of the objects which thus he values most.* Wherever men find some consuming aim that is for them so supreme in worth that they sacrifice all else to win it, we speak of their attitude as a religion. The "religion of science" describes the absolute devotion of investigators to scientific research as the highest good; the "religion of art" describes the consuming passion with which some value beauty. When we say of one that "money is his God" we mean that he estimates it as life's highest treasure, and when with Paul we speak of others, "whose god is the belly" (Phil. 3:19), we mean men whose sensual life is to them the thing worth most. *What men believe in, therefore, is most deeply seen not by any opinions which they profess, but by the things they prize.* Faith, as Ruskin said is "that by which men act while they live; not that which they talk of when they die." Many a man uses pious affirmations of Christian faith, but it is easy to observe from his life that what he really believes in is money. Where a man's treasure is, as Jesus said, his heart is, and there his faith is, too.

Is there any doubt, then, what we most believe in when we are at our best? While in our lower altitudes it may be easy to believe that the physical is the ultimately real, in our upper altitudes we so value the spiritual world, that we tend with undeniable conviction to feel sure that it must be causal and eternal. Materialism is man's "nightview" of his life; but the "day-view" is religion. Tyndall the scientist was regarded by the Christians of his generation as the enemy of almost everything that they held dear. Let him, then, be witness for the truth which we have stated. "I have noticed," he said, speaking of materialism, "during years of self-observation, that it is not in hours of clearness and vigor that this doctrine commends itself to my mind."

The challenge, therefore, presented to every one of us by Christian faith is ultimately this: *Shall I believe the testimony of my better hours or of my worse?* Many who deny the central affirmations of the Gospel put the object of their denial far away from them as though it were an external thing; they say that they deny the creed or the Bible or the doctrine about God. Such a description of a man's rejection of religious faith is utterly inadequate—the real object of his denial is inward. One may, indeed, discredit forms of doctrine and either be unsure about or altogether disbelieve many things that Christians hold, but when one makes a clean sweep of religion and banishes the central faiths of Christianity *he is denying the testimony of his own finest days.* From such rejection of faith one need not appeal to creed or Bible, or to anything that anybody ever said. Let the challenge strike inward to the man's own heart. From his denial of religious faith we may appeal to the hours that he has known and yet will know again, when the road rose under his feet and from a height he looked on wide horizons and knew that he was at his best. To those hours of clear insight, of keen thought, of love and great devotion, when he knew that the spiritual is the real and the eternal, we may appeal. They were his best. He *knows* that they were his best. And as long as humanity lives upon the earth this conviction must underlie great living—that *we will not deny the validity of our own best hours.*

CHAPTER IX

Faith in the Earnest God

DAILY READINGS

Throughout our studies we have been thinking of the effect of faith on the one who exercises it. As an introduction to this week's thought on the earnestness of God, let us approach the effect of faith from another angle. Faith has enormous influence on the one in whom it is reposed; not only the believer but the one in whom he believes is affected by his faith.

Ninth Week, First Day

I commend unto you Phoebe our sister, who is a servant of the church that is at Cenchreae: that ye receive her in the Lord, worthily of the saints, and that ye assist her in whatsoever matter she may have need of you: for she herself also hath been a helper of many, and of mine own self.

Salute Prisca and Aquila my fellow-workers in Christ Jesus, who for my life laid down their own necks; unto whom not only I give thanks, but also all the churches of the Gentiles: and salute the church that is in their house. Salute Epaenetus my beloved, who is the first-fruits of Asia unto Christ. Salute Mary, who bestowed much labor on you. Salute Andronicus and Junias, my kinsmen, and my fellow-prisoners, who are of note among the apostles, who also have been in Christ before me. Salute Ampliatus my beloved in the Lord.—Rom. 16:1-8.

This series of personal commendations is only the beginning of the last chapter of Paul's letter to the Romans.

All the way through one hears the individual names of Paul's friends and fellow-laborers, with his discriminating and hearty praise of each. It is clear that he has faith in these men and women; he believes in them and relies on them. Consider the effect on them that Paul's confidence in their Christian fidelity would naturally have. There is no motive much more stirring than the consciousness that somebody believes in us, is trusting and counting on us. Whatever is fine and noble in human life responds to that appeal. Soldiers who feel that their country is relying upon their fidelity, children who are conscious that their parents believe in them, friends who are heartened by the assurance that some folk completely trust them—how much of the best in all of us has come because we have been the objects of somebody's faith! A Connecticut volunteer in the American Revolution has written that George Washington once paused for a moment in front of his company and said simply, "I am counting on you men from Connecticut." And the recruit clasped his musket in his arms and wept with the devotion which Washington's confidence evoked. Would not the sixteenth chapter of Romans have a similar effect on those who read it?

O Thou loving and tender Father in heaven, we confess before Thee, in sorrow, how hard and unsympathetic are our hearts; how often we have sinned against our neighbors by want of compassion and tenderness; how often we have felt no true pity for their trials and sorrows, and have neglected to comfort, help, and visit them. O Father, forgive this our sin, and lay it not to our charge. Give us grace ever to alleviate the crosses and difficulties of those around us, and never to add to them; teach us to be consolers in sorrow, to take thought for the stranger, the widow, and the orphan; let our charity show itself not in words only, but in deed and truth. Teach us to judge as Thou dost, with forbearance, with much pity and indulgence; and help us to avoid all unloving judgment of others; for the sake of Jesus Christ Thy Son, who loved us and gave Himself for us. Amen.—Johann Arndt, 1555.

Ninth Week, Second Day

And it came to pass in these days, that he went out into the mountain to pray; and he continued all night in prayer to

God. And when it was day, he called his disciples; and he chose from them twelve, whom also he named apostles: Simon, whom he also named Peter, and Andrew his brother, and James and John, and Philip and Bartholomew, and Matthew and Thomas, and James the son of Alphaeus, and Simon who was called the Zealot, and Judas the son of James, and Judas Iscariot, who bcame a traitor.—Luke 6:12-16.

The power that comes to men when someone believes in them must have come to these disciples whom Jesus trusted with his work. We often note the power that was theirs through their faith in Christ; consider today the inspiration that came from Christ's faith in them. He picked them out, commissioned them, relied on them, and believed in their ability with God's help to carry his work to a successful issue. All that is most distinctive and memorable in their character came from their response to that divine trust. How they must have encouraged themselves in times of failure and disheartenment by saying: he believes in us; even though we are ignorant and sinful, he believes in us; he has trusted his work to us, and for all our inability he has faith that we can carry it to triumph! Their faith in themselves and what they could do with God's help must have been almost altogether a reflex of his faith in them. Our contention, therefore, that faith is the dynamic of life has now a new confirmation: *the faith that lifts and motives life is not simply our faith in the Divine, but the faith of the Divine in us.* One of the most glorious results of believing in God is that a man can press on to the further confidence that God believes in us. If he did not, he would never have made us. The very fact that we are here means that he does believe in us, in our possibilities of growth, in our capacities of service, in what he can do in and for and through us before he is done. Man's faith in God and God's faith in)an together make an unequaled motive for great living. Yet there is always a sad appendix to every list of trusted men, with somebody's blighted name: "Judas Iscariot, who became a traitor."

Loving Father, our hearts are moved to gratitude and trust when we look up to Thee. We rejoice that through our fleeting days there runs Thy gracious purpose. We praise Thee that we are not the creatures of chance, nor the victims of iron fate, but that out from Thee we have come and into Thy bosom we shall return. We would not, even if we could, escape Thee. Thou alone art good, and to escape from Thee is to fall into infinite evil. Thy hand is upon us moving us on to some far-off spiritual event, where the meaning and the mystery of life shall be made plain and Thy glory shall be revealed. Look in pity upon our ignorance and childishness. Forgive us our small understanding of Thy purpose of good concerning us. Be not angry with us, but draw us from the things of this world which cannot satisfy our foolish hearts. Fill us with Thyself, that we may no longer be a burden to ourselves. So glorify the face of goodness that evil shall have no more dominion over us. Amen.—Samuel McComb.

Ninth Week, Third Day

The fact that God has faith in us is not alone a source of comfort; it presents a stirring challenge. It means that he is in earnest about achieving his great purposes in human life and that he is counting upon us to help. He has set his heart on aims, about which he cares, and to whose achievement he is calling us; he is confident that with him we can work out, if we will, loftier character and a better world. Let us consider some of the purposes which God is counting on us, in fellowship with him, to achieve. The prophet Micah, in a brief but perfect drama, gives one clue. First the Lord summons his people to a trial, with the eternal mountains for judges:

Hear ye now what Jehovah saith: Arise, contend thou before the mountains, and let the hills hear thy voice. Hear, O ye mountains, Jehovah's controversy, and ye enduring foundations of the earth; for Jehovah hath a controversy with his people, and he will contend with Israel.—Mic. 6:1-2.

Then, the Lord presents his case:

O my people, what have I done unto thee? and wherein have I wearied thee? testify against me. For I brought thee

up out of the land of Egypt, and redeemed thee out of the house of bondage; and I sent before thee Moses, Aaron, and Miriam. O my people, remember now what Balak king of Moab devised, and what Balaam the son of Beor answered him; remember from Shittim unto Gilgal, that ye may know the righteous acts of Jehovah.—Mic. 6:3-5.

Then the people put in their hesitant, questioning plea.

Wherewith shall I come before Jehovah, and bow myself before the high God? shall I come before him with burnt-offerings, with calves a year old? will Jehovah be pleased with thousands of rams, or with ten thousands of rivers of oil? shall I give my first-born for my transgression, the fruit of my body for the sin of my soul?—Mic. 6:6-7.

Then the mountains pronounce judgment:

He hath showed thee, O man, what is good; and what doth Jehovah require of thee, but to do justly, and to love kindness, and to walk humbly with thy God?—Mic. 6:8.

God, then, is in earnest about *just, kind, and humble character*. He believes in it as a possibility; he sees the making of it now in human hearts; he is pledged to further and establish it with all his power; and he is counting on us for loyal cooperation with all our powers of choice. Vital faith means a transforming partnership with a God who is in earnest about character.

O Thou who art the Father of that Son which hast awakened us and yet urgeth us out of the sleep of our sins, and exhorteth us that we become Thine, to Thee, Lord, we pray, who art the supreme Truth, for all truth that is, is from Thee. Thee we implore, O Lord, who art the highest Wisdom, through Thee are wise, all those that are so. Thou art the supreme Joy, and from Thee all have become happy that are so. Thou art the highest Good and from Thee all beauty springs. Thou art the intellectual Light, and from Thee man derives his understandings. To Thee, O God, we call and speak. Hear us, O Lord for Thou art our God and our Lord, our Father and our Creator, our Ruler and our

Hope, our Wealth and our Honor, our Home, our Country, our Salvation, and our Life; hear, hear us, O Lord. Few of Thy servants comprehend Thee, but at least we love Thee—yea, love Thee above all other things. We seek Thee, we follow Thee, we are ready to serve Thee; under Thy power we desire to abide, for Thou art the Sovereign of all. We pray Thee to command us as Thou wilt; through Jesus Christ Thy Son our Lord. Amen.—King Alfred, 849.

Ninth Week, Fourth Day

God also is in earnest about *social righteousness*.

I hate, I despise your feasts, and I will take no delight in your solemn assemblies. Yea, though ye offer me your burnt-offerings and meal-offerings, I will not accept them; neither will I regard the peace-offerings of your fat beasts. Take thou away from me the noise of thy songs; for I will not hear the melody of thy viols. But let justice roll down as waters, and righteousness as a mighty stream.—Amos 5:21-24.

Anyone who cares about character must care about social conditions, for every unfair economic situation, every social evil left to run its course means ruin to character. And the God of the Bible, because he cares supremely for personal life at its best, is zealously in earnest about social justice; his prophets blazed with indignation at all inequity, and his Son made the coming Kingdom, when God's will would be done on earth, the center of his message. To fellowship with this earnest purpose of God we all are summoned; God believes in the glorious possibilities of life on earth; he is counting on us to put away the sins that hold the Kingdom back and to fight the abuses that crush character in men. To believe in God, therefore—the God who is fighting his way with his children up through ignorance, brutality, and selfishness to "new heavens and a new earth wherein dwelleth righteousness"—is no weakly comfortable blessing. It means joining a moral war; it means devotion, sacrifice; its spirit is the Cross and its motive an undiscourageable faith. And our underlying assurance that this war for a better world can be won is not simply our belief that it can be done, but *our faith that God is, and that he believes that it can be done.* When we pray we say, "Thy Kingdom come," and we are full of hope about the long, sacrificial struggle, for the purpose behind and through it all is first of all God's. Our earnestness is but an echo of his.

O Thou Eternal One, we adore Thee who in all ages hast been the great companion and teacher of mankind; for Thou hast lifted our race from the depths, and hast made us to share in Thy conscious intelligence and Thy will that makes for righteousness and love. Thou alone art our Redeemer, for Thy lifting arms were about us and Thy persistent voice was in our hearts as we slowly climbed up from savage darkness and cruelty. Thou knowest how often we have resisted Thee and loved the easy ways of sin rather than the toilsome gain of self-control and the divine irritation of Thy truth. . . .

We pray Thee for those who amid all the knowledge of our day are still without knowledge; for those who hear not the sighs of the children that toil, nor the sobs of such as are wounded because others have made haste to be rich; for those who have never felt the hot tears of the mothers of the poor that struggle vainly against poverty and vice. Arouse them, we beseech Thee, from their selfish comfort and grant them the grace of social repentance. Smite us all with the conviction that for us ignorance is sin, and that we are indeed our brother's keeper if our own hand has helped to lay him low. Though increase of knowledge brings increase of sorrow, may we turn without flinching to the light and offer ourselves as instruments of Thy spirit in bringing order and beauty out of disorder and darkness. Amen.—Walter Rauschenbusch.

Ninth Week, Fifth Day

The thought which we have been pursuing leads us to a truth of major importance: if God is thus in earnest, believing in man's possibilities and laboring for them, then he cannot be known by anyone who does not share his purpose and his labor. *Action is a road to knowledge and some things never can be known without it.* If one would know the business world, he must be an active businessman; no amount of abstract study and speculation can take the place of vital participation in business struggle. The way to understand any movement or enterprise is to go into it, share its enthusiasms and hopes, labor sacrificially for its success, bear its defeats as though they were our own, and rejoice in its achievements as though nothing so much mattered to our happiness. Such knowledge is thorough and vital; when one who so has learned what war is, or the missionary enterprise, or the fight against the liquor traffic, stands up to speak, a merely theoretical student of these movements sounds unreal and tame. If therefore God is earnest Purpose, with aims in which he calls us to share, no one can thoroughly know him merely by *thinking;* he must know him by *acting.*

But he that doeth the truth cometh to the light, that his works may be made manifest, that they have been wrought in God.—John 3:21.

Jesus therefore answered them, and said, My teaching is not mine, but his that sent me. If any man willeth to do his will he shall know of the teaching, whether it is of God, or whether I speak from myself.—John 7:16-17.

Many people endeavor to reach a satisfactory knowledge of God by clarifying their thought and working out a rational philosophy. But, by such intellectual means alone, they could not gain satisfactory knowledge of so familiar a thing as home life. To know home life one elemental act is essential: get into a home and share its problems, its satisfactions, and its hopes. So the most adequate philosophy by itself can bring no satisfactory knowledge of God; only by working with God, sharing his purposes for the world, sacrificially laboring for the aims he has at heart can men know him.

Eternal God, who hast formed us, and designed us for companionship with Thee; who hast called us to walk with Thee and be not afraid; forgive us, we pray Thee, if craven fear, unworthy thought, or hidden sin has prompted us to hide from Thee. Remove the suspicion which regards Thy service as an intrusion on our time and an interference with our daily task. Shew to us the life that serves Thee in the quiet discharge of each day's duty, that ennobles all our toil by doing it as unto Thee. We ask for no far-off vision which shall set us dreaming while opportunities around slip by; for no enchantment which shall make our hands to slack and our spirits to sleep, but for the vision of Thyself in common things for every day; that we may find a Divine calling in the claims of life, and see a heavenly reward in work well done. We ask Thee not to lift us out of life, but to prove Thy power within it; not for tasks more suited to our strength, but for strength more suited to our tasks. Give to us the vision that moves, the strength that endures, the grace of Jesus Christ, who wore our flesh like a monarch's robe and walked our earthly life like a conqueror in triumph. Amen.—W. E. Orchard.

Ninth Week, Sixth Day

Because action with God is essential to any satisfying knowledge of him, action is one of the great resolvers of doubt. Many minds, endeavoring to think through the mystifying problems of God's providence, find themselves in a clueless labyrinth. The more they think the more entangled and confused their minds become. Their thoughts strike a fatal circle, like wanderers lost in the woods, and return upon their course, baffled and disheartened. To such perplexed minds the best advice often is: Cease your futile thinking and go to work. Let action take the place of speculation. Break the fatal round of circular thought that never will arrive, and go out to act on the basis of what little you do believe. Your mind like a dammed stream is growing stagnant; set it running to some useful purpose, if only to turn mill-wheels, and trust that activity will bring it cleansing in due time. Horace Bushnell, the great preacher, while a skeptical tutor at Yale, was disturbed because so may students were unsettled by his disbelief. In the midst of a revival he said that like a great snag he caught and stopped the newly launched boats as fast as they came down. Unable to think his way out of his

241

intellectual perplexity, he faced one night this arresting question: "What is the use of my trying to get further knowledge, so long as I do not cheerfully yield to what I already know?" And kneeling he prayed after this fashion: "O God, I believe there is an eternal difference between right and wrong, and I hereby give myself up to do the right and to refrain from the wrong. I believe that Thou dost exist, and if Thou canst hear my cry and wilt reveal Thyself to me, I pledge myself to do Thy will, and I make this pledge fully, freely, and forever." What wonder that in time the light broke and that Bushnell became a great prophet of the faith!

Even Paul, finishing his laborious discussion of God's providence toward Israel, acknowledges his baffled thought:

O the depth of the riches both of the wisdom and the knowledge of God! how unsearchable are his judgments, and his ways past tracing out! For who hath known the mind of the Lord? or who hath been his counsellor? or who hath first given to him, and it shall be recompensed unto him again? For of him, and through him, and unto him, are all things. To him be the glory for ever. Amen.—Rom. 11:33-36.

And then, as if he turned from philosophy to action with gratitude, he begins the twelfth chapter:

I beseech you therefore, brethren, by the mercies of God, to present your bodies a living sacrifice, holy, acceptable to God, which is your spiritual service. And be not fashioned according to this world: but be ye transformed by the renewing of your mind, that ye may prove what is the good and acceptable and perfect will of God.—Rom. 12:1-2.

O God, we thank Thee for the sweet refreshment of sleep and for the glory and vigor of the new day. As we set our faces once more toward our daily work, we pray Thee for the strength sufficient for our tasks. May Christ's spirit of duty and service ennoble all we do. Uphold us by the consciousness that our work is useful work and a blessing to all. If there has been anything in our work harmful to others and dishonorable to ourselves, reveal it to our inner eye with such clearness that we shall hate it and put it away, though it be at a loss to ourselves. When we work with others, help us to regard them, not as servants to our will, but as brothers equal to us in human dignity, and equally worthy of their full reward. May there be nothing in this day's work of which we shall be ashamed when the sun has set, nor in the eventide of our life when our task is done and we go to our long home to meet Thy face. Amen.—Walter Rauschenbusch.

Ninth Week, Seventh Day

Then shall the King say unto them on his right hand, Come, ye blessed of my Father, inherit the kingdom prepared for you from the foundation of the world: for I was hungry, and ye gave me to eat; I was thirsty, and ye gave me drink; I was a stranger, and ye took me in; naked, and ye clothed me; I was sick, and ye visited me; I was in prison, and ye came unto me. Then shall the righteous answer him, saying, Lord, when saw we thee hungry, and fed thee? or athirst, and gave thee drink? And when saw we thee a stranger, and took thee in? or naked, and clothed thee? And when saw we thee sick, or in prison, and came unto thee? And the King shall answer and say unto them, Verily I say unto you, Inasmuch as ye did it unto one of these my brethren, even these least, ye did it unto me.—Matt. 25:34-40.

The earnestness of God is not about any diffuse generality; it is about persons. His purposes concern them, and he believes in them and in their capacities for fellowship with him, for growing character and for glorious destiny. If, therefore, one wishes the sense of God's reality which comes from active co-partnership, let him serve persons, believe in them, and be in earnest about them. A woman, troubled by invincible doubts, was given by a wise minister the Gospel of John and a calling-list of needy families, and was told to use them both. She came through into a luminous faith, and which helped her more, her reading or her service, she could never tell. When the Master said that the good we did to the least of his brethren, we did to him, he indicated a road to vital knowledge of him; he said in effect that we can always find him in the lives of people to whom we give love and help. Many will never find him at all unless they find him there. The great believers have been the great servants; and the reason for this is not simply that faith produced service, but also that *service produced faith.* The life of Sir Wilfred Grenfell, for example, makes convincingly plain that his faith sent him to Labrador for service, and that then he drew out of service a compound interest on his original investment of faith.

O God, the Father of the forsaken, the Help of the weak, the Supplier of the needy, who hast diffused and proportioned Thy gifts to body and soul, in such sort that all may acknowledge and perform the joyous duty of mutual service; Who teachest us that love towards the race of men is the bond of perfectness, and the imitation of Thy blessed Self; open our eyes and touch our hearts, that we may see and do, both for this world and for that which is to come, the things which belong to our peace. Strengthen us in the work we have undertaken; give us counsel and wisdom, perseverance, faith, and zeal, and in Thine own good time, and according to Thy pleasure, prosper the issue. Pour into us a spirit of humility; let nothing be done but in devout obedience to Thy will, thankfulness for Thine unspeakable mercies, and love to Thine adorable Son Christ Jesus. . . .Amen.—Earl of Shaftesbury, 1801.

COMMENT FOR THE WEEK

I

Throughout our studies we have been asserting that faith in God involves confidence that creation has a purpose. But we shall not see the breadth and depth of the affirmation, or its significant meaning for our lives, unless more carefully we face a question, which, as keenly as any other, pierces to the marrow of religion: *Is God in earnest?*

That the God of the Bible is in earnest is plain. If we open the Book at the Exodus, we hear him saying, "I have surely seen the affliction of my people, . . . and have heard their cry, . . . and I am come down to deliver them" (Exod. 3:7-8). If we turn to the prophets, we find Hosea, interpreting the beating of God's heart: "How am I to give thee up, O Ephraim? How am I to let thee go, O Israel? How am I to give thee up? My heart is turned upon me, my compassions begin to boil" (Hos. 11:8, George Adam Smith's Translation). Everywhere in the Old Testament, God is in earnest: about personal character—"What doth Jehovah require of thee, but to do justly, and to love kindness, and to walk humbly with thy God?" (Mic. 6:8); about social righteousness—"Let justice roll down as waters, and righteousness as a mighty stream" (Amos 5:24); about the salvation of the world—"It is too light a thing that thou shouldest be my servant to raise up the tribes of Jacob and to restore the preserved of Israel: I will also give thee for a light to the Gentiles, that thou mayest be my salvation unto the end of the earth" (Isa. 49:6). When from the Old Testament one turns to the New, he faces an assertion of God's earnestness that cannot be surpassed: "God so loved the world that he gave his only begotten Son." God in the New Testament is as much in earnest as that, and all the major affirmations of the Book cluster about the magnetism of this central faith. God is even like a shepherd with a hundred sheep, who having lost one, leaves the ninety and nine and goes after that which is lost, until he finds it (Luke 15:4). From the earliest Hebrew seer dimly perceiving him, to the last apostle of the New Covenant, the God of the Bible is tremendously in earnest.

How profoundly the acceptance of this faith deepens the meaning and value of life is evident. For a moment some might think that the major question is not whether *God* is in earnest but whether *we* are; but when a man considers the hidden fountains from which the streams of his human earnestness must flow, he sees how necessary is at least the hope that at the heart of it creation is in earnest too. Von Hartmann, the pessimist, makes one of his characters say, "The activities of the busy world are only the shudderings of a fever." How shall a man be seriously in earnest about great causes in a world like that? The men whose devoted lives have made history great have seen in creation's busyness more than aimless shuddering. Moses was in earnest, but behind his consecration was his vision of the Eternal, saying to Pharaoh, "Let my people go!" The Master was in earnest, but with a motive that took into its account the purposefulness of God, "My Father worketh hitherto, and I work" (John 5:17).

Indeed, no satisfying meaning, no real unity are conceivable in a purposeless universe. The plain fact is that *within* the universe nobody explains anything without the statement of its purpose. A chair is something to sit down on; a watch is something to tell time by; a lamp is something to give illumination in the dark—and lacking this purposive description, the story of the precedent history of none of these things, from their original materials to their present shape, would in the least tell what they really are. One who knows all else about a telephone, practically knows nothing, unless he is aware of what it is *for*. Nor is the necessity of such explanation lessened when scientists endeavor descriptions in their special realms. Huxley, narrating the growth of a salamander's egg, writes, "Let a moderate supply of warmth reach its watery cradle, and the plastic matter undergoes changes so rapid, and yet so steady and so purposelike in their succession, that one can only compare them to those operated by a skilled modeler upon a formless lump of cláy. As with an invisible trowel, the mass is divided and subdivided into smaller and smaller portions, until it is reduced to an aggregation of granules not too large to build withal the finest fabrics of the nascent organism. And, then, it is as if a delicate finger traced out the line to be occupied by the spinal column and moulded the contour of the body; pinching up the head at one end, the tail at the other, and fashioning flank and limb into the due salamandrine proportions, in so artistic a way, that, after watching the process hour by hour, one is almost involuntarily possessed by the notion that some more subtle aid to vision than an achromatic, would show the hidden artist, with his plan before him, striving with skilful manipulation to perfect his work." The obvious fact is that salamanders' eggs act as though they were seriously intent on making salamanders; and lions' cells as though they were tremendously in earnest about making lions. As Herbert

Spencer said of a begonia leaf, "We have therefore no alternative but to say, that the living particles composing one of these fragments, have an innate tendency to arrange themselves into the shape of the organism to which they belong." *But if this is so, purpose is essential in the description of every living thing.* All about us is a world of life with something strikingly like purposeful action rampant everywhere, so that in describing an elm tree it will not do to say only that forces from behind pushed it into being; one must say, too, that from our first observation of its cells they acted as though they were intent on making nothing else but elm. They went about their business as though they had a purpose. The tree's cause is not alone the forces from behind; it is as well the aim that in the cells' action lay ahead.

Men can describe nothing in heaven above or on the earth beneath without the use of purposive terminology. How shall they try otherwise to describe the universe? *A world in which the minutest particles and cells all act as though they were eagerly intent on achieving aims, can only with difficulty be thought of as an aimless whole.* Man's conviction is insistent and imperious that creation, so surcharged with purposes, must have Purpose. The greatest scientists themselves are often our best witnesses here. Charles Darwin and Alfred Russel Wallace are the twin discoverers of evolution. Said the former: "If we consider the whole universe the mind refuses to look at it as the outcome of chance." Said the latter: the world is "a manifestation of creative power, directive mind, and ultimate purpose."

What such men have coldly said, the men of devout religion have set on fire with passionate faith. They have been sure that this world is not

"A tale

Told by an idiot, full of sound and fury,
Signifying nothing."

In every cause that makes for man's salvation they have seen the manifest unveiling of divine intent. *God is in earnest*—this conviction has possessed them utterly, and to live and die for those things on behalf of which the Eternal is tremendously concerned has been the aim, the motive, and the glory of their lives.

II

One need only watch with casual observance the multitudes who say that they believe in God, to see how few of them believe in this God who is in earnest. When they confess their faith in deity they have something else in mind beside the God of the Bible, compassionately purposeful about his world and calling men to be his fellow-workers. Let us therefore consider some of the fallacies that enable men to believe in a God who is *not* in earnest.

For one thing, some *put God far away*. Missionaries in Africa's interior find tribes worshiping stocks, stones, demons, ghosts, but this does not mean that no idea of a great original god is theirs. Often they are not strangers to that thought, but, as an old Afrikander woman said, "He never concerned himself with me; why should I concern myself with him?" To such folk a great god exists, but he does not care; he dwells apart, an indifferent deity, who has left this world in the hands of lesser gods that really count. The task of the missionary, therefore, is not to prove the existence of a creator—"No rain, no mushrooms," said an African chief; "no God, no world"—but it is to persuade men that the God who seems so far away is near at hand, that he really cares, and over each soul and all his world is sacrificially in earnest.

Such missionary work is not yet needless among Christian people. Said a Copenhagen preacher in a funeral discourse, "God cannot help us in our great sorrow, because he is so infinitely far away; we must therefore look to Jesus." One feels this Siberian exile of God from all vital meaning for our humanity, when he is called the "Absolute," the "Great First Cause," the "Energy from which all things proceed." Like the man, examined by the Civil Service, who, asked the distance from sun to earth, answered, "I do not know how far the sun is from the earth; but it is far enough so that it will not interfere with the proper performance of my duties at the Customs Office," so men with phrases like the "Great First Cause" put God an immeasurable distance off. No man has dealings with a "Great First Cause," no "Great First Cause" ever had vital, personal, constraining meanings for a man. Rather across infinite distance and time unthinkable, we vaguely picture a dim Figure, who gave this toboggan of a universe its primal shove and has not thought seriously of it since. So a wanderer down the street might put a child upon her sled and giving her a start downhill, go on his way. She may have a pleasant slide, but he will not know; she may fall off, but he will not care; there may be a tragic accident, but that will not be his concern—he has gone away off down the street. Multitudes of nominal believers have a god like that.

In comparison with such, one thinks of men like Livingstone. His God was compassionately concerned for Africa, spoke about black folk as Hosea heard him speak concerning Israel, "How can I give thee up? How can I let thee go?" until the fire of the divine earnestness lit a corresponding ardor in Livingstone's heart and he went out to be God's man in the dark continent. Such men have smitten the listless world as winds fill flapping sails, crying "Move!" And the God of such has been tremendously in earnest.

III

Some gain a God lacking serious purpose, not by putting him afar off, but by endeavoring to bring him so near that they *diffuse him everywhere*. Writers tell us that God is in every rustling leaf and in every wave that breaks upon the beach; we are assured that God is in every gorgeous flower and in every flaming sunset. And the poetry of this is so alluring that we cannot bear to have God specially anywhere, because we are so anxious to keep him everywhere. Preachers delight to illustrate their thought of God with figures drawn from nature's invisible energies—

"Who has seen the wind?
  Neither I nor you:
But when the leaves hang trembling
  The wind is passing through.

Who has seen the wind?
    Neither you nor I:
But when the trees bow down their heads
    The wind is passing by."

By such comparisons are we taught to see that God invisibly is everywhere.

For all the valuable truth that such speech contains, its practical issue, in many minds today, is to strip God of the last shred of personality, and with that loss to end the possibility of his being in earnest about anything. He has become refined Vapor thinly diffused through space. Folk say they love to meditate on him, and well they may! For such a god asks nothing of anybody except meditation; he has no purposes that call for earnestness in them. When little children are ruined in a city's tenements, when the liquor traffic brutalizes men, when economic inequity makes many poor that a few may be made rich, when war clothes the world with unutterable sorrow, such a god does not care. He is not in earnest about anything. For the only thing in the universe that can be consciously in earnest is personality, and when one depersonalizes God, the remainder is a deity who has no love, no care, no purpose. Thousands do obeisance to such a gaseous idol.

From this fallacy spring such familiar confessions of faith as this, "God is not a person; he is spirit." If by this negation one intends to say that God is not a limited individual, that is obviously true; but *the contrast between personality and spirit is impossible.* One may as well speak of dry water as of impersonal spirit. Rays of radium are unimaginably minute and swift, but they are not spirit. Nothing in the impersonal realm can be conceived so subtle and refined that it is spirit. Spirit begins only where love and intelligence and purpose are, and these all are activities of personality. No one can *really* believe what Jesus said, "God is a Spirit," without being ready to pray as Jesus prayed, "Our Father."

Between an impersonal, diffused, and gaseous god, and the God of the Bible, how great the difference! God's pervading omnipresence is indeed affirmed in Scripture. There, as much as in any modern thought, the heavens declare his glory, the flowers of the field are illustrations of his care, and the influences of his spirit are like the breeze across the hills. To the ancient Hebrew, heaven and Sheol were the highest and the lowest, but of each the psalmist says to God, "Thou art there," and as for the uttermost parts of the sea, "even there shall thy hand lead me" (Ps. 139:7-10). Cries Jeremiah from the Old Testament, "Am I a God at hand, saith Jehovah, and not a God afar off? Can any hide himself in secret places so that I shall not see him? saith Jehovah. Do not I fill heaven and earth?" (Jer. 23:23-24). And Paul answers from the New Testament, "Not far from every one of us: for in him we live, and move, and have our being" (Acts 17:27-28). But the God of the Bible who so pervades and sustains all existence never degenerates into a Vapor. When Egyptian taskmasters crack their whips over Hebrew slaves, he cares. When exiles try in vain to sing the songs of Zion in a strange land, he cares. When evil men build Jerusalem with blood, and rapacious men pant after the dust on the head of the poor, he cares. He is prodigiously in earnest, and those who best represent him, from the great prophets to the sacrificial Son, are like him in this, that they are mastered by consuming purpose. The God of the Bible is sadly needed by his people. For lack of him religion grows often listless and churches become social clubs.

IV

By another road men travel to believe in a God who is not in earnest: *they think of him as a historic being.* It was said of Carlyle, shrewdly if unjustly, that his God lived until the death of Oliver Cromwell. Whatever may be the truth about Carlyle, it is easy to find folk whose God to all intents and purposes is dead. Long since he closed his work, spoke his last word, and settled down to inactivity and silence. He made the world, created man, thundered from Sinai, established David's kingdom, brought back the exiles, inspired the prophets, and sent his Son. He *once* was earnest; the record of his ancient acts is long and glorious, and men find comfort in reading what he used to do. They would not explicitly confess it, but in fact they habitually think of God in the past tense. They cannot conceive the universe as happening by chance, and they posit God as

251

making it; they cannot believe that the transcendent characters of olden times were uninspired, so God becomes the explanation of their power. When such believers wish to assure themselves of God they go to the stern of humanity's ship and watch the wake far to the rear; but they never stand on the ship's bridge, and feel it sway and turn at the touch of a present Captain in control. They have not risen to the meaning of the Bible's reiterated phrase, *"the living God."*

Höffding tells us that in a Danish Protestant church, well on into the nineteenth century, worshipers maintained the custom of bowing, when they passed a certain spot upon the wall. The reason, which no one knew, was discovered when removal of the whitewash revealed a Roman Catholic Madonna. Folk had bowed for three centuries before the place where the Madonna *used to be.* So some folk worship deity; he is not a present reality but a tradition; their faith is directed not toward the living God himself, but toward what someone else has written about a God who used to be alive. They do not feel now God's plans afoot, his purposes as certainly in progress now as ever in man's history. They stand rather like unconverted Gideon, facing backwards and lamenting, "Where are all his wondrous works which our fathers told us of?" (Judg. 6:13).

Not by what we say, but by our practical attitudes we most reveal how little we believe in an earnest, living God whose voice calls *us,* whose plans need *us,* as much as ever Moses or David or Paul was summoned and required. If we say that we do believe in this living God we are belied by our discouragements, deserving as we often do the rebuke which Luther's wife administered to the Reformer. "From what you have said," she remarked, standing before him clothed in deep, mourning black, "and from the way you feel and act I supposed that God was dead." If we say that we believe in a living, earnest God, we are belied by our reluctance to expect and welcome new revelations of God's truth and enlarging visions of his plan. Willing to believe what the astronomers say, that light from a new star reaches the earth each year, we act as though God's spiritual universe were smaller than his physical, and do not eagerly await the new light perpetually breaking from his heavens. But most of all the little influence which our faith in God has upon our practical service is a scathing indictment of its vitality and power. No one who really believes in an earnest, living God can have an undedicated life. He may not think of the Divine in the past tense chiefly; the present and the future even more belong to God; and through each generation runs the earnest purpose of the Eternal, who has never said his last word on any subject, nor put the final hammer blow on any task. A faith like this, deeply received and apprehended, is a masterful experience. It changes the inner quality of life; it makes the place whereon we stand holy ground; it urgently impresses us into the service of those causes that we plainly see have in them the purpose of God. No outlook upon life compares with this in grandeur; no motive for life is at once so weighty and so fine.

V

One of the subtlest fallacies by which we miss believing in an earnest God is not describable as an opinion. Men fall into it, who neither reduce God to a Great First Cause, nor diffuse him into a vapor, nor regard him as a historic being. *They rather allow their superstitious sentiments to take the place of worthy faith.* Plenty of people who warmly would insist on their religion, reveal in their practical attitudes how utterly bereft of serious moral purpose their God is. They think their fortune will be better if they do not sit thirteen at a table or occupy room thirteen at a hotel; on occasion they throw salt or look at the moon over their right shoulders and rap on wood to assure their safety or their luck; and to be quite certain of divine favor they hang fetishes, like rabbits' feet, about their necks. Their attitude toward such surviving pagan superstitions is like Fontenelli's toward ghosts. "I do not believe in them," he said, "but I am afraid of them." That this is a law-abiding universe with moral purpose in it, such folk obviously do not believe. Their God is not in earnest. He spends his time watching for dinner parties of thirteen or listening for folk who forget to rap on wood when they boast that they have not been ill all winter. The utter poverty to which great words may be reduced by meager minds is evident when such folk say that they believe in God.

Even when these grosser forms of superstition are not

present, others hardly more respectable may take their place. God is pictured as a King, surrounded with court ritual, in the complete and proper observance of which he takes delight, and any rupture in whose regularity awakes his anger. To go to church, to say our prayers, to read our Bibles, to be circumspect on Sunday, to help pay the preacher's salary and to contribute to the missionary cause—such things as these comprise the court ritual of God. These Christian acts are not presented as gracious privileges, opportunities, like fresh air and sunshine and friendship, to make life rich and serviceable; they are presented as works of merit, by which we gain standing in God's favor and assure ourselves of his benignity. For with those who so conform to his ordinances and respect his taboos, he is represented as well-pleased, and he blesses them with special favors. But any infraction of these rituals is sure to bring terrific punishment. God watches those who do not sing his praises or who fail in praying, and he marks them for his vengeance! Dr. Jowett tells us that in the Sunday school room of the English chapel where as a child he worshiped, a picture hung that to his fascinated and frightened imagination represented the character of God: a huge eye filled the center of the heavens, and from it rays of vision fell on every sort of minute happening and small misdeed on earth. As such a monstrous Detective, jealous of his rights and perquisites, God is how often pictured to the children! So H. G. Wells indignantly interprets his experience: "I, who write, was so set against God, thus rendered. He and his Hell were the nightmare of my childhood; I hated him while I still believed in him, and who could help but hate? I thought of him as a fantastic monster, perpetually spying, perpetually listening, perpetually waiting to condemn and to strike me dead; his flames as ready as a grill-room fire. He was over me and about my feebleness and silliness and forgetfulness as the sky and sea would be about a child drowning in mid-Atlantic. When I was still only a child of thirteen, by the grace of the true God in me, I flung this lie out of my mind, and for many years, until I came to see that God himself had done this thing for me, the name of God meant nothing to me but the hideous sear in my heart where a fearful demon had been."

This "bogey God" is in earnest about nothing except the

observance of his little rituals; he is unworthy of a good man's worship, he has no purpose that can capture the consent and inspire the loyalty of serious folk. How many so-called unbelievers are in revolt against this perversion of the idea of God, taught them in childhood! The deity whom they refuse to credit is not the Father, with "the eternal purpose which he purposed in Christ" (Eph. 3:11); often they have not heard of him. Their denial is directed against another sort of God. "I wish I could recall clearly," writes one, "the conception of God which I gained as a boy in Sunday school. He was as old as grandfather, I know, but not so kind. We were told to fear him." Surely the real God must sympathize with those who hate his caricature. A vindictive Bogey, querulous about the mint, anise, and cummin of his ritual, in earnest about nothing save to reward obsequious servants and to have his vengeance out on the careless and disobedient, is poles asunder from the God and Father of our Lord Jesus Christ with his majestic purpose for the world's salvation.

VI

Of all the sentiments, however, by which a worthy faith is made impossible, none is so common, in these recent years, *as the ascription to God of a weak and flaccid affectionate-ness.* God's love is interpreted by love's meaning in hours when we are gentle with our children or tender with our friends. The soft and cozy aspects of love, its comforts, its pities, its affections, are made central in our thought of God. We are taught, as children, that he loves us as our mothers do; and as from them we look for coddling when we cry for it, so are our expectations about God. Our religion becomes a selfish seeking for divine protection from life's ills, a recipe for ease, an expectant trust, that as we believe in God he in return will nurse us, unharmed and happy, through our lives. No one intimately acquainted with the religious life of men and women can be unaware of this widespread, ingrained belief in a soft, affectionate, grandmotherly God. What wonder that life brings fearful disillusionment! What wonder that in a world where all that is valuable has been

> "Battered with the shocks of doom
> To shape and use,"

the God of coddling love seems utterly impossible!

The lack in this fallacious faith is central; there is no place in it for the movement of God's moral purpose. *To ascribe love to God without making it a quality of his unalterable purpose, which must sweep on through costs in suffering however great, is to misread the Gospel.* Many kinds of love are known in our experience, from a nursing mother with her babe to a military leader with his men. In Donald Hankey's picture of "the Beloved Captain" we see affection and tenderness, as beautiful as they are strong: "It was a wonderful thing, that smile of his. It was something worth living for, and worth working for. . . . It seemed to make one look at things from a different point of view, a finer point of view, his point of view. There was nothing feeble or weak about it. . . . It meant something. It meant that we were his men and that he was proud of us. . . . When we failed him, when he was disappointed in us, he did not smile. He did not rage or curse. He just looked disappointed, and that made us feel far more savage with ourselves than any amount of swearing would have done. . . . The fact was that he had won his way into our affections. We loved him. And there isn't anything stronger than love, when all's said and done."

Yet, this Captain, loving and beloved, will lead his men in desperate charges, where death falls in showers, but where the purpose which their hearts have chosen forces them to go. The love of God must be like that; it surely is if Jesus' love is its embodiment. His affection for his followers, his solicitude and tenderness have been in Christian eyes, how beautiful! They shine in words like John's seventeenth chapter where love finds transcendent utterance. Yet this same Master said: "Behold, I send you forth as sheep in the midst of wolves" (Matt. 10:16); "Blessed are ye when men shall reproach you, and persecute you, and say all manner of evil against you falsely for my sake" (Matt. 5:11); "Then shall they deliver you up into tribulation, and shall kill you; and ye shall be hated of all the nations for my name's sake" (Matt. 24:9); "They shall put you out of the synagogues; yea, the hour cometh, that whosoever killeth you shall think that he offereth service unto God" (John 16:2); "If any man cometh unto me, and hateth not his own father, and mother, and wife, and children, and brethren, and sisters, yea, and his own life also, he cannot be my disciple" (Luke 14:26). The love of Jesus was no coddling affection; it had for its center a moral purpose that balked at no sacrifice. He took crucifixion for himself, and to his beloved he cried, "If any man would come after me, let him deny himself, and take up his cross, and follow me" (Matt. 16:24). Such love is God's; and *preachers who advertise his Fatherhood as a gentle nurse that shelters us from suffering have sapped the Gospel of its moral power*. God's love is austere as well as bountiful; he is, as Emerson said, the "terrific benefactor."

Indeed, faith in a God of coddling love may be one of the most pernicious influences in human life. Our trust, so misinterpreted, becomes a cushion on which to lie, a sedative by which to sleep. When ills afflict the world that men could cure, such misbelievers merely trust in God; when tasks await man's strength, they quietly retreat upon their faith that God is good and will solve all, until religion becomes a by-word and a hissing on the lips of earnest men. Such misbelievers have not dimly seen the Scripture's meaning, where faith is not a pillow but a shield, from behind which plays a sword (Eph. 6:16) and where men do not sleep by faith, but "fight the good fight of faith" instead (I Tim. 6:12). Or if such misbelievers do rouse themselves to lay hold on their Divinity, it is to demand God's love for them and not to offer their lives to God. As Sydney Smith exclaimed about some people's patriotism, "God save the King! in these times too often means, God save my pension and my place. God give my sisters an allowance out of the Privy Purse, let me live upon the fruits of other men's industry and fatten upon the plunder of the public."

Faith in God never is elevated and ennobling until we overpass *"God for our lives!"* to cry *"Our lives for God!"* Then at the luminous center of our faith shines the divine purpose, costly but wonderful, that binds the ages together in spiritual unity. To that we dedicate our lives in that we exceedingly rejoice. No longer do we test God's goodness by our happiness or our ill-fortune; we are *his* through fair weather and through foul. No longer do we merely hold beliefs, we are held by them, captured now and not simply consoled by faith. Only so are we learning discipleship to Christ and are beginning really to believe in the Christian God.

VII

From all these common fallacies of thought and sentiment one turns to the New Testament to find the God of the Gospel. The very crux of the Good Tidings is that God is so much in earnest that he is the eternal Sufferer. The ancient Greeks had a god of perfect bliss; he floated on from age to age in undisturbed tranquillity; no cry of man ever reached his empyrean calm; his life was an endless stream of liquid happiness. How different this Greek deity is from ours may be perceived if one tries to say of him those things which the Scripture habitually says of God. "In all their affliction he was afflicted" (Isa. 63:9); "Can a woman forget her sucking child, that she should not have compassion on the son of her womb? yea, these may forget, yet will not I forget thee" (Isa. 49:15); "God, being rich in mercy, for his great love wherewith he loved us even when we were dead through our trespasses" (Eph. 2:4-5); "God so loved the world that he gave his only begotten Son" (John 3:16). None of these things that Christians say about their God can be said of a deity who dwells in tranquil bliss.

Indeed let one stand over against a war-torn, unhappy world and try to think that God does not suffer in man's agony, and he will see how useless and incredible such a God would be. God looks on Belgium and he does not care; he looks on Armenia desolate and Poland devastated, and he does not care; he sits in heaven and sees his children wounded and alone in No-man's land, watches the deaths, the heartbreaks, the poverty of war, its ruined childhood and its shattered families, and he does not care—how impossible it is to believe in such a God! A God who does not care does not count.

Christians, therefore, have the God who really meets the needs of men. He cares indeed, and, with all the modesty that words of human emotion must put on when they are applied to him, he suffers in the suffering of men and is crucified in his children's agonies. God limited himself in making such a world as this; in it he cannot lightly do what he will; he has a struggle on his heart; he makes his way upward against obstacles that man's imagination cannot measure. There is a cross forever at the heart of God. He climbs his everlasting Calvary toward the triumph that must come, and he is tremendously in earnest.

One important consequence follows such faith as this. Confidence in such an earnest, sacrificial God makes inevitable the Christian faith in immortality. Our solar system is no permanent theater for God's eternal purposes; it is doomed to dissolution as certainly as any human body is doomed to die. In the Lick observatory one reads this notice under a picture of the sun: "The blue stars are considered to be in early life, the yellow stars in middle life, the red stars in old age. . . . From the quality of its spectrum the sun is classified as a star in middle age." Those, therefore, who, denying their own immortality, comfort themselves with prophesying endless progress for the race upon the earth, have no basis for their hopes. "We must therefore renounce those brilliant fancies," says Faye the scientist, "by which we try to deceive ourselves in order to endow man with unlimited posterity, and to regard the universe as the immense theater on which is to be developed a spontaneous progress without end. On the contrary, life must disappear, and the grandest material works of the human race will have to be effaced by degrees under the action of a few physical forces which will survive man for a time. Nothing will remain—'Even the ruins will perish.'"

If one believes, therefore, in the God who is in earnest, he cannot content himself with such a universe—lacking any permanent element, any abiding reality in which the moral gains of man's long struggle are conserved. God's purpose cannot be so narrow in horizon that it is satisfied with a few million years of painful experiment, costly beyond imagination, yet with no issue to crown its sacrifice. In such a universe as Faye pictures, lacking immortality, generation after generation of men suffer, aspire, labor, and die, and this shall be the history of all creation, until at last Shakespeare's prophecy shall be fulfilled,

"The cloud-capp'd towers, the gorgeous palaces,
The solemn temples, the great globe itself,
Yea, all which it inherit, shall dissolve
And, like this insubstantial pageant faded,
Leave not a rack behind."

If such is to be the story of creation, there is no purpose in it and the Christian faith in an earnest God is vain.

Only one truth is adequate to crown our confidence in a purposeful universe and to make it reasonable: *personality must persist*. We believe in immortality, not because we meanly want rewards ahead, but because in no other way can life, viewed as a whole, find sense and reason. If personality persists, this transient theater of action and discipline may serve its purpose in God's time, and disappear. He is in earnest, but not for rocks and suns and stars, he is in earnest about persons—the sheep of his pasture are men. They are not mortal; they carry over into the eternal world the spiritual gains of earth; and all life's struggle—its vicarious sacrifice, its fearful punishments, its labor for better circumstance and worthier life—is justified in its everlasting influence on personality. When we say that God cares, we mean no vague, diffusive attitude toward a system that lasts for limited millenniums and then comes to an uneventful end in a cold sun and a ruined earth. We mean that he cares for personality which is his child, that he suffers in the travail of his children's character, and that this divine solicitude has everlasting issues when the heavens "wax old like a garment." Still Paul's statement stands, one of the most worthy summaries of God's earnestness that ever has been written: "The creation waits with eager longing for the sons of God to be revealed" (Rom. 8:19, Moffatt's Translation).

CHAPTER X

Faith in Christ the Savior: Forgiveness

DAILY READINGS

During the next two weeks we are to consider some of the distinctive meanings which faith in Christ has had for his disciples. They have found in that faith unspeakable blessing and have uttered their gratitude in radiant language. But, just because of this, many folk find themselves in difficulty. Their expectations concerning the Christian life have been lifted very high, and in their experience of it they have been disappointed. Their problem is not theoretical doubt, but practical disillusionment. Their difficulty lies in their experience that the Christian life, while it may be theoretically true, is not practically what it is advertised to be. At this common problem let us look in the daily readings.

Tenth Week, First Day

Many expect in the Christian experience an emotional life of joy and quietude which they have not found. They are led to expect this by many passages of Scripture about "peace in believing," by many hymns of exultation where a mood of unqualified spiritual triumph finds voice, and by testimonies of men who speak of living years without any depressed hours or flagging spirits. Such a wonderful life of elevated emotion many crave for themselves; they came into the Christian fellowship expecting it; and they neither have it, nor are likely to achieve it. Now the beauty of a clear, high emotional life no one can doubt, but *we must not demand it as a condition of our keeping faith.* We ought not to seek God simply for the sake of sensational experiences, no matter how desirable they may be. In all the ages before Christ, the outstanding example of deep personal religion, expressing itself in over forty years of splendidly courageous prophetic ministry, is Jeremiah, and his temperament was never marked by quietude and joy. His emotional life was profoundly affected by his faith: *courage was substituted for fear.* But if he had demanded the mood of Psalm 103 as a price for continued faith, he would have lost his faith. He was not temperamentally constructed like the psalmist—and he was a far greater personality. We must not be too much concerned about our spiritual sensations. Consider the Master's parable about the two sons: one had amiable feelings, but his will was wrong, the other lacked satisfactory emotions, but he did the work.

But what think ye? A man had two sons; and he came to the first, and said, Son, go work to-day in the vineyard. And he answered and said, I will not: but afterward he repented himself, and went. And he came to the second, and said likewise. And he answered and said, I go, sir: and went not. Which of the two did the will of his father? They say, The first.—Matt. 21:28-31.

Ah, Lord, unto whom all hearts are open; Thou canst govern the vessel of our souls far better than we can. Arise, O Lord, and command the stormy wind and the troubled sea of our hearts to be still, and at peace in Thee, that we may look up to Thee undisturbed, and abide in union with Thee, our Lord. Let us not be carried hither and thither by wandering thoughts, but, forgetting all else, let us see and hear Thee. Renew our spirits; kindle in us Thy light, that it may shine within us, and our hearts may burn in love and adoration towards Thee. Let Thy Holy Spirit dwell in us continually, and make us Thy temples and sanctuary, and fill us with Divine love and light and life, with devout and heavenly thoughts, with comfort and strength, with joy and peace. Amen.—Johann Arndt, 1555.

Tenth Week, Second Day

Many came into the Christian life because they needed conquering power in their struggle against sin. They were told that absolute victory could be theirs through Christ, and they set their hearts on that in ardent hope and expectation. But they are disappointed. That they have been helped they would not deny, but they find that the battle with besetting sin is a running fight; it has not been concluded by a final and resounding victory. This seems to them a denial of what Christian preachers and Christian hymns have promised, and perhaps it is. Hymns and preachers are not infallible. Christian experience, however, is plainly aligned against their disappointment. Some men under the power of Christ are immediately transformed so that an old sin becomes thenceforth utterly distasteful; even the desire for it is banished altogether. But a great preacher, only recently deceased, no less really under the power of Christ, had all his life to fight a taste for drink which once had mastered him. His battle never ceased. His victory consisted not in the elimination of his appetite, but in abiding power to keep up the struggle, to refuse subjugation to it, and at last gloriously to fall on sleep, admired and loved by his people who had seen in him steadfast, unconquerable will, sustained by faith. To have done with a sinful appetite in one conclusive victory is glorious; but we must not demand it as a price of keeping faith. Perhaps our victory must come through the kind of patient persistence which James the Apostle evidently knew.

Count it all joy, my brethren, when ye fall into manifold temptations; knowing that the proving of your faith worketh patience. And let patience have its perfect work, that ye may be perfect and entire, lacking in nothing.

But if any of you lacketh wisdom, let him ask of God, who giveth to all liberally and upbraideth not; and it shall be given him. But let him ask in faith, nothing doubting: for he that doubteth is like the surge of the sea driven by the wind and tossed. For let not that man think that he shall receive anything of the Lord; a double-minded man, unstable in all his ways.—James 1:2-8.

THE MEANING OF FAITH

O Lord God Almighty, who givest power to the faint, and increasest strength to them that have no might; without Thee we can do nothing, but by Thy gracious assistance we are enabled for the performance of every duty laid upon us. Lord of power and love, we come, trusting in Thine almighty strength, and Thine infinite goodness, to ask from Thee what is wanting in ourselves; even that grace which shall help us such to be, and such to do, as Thou wouldst have us, O our God, let Thy grace be sufficient for us, and ever present with us, that we may do all things as we ought. We will trust in Thee, in whom is everlasting strength. Be Thou our Helper, to carry us on beyond our own strength, and to make all that we think, and speak, and do, acceptable in Thy sight; through Jesus Christ. Amen.—Benjamin Jenks, 1646.

Tenth Week, Third Day

Jehovah is my shepherd; I shall not want.
He maketh me to lie down in green pastures;
He leadeth me beside still waters.
He restoreth my soul:
He guideth me in the paths of righteousness for his name's sake.
Yea, though I walk through the valley of the shadow of death,
I will fear no evil; for thou art with me;
Thy rod and thy staff, they comfort me.

—Ps. 23:1-4.

What expectations are awakened by such a passage! Many have come into the Christian life because in experience they have found that "it is not in man that walketh to direct his steps." They wanted a Guide in the mysterious pilgrimage of life, and in the words of hymns like, "He leadeth me, O blessed thought!" they saw the promise of a God-conducted experience. But they are disappointed. They have the same old puzzles to face about what they ought to do; they have no divine illumination that clears up in advance their uncertainty as to the wisdom of their choices; they are not vividly aware of any guidance from above to save them from the perplexities which their companions face about conduct and career. Of course part of their difficulty is due to false expectation. Not even Paul or John was given mechanical guidance, infallible and unmistakable; they never had a syllabus of all possible emergencies with clear directions as to what should be done in every case; they were guided through their normal faculties made sensitive to divine suggestion, and doubtless they never could clearly distinguish between their thought and their inspirations. Divine guidance did not save them from puzzling perplexities and unsure decisions. But it did give them certainty that they were in God's hands; that he had hold of the reins behind their human grasp; that when they did wisely and prayerfully the best they knew, he would use it somehow to his service. And so far as the vivid consciousness of being guided is concerned, that probably came *in retrospect;* when they saw how the road came out, they agreed that God's hand must have been in the journey. Such an experience it is reasonable to expect and possible to have.

O God our Lord, the stay of all them that put their trust in Thee, wherever Thou leadest we would go, for Thy ways are perfect wisdom and love Even when we walk through the dark valley, Thy light can shine into our hearts and guide us safely through the night of sorrow. Be Thou our Friend, and we need ask no more in heaven or earth, for Thou art the Comfort of all who trust in Thee, the Help and Defence of all who hope in Thee. O Lord, we would be Thine; let us never fall away from Thee. We would accept all things without murmuring from Thy hand, for whatever Thou dost is right. Blend our wills with Thine, and then we need fear no evil nor death itself, for all things must work together for our good. Lord, keep us in Thy love and truth, comfort us with Thy light, and guide us by Thy Holy Spirit; through Jesus Christ our Lord. Amen.—S. Weiss, 1738.

Tenth Week, Fourth Day

Many folk grow up into the Christian life, and so interpret the love of God that they expect from him affectionate mothering; they look to him to keep them from trouble. In childhood, sheltered from life's tragic incidents, this expectation was more or less realized; but now in maturity they are disappointed. God has not saved them from trouble; he has not dealt with them in maternal tenderness. Rather Job's complaint to God is on their lips:

I cry unto thee, and thou dost not answer me:
I stand up, and thou gazest at me.
Thou art turned to be cruel to me;
With the might of thy hand thou persecutest me.

•   •   •   •   •   •   •   •   •   •   •

Did not I weep for him that was in trouble?
Was not my soul grieved for the needy?
When I looked for good, then evil came;
And when I waited for light, there came darkness.
My heart is troubled, and resteth not;
Days of affliction are come upon me.
                                      —Job 30:20-21, 25-27.

One such disappointed spirit says that in youth, even if she hurt her finger, she was told to pray to God and he would take away the bruise; but now life does not seem to be directed by that kind of a God at all. It isn't! A pregnant source of lost faith is to be found in this unscriptural presentation of God's love. In Scripture God's love for his people and their tragic suffering are put side by side, and the Cross where the well-beloved Son is crucified is typical of the whole Book's assertion that God does not keep his children from trouble. Sometimes he leads them into it; and always he lets the operation of his essential laws sweep on, so that disease and accident and death are no respecters of character. When Ananias was sent with God's message to the newly converted Paul, that greeting into the Christian life concerned "how many things he must suffer" (Acts 9:16). Whatever else our faith must take into account, this is an unescapable fact: we are seeking the impossible when we ask that our lives be arranged on the basis that we shall not face trouble. Faith means a conquering confidence that good will, a purpose of eternal love, runs through the whole process. It says, not apart from suffering, but in the face of it:

> "I'm apt to think the man
> That could surround the sum of things, and spy
> The heart of God and secrets of his empire,
> Would speak but love—with him the bright result
> Would change the hue of intermediate scenes,
> And make one thing of all Theology."

Almighty God to whom all things belong, whose is light and darkness, whose is good and evil, Master of all things, Lord of all; who hast so ordered it, that life from the beginning shall be a struggle throughout the course, and even to the end; so guide and order that struggle within us, that at last what is good in us may conquer, and all evil be overcome, that all things may be brought into harmony, and God may be all in all. So do Thou guide and govern us, that every day whatsoever betide us, some gain to better things, some more blessed joy in higher things may be ours, that so we, though but weaklings, may yet, God-guided, go from strength to strength, until at last, delivered from that burden of the flesh, through which comes so much struggling, we may enter into the land of harmony and of eternal peace. Hear us, of Thy mercy; through Jesus Christ our Lord. Amen.—George Dawson, 1877.

Tenth Week, Fifth Day

Till we all attain unto the unity of the faith, and of the knowledge of the Son of God, unto a fullgrown man, unto the measure of the stature of the fulness of Christ: that we may be no longer children, tossed to and fro and carried about with every wind of doctrine, by the sleight of men, in craftiness, after the wiles of error; but speaking truth in love, may grow up in all things into him, who is the head, even Christ.—Eph. 4:13-15.

Many came into the Christian life familiar with such an idea of growth. They expected the new life to be an enlarging experience, with new vistas, deepening satisfactions, increasing certitude. If at the beginning the Christian way did not content them, they blamed their immaturity for the unsatisfactory experience; they appealed to the days ahead for fuller light. But they are disappointed. They have not grown. The most they can claim is that they are stationary; the haunting suspicion cannot altogether be avoided that their faith is dwindling and their fervor burning down. This difficulty is not strange—with many folk it is inevitable; for they have never grasped the fact that the Christian life, like all life whatsoever, is law-abiding, and that to expect effects without cause is vain. That a Christian experience has begun with promise does not mean that it will magically continue; that the spirit will naturally drift into an enlarging life. An emotional conversion, like a flaming meteor, may plunge into a man's heart, and soon cool off, leaving a dead, encysted stone. But to have a real life in God, that begins like a small but vital acorn and grows like an aspiring oak, one must obey the laws that make such increasing experience possible. To keep fellowship with God unimpeded by sin, uninterrupted by neglect; to think habitually as though God were, instead of casually believing that he is; to practice love continually until love grows real; and to arrange life's program conscientiously as though the doing of God's will were life's first business—such things alone make spiritual growth a possibility.

We desire to confess, O Lord, that we have not lived according to our promises, nor according to the thoughts and intents of our hearts. We have felt the gravitation of things that drew us downward from things high and holy. We have followed right things how feebly! Weak are we to resist the attraction of evils that lurk about the way of goodness; and we are conscious that we walk in a vain show. We behold and approve Thy law, but find it hard to obey; and our obedience is of the outside, and not of the soul and of the spirit, with heartiness and full of certainty. We rejoice that Thou art a Teacher patient with Thy scholars, and that Thou art a Father patient with Thy children. Thou art a God of long-suffering goodness, and of tender mercies, and therefore we are not consumed.

And now we beseech of Thee, O Thou unwearied One,

*that Thou wilt inspire us with a heavenly virtue. Lift before us
the picture of what we should be and what we should do, and
maintain it in the light, that we may not rub it out in
forgetfulness; that we may be able to keep before ourselves
our high calling in Christ Jesus. And may we press forward,
not as they that have attained or apprehended; may we press
toward the mark, for the prize of our high calling in Christ
Jesus, with new alacrity, with growing confidence, and with
more and more blessedness of joy and peace in the soul.
Amen.*—Henry Ward Beecher.

Tenth Week, Sixth Day

The Christian experience which disappoints its possessor
by lack of growth is common, because so many leave the
idea of growth vague and undefined. They expect in general
to grow, but in what direction, to what describable results,
they never stop to think. If we ran our other business as
thoughtlessly, with as little determinate planning and
discipline, as we manage our Christian living, any progress
would be impossible. What wonder that as Christians we
often resemble the child who fell from bed at night, and
explained the accident by saying, "I must have gone to sleep
too near the place where I got in"!

Growth is always in definite directions, and folk will do
well at times, without morbid self-examination, to forecast
their desired courses. Becoming Christians from motives of
fear, as many do, we should press on to a fellowship with
God in which fear vanishes in divine friendship and
cooperation. Choosing the Christian life for self-centered
reasons, because it can do great things for us, we should
press on to glory in it as a Cause on which the welfare of the
race depends and for which we willingly make sacrifice.
Beginning with narrow ideas of service to our friends and
neighborhood, we should press on to genuine interest in the
world-field, in international fraternity, and in Christ's
victory over all mankind. Such definite lines of progress we
well may set before us. And a life that does grow, so that
each new stage of maturing experience finds deeper levels
and greater heights, is never disappointing; it is life
becoming endlessly interesting and worth while.

Not that I have already obtained, or am already made perfect: but I press on, if so be that I may lay hold on that for which also I was laid hold on by Christ Jesus. Brethren, I count not myself yet to have laid hold: but one thing I do, forgetting the things which are behind, and stretching forward to the things which are before, I press on toward the goal unto the prize of the high calling of God in Christ Jesus. Let us therefore, as many as are perfect, be thus minded: and if in anything ye are otherwise minded, this also shall God reveal unto you: only, whereunto we have attained, by that same rule let us walk.—Phil. 3:12-16.

Our Father, we pray Thee that we may use the blessings Thou hast given us, and never once abuse them. We would keep our bodies enchanted still with handsome life, wisely would we cultivate the intellect which Thou hast throned therein, and we would so live with conscience active and will so strong that we shall fix our eye on the right, and, amid all the distress and trouble, the good report and the evil, of our mortal life, steer straightway there, and bate no jot of human heart or hope. We pray Thee that we may cultivate still more these kindly hearts of ours, and faithfully perform our duty to friend and acquaintance, to lover and beloved, to wife and child, to neighbor and nation, and to all mankind. May we feel our brotherhood to the whole human race, remembering that nought human is strange to our flesh but is kindred to our soul. Our Father, we pray that we may grow continually in true piety, bringing down everything which would unduly exalt itself, and lifting up what is lowly within us, till, though our outward man perish, yet our inward man shall be renewed day by day, and within us all shall be fair and beautiful to Thee, and without us our daily lives useful, our whole consciousness blameless in Thy sight. Amen.—Theodore Parker.

Tenth Week, Seventh Day

While some, for reasons such as we have suggested, have made at least a partial failure of the Christian life, and are tempted to feel that their experience is an argument against it, we may turn with confidence to the multitude who have found life with Christ an ineffable blessing.

> There is therefore now no condemnation to them that are in Christ Jesus. For the law of the Spirit of life in Christ Jesus made me free from the law of sin and of death. For what the law could not do, in that it was weak through the flesh, God, sending his own Son in the likeness of sinful flesh and for sin, condemned sin in the flesh: that the ordinance of the law might be fulfilled in us, who walk not after the flesh, but after the Spirit. For they that are after the flesh mind the things of the flesh; but they that are after the Spirit the things of the Spirit. For the mind of the flesh is death; but the mind of the Spirit is life and peace.—Rom. 8:1-6.

Innumerable disciples of Jesus can subscribe to this Pauline testimony, and the center of their gratitude, as of his, is the victory over sin which faith in Christ has given them. The farther they go with him the more wonderful becomes the meaning of his Gospel. What Thomas Fuller, in the seventeenth century, wrote about the Bible, they feel about their whole relationship with Christ: "Lord, this morning I read a chapter in the Bible, and therein observed a memorable passage, whereof I never took notice before. Why now, and no sooner, did I see it? Formerly my eyes were as open, and the letters as legible. Is there not a thin veil laid over Thy Word, which is more rarified by reading, and at last wholly worn away? I see the oil of Thy Word will never leave increasing whilst any bring an empty barrel." As for the consciousness of filial alliance with the God and Father of Jesus, that has been a deepening benediction. How many can take over the dual inscription on an ancient Egyptian temple, as an expression of their own experience! A priest had written, in the name of the Deity, "I am He who was and is and ever shall be, and my veil hath no man lifted." But near at hand, some man of growing life and deepening faith has added: "Veil after veil have we lifted, and ever the Face is more wonderful."

Eternal and Gracious Father, whose presence comforteth like sunshine after rain; we thank Thee for Thyself and for all Thy revelation to us. Our hearts are burdened with thanksgiving at the thought of all Thy mercies; for all the blessings of this mortal life, for health, for reason, for learning, and for love; but far beyond all thought and thankfulness, for Thy great redemption. It was no painless travail that brought us to the birth, it has been no common patience that has borne with us all this while; long-suffering love, and the breaking of the eternal heart alone could reconcile us to the life to which Thou hast ordained us. We have seen the Son of Man sharing our sickness and shrinking not from our shame, we have beheld the Lamb of God bearing the sins of the world, we have mourned at the mysterious passion and stood astonished at the cross of Jesus Christ; and behind all we have had the vision of an altar-throne and one thereon slain from the foundation of the world; heard a voice calling us that was full of tears; seen beyond the veil that was rent, the agony of God.

O for a thousand tongues to sing the love that has redeemed us. O for a thousand lives that we might yield them all to Thee. Amen.—W. E. Orchard.

COMMENT FOR THE WEEK

I

Hitherto in our studies we have thought of God as the object of our faith. From the beginning, to be sure, we have been using the Master as the Way. The God who is in earnest about immortal personalities is supremely revealed in Jesus Christ. But through Christ's mediation we have been trying to pierce to the Eternal character and purpose; we have been taking Jesus at his word, "He that believeth on me, believeth not on me but on him that sent me" (John 12:44).

The meaning of faith for the Christian, however, cannot be left as though Christ were an instrument which God used for his revealing and then thrust aside, a symbol in terms of whom we may poetically picture God. Christ has been for his people more than a transparent pane, itself almost forgettable, through which the divine light shone. His personality has been central and dominant, and when his disciples have most vividly expressed the meaning of their faith they have said that they believed in him. The first Christians whose experience is enshrined in the New Testament did not deal with faith in God alone. They adored Jesus; they were illimitably thankful to him; they rejoiced to call themselves his bondservants and to suffer for him; they claimed him as a brother, but they acknowledged him their Lord as well; and they bowed before him with inexpressible devotion. "They all set him in the same incomparable place. They all acknowledged to him the same immeasurable debt."

One need not read far in the New Testament to see why these first disciples so adored their Lord. He was their Savior. They called him by many other names—Messiah, *Logos*, Son of Man, and Son of God—in their endeavor to do justice to his work and character, but one name shines among all the rest and swings them about it like planets round a sun. He is the Savior. From the annunciation to Joseph, "Thou shalt call his name Jesus; for it is he that shall save his people from their sins" (Matt. 1:21), to the New Song of the Apocalypse (Rev. 5:5-13), the New Testament is written around the central theme of saviorhood. These first disciples were vividly aware of an abysmal need, which had been met in Christ, a great peril from which through him they had escaped; and throughout the New Testament one never loses the accent of astonished gratitude, from folk who were once slaves and now are free, who from victims have been turned to victors. When Wilberforce's long campaign for the freeing of British slaves was at its climax, the population of Jamaica lined the shore for days awaiting the ship that should bring news of Parliament's decision. And when from a boat's prow the messenger cried "Freedom," the island rang with the thanksgiving of the liberated. Such rejoicing one hears in the New Testament. The disciples speak of the freedom wherewith Christ has set them free (Gal. 5:1); they say that they were dead and now are made alive (Rom. 6:11-13); once overwhelmed by sin, they now cry, "More than conquerors" (Rom. 8:37). Nor have they any doubt who is the agent or what is the agency of their salvation: Christ is the Savior and faith the means. "This is the victory that hath overcome the world," they cry, "even our faith" (I John 5:4).

If we are to understand this attitude of the first disciples toward Christ the Savior, *we must appreciate as they did the peril from which he rescued them.* One cannot understand the meaning of any character who, like Moses, delivered a people from their bondage, unless he deeply feels the importance of the problem to whose solution the man contributed. Moses shines out against the background of a nation's trouble like a star against the midnight sky. When the blackness of the night is gone, the star has vanished, too. The race's deliverers never can retain their brightness in our gratitude unless we keep alive in our remembrance the evil against which they fought. If we would know Moses, we must know Pharaoh; if we would know Wellington, we must know Napoleon. If we are to value truly the great educators, we must estimate aright the blight that ignorance lays on human life. John Howard will be nothing to us, if we do not know the ancient prison system in comparison with which even our modern jails are paradise; and Florence Nightingale will be an empty name, if we cannot imagine the terrors of war without a nurse. Always we must see the stars against the night.

Nor is there any other way in which a Christian can keep alive a vital understanding of his Lord. Many modern Christians seem to have lost vision of the problem that Jesus came to solve, of the human peril to whose conquest he made the supreme contribution. They think that the Church has adored Jesus because of a metaphysical theory about him, but all theories concerning Christ have arisen from a previous devotion to him. Or they think that Jesus is adored because he was so uniquely beautiful in character. But while without this his people never would have called him Lord, not on this account chiefly have they looked on him with inexpressible devotion. No one can understand the Christian attitude toward Jesus except in terms of the bondage from which he came to rescue us. There is a human cry that makes his advent meaningful; it is like the night behind the star of Bethlehem. Long ago a psalmist heard that cry and every age and land and soul has echoed it, "My sins are mightier than I" (Ps. 65:3).[1]

---

[1] "Iniquities prevail against me."

II

The peril of sin as the innermost problem of human life is in these days obscure to many minds. For one thing, sin has been so continuously preached about, that it seems to some an ecclesiastical question, fit for discussion, it may be, in a church on Sunday, but otherwise not often emerging in ordinary thought. But sin is no specialty of preaching. If a man, forgetting churches and sermons, seriously ponders human life as he knows it actually to be, if he gathers up in his imagination the deepest heartaches of the race, its worst diseases, its most hopeless miseries, its ruined childhood, its dissevered families, its fallen states, its devastated continents, he soon will see that the major cause of all this can be spelled with three letters—sin. To make vivid this peril as the very crux of humanity's problem on the earth, one needs at times to leave behind the customary thoughts and phrases of religion and to seek testimony from sources that the Church frequently forgets. When governments try to build social states where equity and happiness shall reign, their prison systems, their criminal codes, their courts of law loudly advertise that their problem lies in sin. When jurists plan leagues of nations and sign covenants to make the world a more fraternal place, only to find greed, hate, and cruelty demolishing their well-laid schemes, their failure uncovers the crucial problem of man's sin. When philanthropists try to lift from man's bent back the burdens that oppress him, it becomes plain how infinitely their task would be lightened, if it were not for sin. As for literature—where the seers, regardless of religious prejudice, have tried to see into the human heart and truly to report their insights—its witness is overwhelming as to what man's problem is. No great book of creative literature was ever written without sin at the center. *Macbeth, Hamlet, Othello, Faust, Les Misérables, Romola, The Scarlet Letter*—let the list be extended in any direction and to any length! Always the insight of the creative seers reports one inner peril of the race. Sin is no bogey erected by the theologians, no ghost imagined by minds grown morbid with the fear of God. Sin to every seeing eye is the one most real and practical problem of mankind.

For another reason this crucial problem is dimly seen by many minds: we do not often use the word about ourselves.

The hardest thing that any man can ever say is "I have sinned." We make mistakes, we have foibles of character and conduct, we even fall into error—but we do not often sin. By such devices we avoid the painful consciousness of our inward malady and even the name of our disease is banished from decorous speech. But sin does not go into exile with its name. Sin has many aliases and can swiftly shift its guise to gain a welcome into any company.

Sin in the slums is gross and terrible. It staggers down the streets, blasphemes with oaths that can be heard, wallows in vice unmentionable by modest lips. Then some day prosperity may visit it. It moves to a finer residence, seeks the suburbs, or finds domicile on a college campus. It changes all its clothes. No longer is it indecent and obscene. Its speech is mild, its civility is irreproachable. It gathers a company of friends who minister to pleasure and respectability, and the cry of the world's need dies unheard at its peaceful door. It presses its face continually through the pickets of social allowance, like a bad boy who wishes to trespass on forbidden ground but fears the consequence. Its goodness is superficial seeming; at heart it is as bad as it dares to be. It has completely changed its garments, but it is the same sin—indulgent, selfish, and unclean. Sin, as anyone can easily observe, takes a very high polish.

Neither by calling sin an ecclesiastical concern nor by covering its presence in ourselves with pleasant euphemisms can we hide its deadly bane in human life. The truth and import of this negative statement become clear and convincing when its positive counterpart is faced. The world needs *goodness*. The one thing in which mankind is poor and for the lack of which great causes lag and noble hopes go unfulfilled is character. With each access of that humanity leaps forward; with the sag of that all else is failure. And the one name for every loss and lack and ruin of character is sin. That is our enemy. Upon the defeat of that all our dearest hopes depend, and in its victory every dream of good that the race has cherished comes to an end.

III

The urgency of this truth is manifest when we note the consequence of sin in our own lives. No statement from antiquity has accumulated more confirming evidence in the course of the centuries than the psalmist's cry, "My sins are mightier than I." Let us consider its truth in the light of our experience.

Our sins are stronger than we are *in their power to fasten on us a sense of guilt that we cannot shake off.* Sinful pleasures lure us only in *anticipation,* dancing before us like Salome before her uncle, quite irresistible in fascination. Happiness seems altogether to depend upon an evil deed. But on the day that deed, long held in alluring expectation, is actually done—how swift and terrible the alteration in its aspect! It passes from anticipation, through committal, into memory, and it never will be beautiful again. We lock it in remembrance, as in the bloody room of Bluebeard's palace, where the dead things hung; at the thought of it we shrink and yet to it our reminiscence continually is drawn. Something happens in us as automatic as the dropping of a loosened apple from a tree; all the laws of the moral universe conspire to further it and we have no power to prevent: sin becomes guilt. When on a lonely ocean the floating bell buoys toll, no human hands cause them to ring; the waste of an unpeopled ocean surrounds them everyway. The sea by its own restlessness is ringing its own bells. So tolls remorse in a man's heart and no man can stop it.

Our sins are stronger than we are *in their power to become habitual.* If one who steps from an upper window had only the single act to consider, his problem would be simple. He could step or not as he chose. But when one steps from an upper window he finds himself dealing with a power over which his will has no control. Master of his single act, he is not master of the *gravitation* that succeeds it. Many a youth blithely plays with sin, supposing that separate deeds— which he may do or refrain from as he will—make up the problem. Soon or late he finds that he is dealing with moral laws, built into the structure of the universe as gravitation is—laws which he did not create and whose operation he cannot control. By them with terrific certainty thoughts grow to deeds, deeds to habits, habits to character, character to destiny.

At the beginning sin always comes disguised as liberty. Its lure is the seductive freedom which it promises from the trammels of conscience and the authority of law. But every man who ever yet accepted sin's offer of a free, unfettered life, discovered the cheat. Free to do the evil thing, to indulge the baser moods—so men begin, but they end *not free to stop,* bound as slaves to the thing that they were free to do. They have been at liberty to play with a cuttlefish, and now that the first long arm with its suckers grasps them, and the second arm is waving near, they are not at liberty to get away.

Our sins are mightier than we are *in their power to make us tempt our fellows.* When we picture our sinfulness, even to ourselves, we naturally represent our lives assailed by the allurements of evil and passively surrendering. We are the tempted; we pity ourselves because the outward pressure was too strong for the inward braces. We forget that in sin we are not simply the passive subjects of temptation; sin always makes us active tempters of our fellows. No drug fiend ever is content until he wins a comrade in his vice; a thief would have his friends steal, too; a gossip is not satisfied until other lips are tearing reputations into shreds; and vindictiveness is happiest when other hearts as well are lighted with lurid tempers. Sin always is contagious as disease is; the tempted becomes the tempter on the instant that he falls. Peter weak, lures Jesus to his weakness, and the Master recognizes the active quality of his disciple's sin; "Get thee behind me, Satan!" (Matt. 16:23). Sin satanizes men and sends them out to seduce their fellows. When, therefore, a sensitive man repents of his evil, he abhors himself—not mildly as a victim, but profoundly as a victimizer. He repents of the way he has played Satan to others, sometimes deliberately, sometimes by the unconscious influence of an unworthy spirit. He remembers the times when his words have poisoned the atmosphere which others breathed, when his tempers have conjured up evil spirits in other hearts, when his attitude has made wrongdoing easy for his friends and family, and well-doing hard. And his desperate helplessness in the face of sin is made most evident when he recalls the irrecoverable injury which lives have suffered and are suffering, hurt, perhaps ruined, by his evil.

Our sins are mightier than we are in their power to bring their natural consequences upon other lives. The landlord, of whom President Hyde has told, who without disinfection rented to a new family an apartment where a perilous disease had been, is typical of every evildoer. When the only child of the incoming family fell sick of the disease and died, and the landlord was faced with his guilt, he pleaded his unwillingness to spend the money which the disinfection would have cost. He denied his Lord for ten dollars. Let the law punish him as it can, the crux of his moral problem lies in the fact that however much he may be sorry now, he never can bear all the consequences of his sin. Somewhere there is a childless home bearing part of the result of his iniquity. One who had done a deed like that might well crave death and oblivion. But everyone who ever sinned is in that estate. No man ever succeeded in building around his evil a wall high and thick enough to contain all evil's consequences. They always flow over and seep through; they fall in cruel disaster on those who love us best. One never estimates his sin aright until he sees that no man ever bears all the results of his own evil. Always our sins nail somebody else to a cross; they even "crucify . . . the Son of God afresh" (Heb. 6:6).

Such is the meaning of the peril against whose background the New Testament believers saw the luminous figure of the Savior. Sin brings men into the debt of a great guilt which they cannot pay and into the bondage of tyrannous habits which they cannot break; it makes men tempting satans to their fellows, and it hurls its results like vitriol across the faces of their family and friends. And when one looks on the lamentable evils of the world at large, its sad inequities, its furious wars, he sees no need to deal delicately with sin or to speak of it in apologetic tones. Sin is, as the New Testament saw it, the central problem of mankind. If anyone has ever come with the supreme contribution to its conquest, the face of the world may well be turned toward him today. In the Christian's faith, such a Savior has come. For if the visitor from Mars who so often has been imagined coming to earth, should come again, and amazed at the churches built, the anthems sung, the service wrought in Jesus' name, should curiously inquire what this character had done to awaken such response, we should have to answer: Jesus of Nazareth made no direct contribution to science or art or government or law—with none of these important realms did he concern himself.

Only one thing he did: *he made the indispensable contribution to man's fight for great character against sin*. And because that is man's crucial problem, all science, art, government, and law are under any unpayable indebtedness to him. Because that is man's innermost need, his birthday has become the hinge of history, until one cannot write a letter to his friend without dating his familiar act from the advent of him who came to save us in our struggle for godliness against evil.

IV

Faith in Christ has a double relationship with the problem of man's sin; it concerns the *basis on which we are to be judged* and *the strength by which we are to conquer*. Christ has brought to men a gospel of forgiveness and power. With regard to the first—and with the first alone this chapter is concerned—the opinion of many modern men is swift and summary: folk are to be judged by what they do; the output of a man, as of a machine, is the test of him. Until this popular method of judgment is convicted of inadequacy, there is no hope of understanding what Christians have meant by being "saved through faith" (Eph. 2:8). We must see that men are worth more than they *do*.

A man's deeds alone are an insufficient basis for judgment, because *motives for the same act may be low or high*. No one can be unaware of the Master's meaning when he speaks of those who do their alms before men to be seen of them (Matt. 6:ff), or of Paul's when he says, "If I bestow all my goods to feed the poor . . . but have not love" (I Cor. 13:3). Some men habitually shine to good advantage by such means; they have the facile gift of putting their best foot forward. Like a store at Christmas time, its finest goods in the window and inferior stock for sale upon the counters, they are infinitely skillful in gaining more credit than their worth deserves. One who has dealt with such folk becomes aware that to estimate an isolated deed is superficial; one must know the motive. A cup of cold water or a widow's penny may awake the Master's spirited approval, and millions rung into the temple treasury by showy Pharisees meet only scorn.

Deeds alone are an insufficient basis for judgment because, while we are more than body, *our bodies are the instruments of all that visibly we do*. Many a man in spirit is like a swift mill race, eager for service, but the flesh, a battered mill wheel, ill sustains the spirit's vehemence; it breaks before the shock. One must shut the gates and patch up the wheel, before the spirit, impatient for utterance, may have its way again; and some mill-wheels never can be mended. Says one of Robert Louis Stevenson's biographers: "When a temporary illness lays him on his back, he writes in bed one of his most careful and thoughtful papers, the discourse on 'The Technical Elements in Style.' When ophthalmia confines him to a darkened room, he writes by the diminished light. When after hemorrhage, his right hand has to be held in a sling, he writes some of his 'Child's Garden' with his left hand. When the hemorrhage has been so bad that he dare not speak, he dictates a novel in the deaf and dumb alphabet." When one has lived with handicapped folk, discerning behind the small amount of work the infinite willingness for more, and in the work done a quality that makes quantity seem negligible, he perceives that deeds are no sufficient measure of spiritual value. Only an eye that pierces behind the unwrought work to the *man*, willing while the flesh was weak, can ever estimate how much some spirits are worth.

Deeds alone are an insufficient basis for judgment because *men face unequal opportunities*. Some start with one talent, some with ten. The cherished son of a Christian family ought to live a decent life; how favorable his chance! But if a vagrant wharf-rat by some mysterious vision of decency and determination of character makes a man of himself, how much more his credit! The worth of goodness cannot be estimated without knowledge of the struggle which it cost. When one considers the smug, conventional respectability of some, possessing every favorable help to goodness, and the rough but genuine integrity of others who have fought a great fight against crippling handicaps to character, he sees why, in any righteous judgment, the last will be first, as Jesus said, and the first last. Only God, with power to understand what heredity and circumstance some men have faced, what enticements they have met, what a fight they have really waged even when they may have seemed to fail, can tell how much they are worth.

"What's done we partly may compute,
But know not what's resisted."

Judgment based on deeds alone can never truly estimate a man, because in every important decision of our lives an *"unpublished self" finds no expression in our outward act.* Duty is not always clear; at times it seems a labyrinth without a clue. Perplexed, we balance in long deliberation the opposing reasons for this act or that, until, forced to choose, we obtain only a majority vote for the decision. Yet that uncertain majority alone is published in our deed; man's eyes never see the unexpressed protestant minority behind. And when the choice proves wrong, and friends are grieved and enemies condemn and what we did is hateful to ourselves, only one who knows how much we wanted to do right, and who accounts not only the published but the unpublished self can truly estimate our worth. Peter, who denied his Lord, it may be because he wanted the privilege of being near him at the trial, is not the only one who has appealed from the outward aspect of his deed to the inner intention of his heart: "Lord, thou knowest all things; thou knowest that I love thee" (John 21:17).

Moreover, even when we choose aright, *no deed can ever gather into utterance all that is best and deepest in us.* A mother's love is as much greater than any word she speaks or act she does, as the sunshine is greater than the focused point where in a burning glass we gather a ray of it. We are infinitely more than words can utter or deeds express. No adequate judgment, therefore, can rest on deeds alone. A machine may be estimated by its output, but a man is too subtle and profound, his motives and purposes too inexpressible, his temptations and inward struggles too intimate and unrevealed, his possibilities too great to be roughly estimated by his acts alone.

"Not on the vulgar mass
Called 'work' must sentence pass,
Things done, that took the eye and had the price;
O'er which, from level stand,

The low world laid its hand,
Found straightway to its mind, could value in a trice:

But all, the world's coarse thumb
and finger failed to plumb,
So passed in making up the main account;
All instincts immature,
All purposes unsure,
That weighed not as his work, yet swelled the man's
amount:

Thoughts hardly to be packed
Into a narrow act,
Fancies that broke through language and escaped;
All I could never be,
All, men ignored in me,
This, I was worth to God, whose wheel the pitcher shaped."

V

If, however, we are to understand the Christian's meaning when he speaks of being saved by faith (Rom. 3:28; 5:1; Gal. 3:24), we need to see not only that men are worth more than they *do,* but as well that they are worth more than they *are.* Some things always start large and grow small; some things always start small and grow large; but a man may do either, and his value is determined not so much by the position he is in, as it is by the direction in which he is moving. Even of stocks upon the market in their rise and fall this truth is clear. The figure at which a stock is quoted is important, but the meaning of that figure cannot be understood unless one knows whether it was reached on the way up or the way down. How much more is any static judgment of a man impossible! One starts at the summit, with endowments and opportunities that elevate him far above his fellows, and frittering away his chance, drifts down. Another, beginning at the bottom, by dint of resolute endeavor climbs upward, achieving character in the face of odds before which ordinary men succumb. Somewhere these two men will pass, and, statically judged, will be of equal worth. But one is drifting down; one climbing up. The innermost secret of their spiritual value lies in that hidden fact. *When, therefore, one would judge a man, he must pierce behind the deeds that he can see, behind the present quality that he can estimate, back to the thing the man has set his heart upon, to the direction of his life, to the ideal which masters him—that is, to his faith.* There lies the potential future of the man, his ultimate worth, the seed of his coming fruit. If one has eyes to see what that faith is, he knows the man and what the man is bound to be.

When, therefore, men set their hearts on Christ, lay hold on him by faith as life's Master and its goal, that faith opens the door to God's forgiveness. In Augustine's luminous phrase, "The Christian already has in Christ what he hopes for in himself." He is Christ's brother in the filial life with God, young, immature, undeveloped—but the issue of that life is the measure of the stature of Christ's fullness. God does not demand the end when only the beginning is possible, does not scorn the dawn because it is not noon. He welcomes the first movement of man's spirit toward him, not for the fruit which yet is unmatured, but for the seed which still is in the germ; he takes the will for the deed, because the will is earnest; he sees the journey's end in Christlike character, when at the road's beginning the pilgrim takes the first step by faith. There is no fiction here; God ought to forgive and welcome such a man. All good parents act so toward their children. This divine grace corresponds with truth, for a man is *worth* the central, dominant faith, that determines life's direction and decides its goal. And the Gospel that God so deals with man, announced in the words of Jesus, illustrated in his life, sealed in his death, has been a boon to the race that puts all men under an immeasurable debt to Christ.

VI

This method of judgment which all good men use with their friends and families has been often disbelieved, in its Christian formulations, because it has been misrepresented and misunderstood. But human life, far outside religious boundaries, continually illustrates the wisdom and righteousness of so judging men by faith. Roswell McIntyre deserted during the Civil War; he was caught, court-martialed, and condemned to death. He stood with no defense for his deed, no just complaint against the penalty, and with nothing to plead save shame for his act, and faith that, with another chance, he could play the man. On that, the last recourse of the condemned, President Lincoln pardoned him.

> "Executive Mansion,
> Oct. 4, 1864.
>
> Upon condition that Roswell McIntyre of Co. E, 6th Reg't of New York Cavalry, returns to his Regiment and faithfully serves out his term, making up for lost time, or until otherwise discharged, he is fully pardoned for any supposed desertion heretofore committed, and this paper is his pass to go to his regiment.
>
> Abraham Lincoln."

Was such clemency an occasion for lax character? The answer is written across the face of Mr. Lincoln's letter in the archives: "Taken from the body of R. McIntyre at the Battle of Five Forks, Va., 1865." Five Forks was the last cavalry action of the war; McIntyre went through to the finish.

Any one who knows the experience of being forgiven understands the motives that so remake a pardoned deserter. The relief from the old crushing condemnation, the joy of being trusted again beyond desert, the gratitude that makes men rather die than be untrue a second time, the unpayable indebtedness from which ambition springs, "whether at home or absent, to be well-pleasing unto him" (II Cor. 5:9)—this is the moral consequence of being pardoned. Goodness so begotten reaches deep and high, has in it conscious joy and hope, feels vividly the value of its moral victories, possesses great motives for sacrificial service in the world. The Apocalypse is right. There is a song in heaven that angels cannot sing. Only men like McIntyre will know how to sing it.

The vital and transforming faith that saves is always better presented in a story than in an argument, and in the Scripture the best description of it is Jesus' parable of the Prodigal. As the Master drew that portrait of life in the far country, all the watching Pharisees thought that such a boy was lost. The Prodigal himself must have guessed that his case was hopeless. His friends, his character, his reputation, his will were gone, and in the inner courtroom of his soul with maddening iteration he heard sentence passed. Guilty. Only one hope remained. If he was unspoiled enough by the far country's pitiless brutality to think that at home they might bear no grudge, might find forgiveness possible, might offer him another chance as a hired servant, if he could think that perhaps his father even *wanted* him to come home, then there was hope. With such slender faith the boy turned back from the far country. He had the same lack of character, the same weakened will, the same evil habits. Only one difference had as yet been wrought. Before, he had been facing toward swine, now he was facing toward home. The *direction* of his life was changed by faith. And when the father saw him, homeward bound, *"while he was yet afar off,"* forgiveness welcomed him. No pardon could unload from the lad's life all the fearful consequences of his sin. As long as he lived, the scars on health, repute, and usefulness were there. But forgiveness could take the sin away *as a barrier to personal friendship with the father;* the old relationships of mutual confidence, helpfulness, and love could be restored; the glorious chance could be bestowed of fighting through the battle for character, not hopelessly in the far country, but victoriously at home.

One of the chief glories of the Gospel is that it has so reclaimed the waste of humanity, made sons of Prodigals and patriots of McIntyres. Its Pauls were persecutors, its Augustines the slaves of lust, and its rank and file men and women to whom Christ's message has meant forgiveness, reinstatement, a new chance, and boundless hope. Scientific business conserves its waste and makes invaluable by-products from what once was slag; but Christ has been the conserver of mankind. The lost and sick have been returned to sanity and wholesomeness and service; humanity has been enriched beyond computation, with Bunyans and Goughs and Jerry McAuleys. Tolstoi's simple confession in "My Religion" is typical of multitudes: "Five years ago I came to believe in Christ's teaching, and my life suddenly became changed: I ceased desiring what I had wished before, and began to desire what I had not wished before. What formerly had seemed good to me appeared bad, and what had seemed bad appeared good. . . . The direction of my life, my desires became different: what was good and bad changed places." Tolstoi had indulged, as he acknowledges, in every form of unmentionable vice practiced in Russia; and yet forgiven, reinstated, transformed, he was carried to his burial by innumerable Russian peasants with banners flying. Where Christ's influence has vitally come, the loss and wreck and flotsam of the moral world have been so reclaimed to character and power.

At the beginning of the Christian era, a few desolate sand lagoons lay off the Paduan coast of Italy. There the wild fowl made their nests; the lonely skiffs of fishermen threaded the reedy channels; the storms washed the shifting and uncertain sands. And possibly to this day the lagoons would have been thus barren and deserted, had not the Huns swept down on Italy. The Huns made the building of Venice necessary. They did not intend so fair a consequence of their terrific onslaughts. Their thoughts were on death and pillage. But because they came, the Italians fled to the lagoons, built there, behind the barricade of restless waters, their gleaming city, developed there the commerce that combed the world, built the Doge's palace as the abode of justice, and raised St. Mark's in praise of God. Venice was the city of Salvation; it rose resplendent because the Huns had come. So Christ turns the ruin of sin to victory, and builds in human life character, recovered and triumphant. If his Gospel can have its way, a spiritual Venice will arise to make the onslaught of the moral Huns an evil with a glorious issue. What wonder that inexpressible devotion has been felt for him by all his people?

CHAPTER XI

Faith in Christ the Savior: Power

DAILY READINGS

As we saw in the last week's study, Christian faith has always centered around the person of Jesus himself. This week let us consider some testimonies from the New Testament as to the meaning and effect of this definitely Christian faith.

Eleventh Week, First Day

It must be clear to any observing mind that the world does not suffer from lack of faith. There is faith in plenty; everybody is exercising it on some object. In the Bible we read of folk who "trust in vanity" (Isa. 59:4), who "trust in lying words" (Jer. 7:4), or "in the abundance of riches" (Ps. 52:7); and the Master exclaims over the difficulty which those who "trust in riches" have when they try to enter the kingdom of God (Mark 10:24). Faith, then, is a necessary faculty of the soul: the power by which we commit ourselves to any object that wins our devotion and commands our allegiance. No man avoids its use, and men differ only in the objects toward which their faith is directed. Of all the tragedies caused by the misuse of human powers, none is more frequent and disastrous than the ruin that follows the misuse of faith. With this necessary and powerful faculty in our possession, capable of use on things high or low, to what determination can a man more reasonably set himself than this?—*since I must and do use faith on something, I will choose the highest.* It is with such a rational and worthy choice that the Christian turns to Jesus. He is the best we know; we will direct our faith toward him. This does not mean that in the end our faith does not rest on God; it does, for Jesus is the Way, the Door, as he said, and faith in him moves up through him to the One who sent him. As Paul put it, "Such confidence have we through Christ to God-ward" (II Cor. 3:4). But faith in Jesus is the most vivid, true, and compelling way we have of committing ourselves to the highest and best we know. In the light of this truth, we can understand why John calls such faith the supreme "work" which God demands of us.

Work not for the food which perisheth, but for the food which abideth unto eternal life, which the Son of Man shall give unto you: for him the Father, even God, hath sealed. They said therefore unto him, What must we do, that we may work the works of God? Jesus answered and said unto them, This is the work of God, that ye believe on him whom he hath sent.—John 6:27-29.

Gracious Father! Thou hast revealed Thyself gloriously in Jesus Christ, the Son of Thy love. In Him we have found Thee, or rather, are found of Thee. By His life, by His words and deeds, by His trials and sufferings, we are cleansed from sin and rise into holiness. For in Him Thou hast made disclosure of Thine inmost being and art drawing us into fellowship with Thy life. As we stand beneath His Cross, or pass with Him into the Garden of His Agony, it is Thy heart that we see unveiled, it is the passion of Thy love yearning over the sinful, the wandering, seeking that it may save them. No man hath seen Thee at any time, but out from the unknown has come the Son of Man to declare Thee. And now we know Thy name. When we call Thee Father, the mysteries of existence are not so terrible, our burdens weigh less heavily upon us, our sorrows are touched with joy. Thy Son has brought the comfort that we need, the comfort of knowing that in all our afflictions Thou art afflicted, that in Thy grief our lesser griefs are all contained. Let the light which shines in His face, shine into our hearts, to give us the knowledge of Thy glory, to scatter the darkness of fear, of wrong, of remorse, of foreboding, and to constrain our lives to finer issues of peace and power and spiritual service. And this prayer we offer in Christ's name. Amen.—Samuel McComb.

Eleventh Week, Second Day

The New Testament reveals the experience that *forgiveness* comes in answer to such self-committing faith in Christ as we spoke of yesterday.

And he said unto her, Thy sins are forgiven. And they that sat at meat with him began to say within themselves. Who is this that even forgiveth sins? And he said unto the woman, Thy faith hath saved thee; go in peace.—Luke 7:48-50.

In popular thought forgiveness is often shallowly conceived. It is thought to be an easy agreement to forget offense, a good-natured waving aside of injuries committed as though the evil done were of no consequence. But forgiveness is really a most profound and searching experience; and it takes two persons, each sacrificially desirous of achieving it, before it can be perfected. In the pardoner, the passion for saviorhood must submerge all disgust at the sin in love for the sinner; and in the pardoned, desire for a new life must create sacrificial willingness to hate and forsake the evil and humbly accept a new chance. It follows, therefore, that no one can forgive another, no matter how willing he may be to do so, unless the recipient fulfills the conditions that make pardon possible. Forgiveness is a mutual operation; no forgetting or good will on the part of one person is forgiveness at all; and the attitude in the forgiven man that makes the reception of pardon possible is negatively penitence and positively faith. Any experience of human forgiveness reveals that the offender must detest his sin and turn from it in trust and self-commitment to claim the mercy and choose the ideals of the one whom he has wronged. That God in Christ is willing to forgive is the Christian Gospel; and if we go unforgiven it is for lack of faith. That is the hand which grasps the proffered pardon.

Almighty God, whose salvation is ever nigh to them that seek Thee, we think of our little lives, of their wayward ways, and we remember Thee and are troubled. Our days pass from us and we are heated with strifes, and troubles and restless, with mean temptations and fugitive desires. We spend our years in much carelessness, and too seldom do we think of the greatness of our trust and the wonder and mystery of our being. We are vexed with vain dreams and trivial desires. We live our days immersed in petty passions. We strain after poor uncertainties. We pursue the shadows of this passing life and continually are we visited by our own self-contempt and bitterness. We have known the better and have chosen the worse. We have felt the glory and power of a higher life and yet have surrendered to ignoble temptations and to satisfactions that end with the hour.

Almighty Father, of Thy goodness do Thou save our lives, so smitten with passion, from the failure and misery that else must come to us. Be with us in our hours of self-communion, and inspire us with good purpose and service to Thee. Be with us when heart and flesh faint, and there seems no help or safety near us. Be with us when we are carried into the dry and lonely places, seeking a rest that is not in them. Sustain us, we beseech Thee, under the burden of our many errors and failures. From the confused aims and purposes of our lives may there be brought forth, by the aid of Thy Spirit, and the teaching and discipline of life, lives constant and assured in service and obedience to Thee. Amen.—John Hunter.

Eleventh Week, Third Day

It is clear in the New Testament that all the *free movements of divine help* depend on the presence of man's faith. Words like these are continually on the lips of Jesus: "Be of good cheer; thy faith hath made thee whole" (Matt. 9:22); "According to your faith be it done unto you" (Matt. 9:29); "Great is thy faith: be it done unto thee even as thou wilt" (Matt. 15:28). Human life as a whole confirms the truth which such words suggest: *Man's faith is always the limit of his blessing; he never obtains more than he believes in.* Men live in a world of unappropriated truth and unused power; and the blessings of truth and power can be reached only by ventures of faith. Even electricity withholds its service from a man who, like Abdul Hamid, has not faith enough to try. In personal relationships this fact becomes even more clear. Whatever gifts of good will may be waiting in the heart of any man, we are shut out from them forever, unless we have the grace of faith in the man and open-hearted self-commitment to him. As the Christian Gospel sees man's case, the central tragedy lies here: that God in Christ is willing to do so much more in and for and through us than we have faith enough to let him do. Our unbelief is not a matter of theoretical concern alone; it practically disables God, it handicaps his operation in the world, it is an "evil heart of unbelief, in falling away from the living God" (Heb. 3:12). The divine will is forced to wait upon the lagging faith of man. How often the Master exclaimed, "O ye of little faith!" (Matt. 6:30; 8:26). And the reason for his lament was eminently practical.

And coming into his own country he taught them in their synagogue, insomuch that they were astonished, and said, Whence hath this man this wisdom, and these mighty works? Is not this the carpenter's son? is not his mother called Mary? and his brethren, James, and Joseph, and Simon, and Judas? And his sisters, are they not all with us? Whence then hath this man all these things? And they were offended in him. But Jesus said unto them, A prophet is not without honor, save in his own country, and in his own house. And he did not many mighty works there because of their unbelief.—Matt. 13:54-58.

Almighty God, our Heavenly Father, we desire to come to Thee in all humility and sincerity. We are sinful; pardon Thou us. We are ignorant; enlighten Thou our darkness. We are weak; inspire us with strength. In these times of doubt, uncertainty, and trial, may we ever feel conscious of Thine everlasting light. Soul of our soul! Inmost Light of truth! Manifest Thyself unto us amid all shadows. Guide us in faith, hope, and love, until the perfect day shall dawn, and we shall know as we are known.

Almighty God, teach us, we pray Thee, by blessed experience, to apprehend what was meant of old when Jesus Christ was called the power of God unto salvation, for we stand in need of salvation from sin, from doubt, from weakness, from craven fear; we cannot save ourselves; we are creatures of a day, short-sighted, and too often driven about by every wind of passion and opinion. We need to be stayed upon a higher strength. We need to lay hold of Thee. Manifest Thyself unto us, our Father, as the Saviour of our souls, and deliver us from the bondage of corruption into the glorious liberty of the children of God. Amen.—John Hunter.

Eleventh Week, Fourth Day

Not only is man's power to appropriate the divine blessing dependent on faith; in the experience of the New Testament man's power of achievement has the same source.

Then came the disciples to Jesus apart, and said, Why could not we cast it out? And he saith unto them, Because of your little faith: for verily I say unto you, If ye have faith as a grain of mustard seed, ye shall say unto this mountain, Remove hence to yonder place; and it shall remove; and nothing shall be impossible unto you.—Matt. 17:19-20.

Mountains are symbols of difficulty, and the Master's affirmation here that faith alone can remove them is clearly confirmed in human experience. It may seem at times as though faith, compared with the obstacles, were like a minute mustard seed before the ranges of Lebanon, but faith can overcome even that disproportion in size. Great leaders always must have such confidence. Listen to Mazzini: "The people lack faith . . . the faith that arouses the multitudes, faith in their own destiny, in their own mission, and in the mission of the epoch; the faith that combats and prays; the faith that enlightens and bids men advance fearlessly in the ways of God and humanity, with the sword of the people in their hand, the religion of the people in their heart, and the future of the people in their soul." In any great movement for human good, the ultimate and deciding question always is: How many people can be found who have faith enough to believe in the cause and its triumph? When enough folk have faith, any campaign for human welfare can be won. Without faith men "collapse into a yielding mass of plaintiveness and fear"; with faith they move mountains. And when men have faith in Christ as God's Revealer—faith, not formal and abstract, but real and vital—they begin to feel about the word "impossible" as Mirabeau did, "Never mention to me again that blockhead of a word!"

O God, our Father, our souls are made sick by the sight of hunger and want and nakedness; of little children bearing on their bent backs the burden of the world's work; of motherhood drawn under the grinding wheels of modern industry; and of overburdened manhood, with empty hands, stumbling and falling.

Help us to understand that it is not Thy purpose to do away with life's struggle, but that Thou desirest us to make the conditions of that struggle just and its results fair.

Enable us to know that we may bring this to pass only through love and sympathy and understanding; only as we realize that all are alike Thy children—the rich and the poor, the strong and the weak, the fortunate and the unfortunate. And so, our Father, give us an ever-truer sense of human sisterhood; that with patience and steadfastness we may do our part in ending the injustice that is in the land, so that all may rejoice in the fruits of their toil and be glad in Thy sunshine.

Keep us in hope and courage even amid the vastness of the undertaking and the slowness of the progress, and sustain us with the knowledge that our times are in Thy hand. Amen.—Helen Ring Robinson.

Eleventh Week, Fifth Day

Faith in Christ has always been consummated, in the experience to which the New Testament introduces us, in an inward transformation of life.

I have been crucified with Christ; and it is no longer I that live, but Christ liveth in me: and that life which I now live in

the flesh I live in faith, the faith which is in the Son of God, who loved me, and gave himself up for me.—Gal. 2:20.

Such conversion of life is the normal result of a vital fellowship whose bond is faith. For one thing, a man at once begins to care a great deal more about his own quality when he believes in Christ and in Christ's love. "What a King stoops to pick up from the mire cannot be a brass farthing, but must be a pearl of great price." To be loved by anyone is to enter into a new estimate of one's possible value; to be loved by God in Christ is to come into an experience where our possible value makes us alike ashamed of what we are and jubilant over what we may become. We begin saying with Irenaeus, "Jesus Christ became what we are that he might make us what he is." And then, faith, ripening into fellowship, opening the life sensitively to the influence of the friend, issues in a character infused by the friend's character. He lives in us. Such transformation of life does not happen in a moment; it requires more than instantaneous exposure to take the Lord's picture on a human heart; but time-exposure will do it, and "Christ in us" be alike our hope of glory and our secret of influence.

O Father Eternal, we thank Thee for the new and living way into Thy presence made for us in Christ; the way of trust, sincerity, and sacrifice. Beneath His cross we would take our stand, in communion with His Spirit would we pray, in fellowship with the whole Church of Christ we would seek to know Thy mind and will.

We desire to know all the fulness of Christ, to appropriate His unsearchable riches, to feed on His humanity whereby Thou hast become to us the bread of our inmost souls and the wine of life, to become partakers of Thy nature, share Thy glory, and become one with Thee through Him.

Give unto us fellowship with His sufferings and insight into the mystery of His cross, so that we may be indeed crucified with Him, be raised to newness of life, and be hidden with Christ in Thee.

We desire to make thankful offering of ourselves as members of the body of Christ; in union with all the members may we obey our unseen Head, so that the Body may be undivided, and Thy love, and healing power, and very Self

*may be incarnate on the earth in one Holy Universal Church.
Amen.*—W. E. Orchard.

Eleventh Week, Sixth Day

With faith in Christ so seen as the secret of divine
forgiveness and assistance, of achieving power and inward
transformation, there can be little surprise at the solicitude
which the New Testament shows concerning the disciples'
faith. We find this urgent interest in Paul:

**Wherefore when we could no longer forbear, we thought it
good to be left behind at Athens alone; and sent Timothy, our
brother and God's minister in the gospel of Christ, to
establish you, and to comfort you concerning your
faith; . . . night and day praying exceedingly that we may
see your face, and may perfect that which is lacking in your
faith.—I Thess. 3:1-2, 10.**

**We are bound to give thanks to God always for you,
brethren, even as it is meet, for that your faith groweth
exceedingly, and the love of each one of you all toward one
another aboundeth.—II Thess. 1:3.**

And one of the most appealing revelations of Jesus' habit in
prayer concerns his supplication for Peter's faith.

**Simon, Simon, behold, Satan asked to have you, that he
might sift you as wheat: but I made supplication for thee,
that thy faith fail not; and do thou, when once thou hast
turned again, establish thy brethren.—Luke 22:31-32.**

In all such passages one feels at once that faith is used as
Paul uses it in the thirteenth chapter of First Corinthians—a
comrade and ally of hope and love. It is not a matter of
dogma and does not move in the realm of opinion, although
ideas of the first magnitude may be involved in it. It is
primarily a bond of divine fellowship, which at once keeps
the life receptive to all that God would do for the man and
moves the man to do all that he should for God. If that fails,
even Peter would fall in ruins, and the expression is none
too strong, when in First Timothy the failure of such vital

faith is described as a "shipwreck" (I Tim. 1:19). But when by faith the consciousness of God has grown clear, and alliance with him is so real that we stop arguing about it and begin counting on it in daily living, the increment of power and confidence and stability which a man may win is quite incalculable.

O Thou plenteous Source of every good and perfect gift, shed abroad the cheering light of Thy even-fold grace over our hearts. Yea, Spirit of love and gentleness, we most humbly implore Thy assistance. Thou knowest our faults, our failings, our necessities, the dullness of our understanding, the waywardness of our affections, the perverseness of our will. When, therefore, we neglect to practice our minds, rectify our desires, correct our wanderings, and pardon our omissions, so that by Thy guidance we may be preserved from making shipwreck of faith, and keep a good conscience, and may at length be landed safe in the haven of eternal rest, through Jesus Christ our Lord. Amen.
—Anselm, 1033.

Eleventh Week, Seventh Day

Some who gladly acknowledge the surprising results which faith can work in life, do not see any great importance in the object to which faith attaches itself. They say that faith is merely a psychological attitude, and that faith in one thing does as well as faith in another. Folk are healed, they point out, by all kinds of faith, whether directed toward fetishes, or saints' relics, or metaphysical theories, or God himself. It is the faith, they say, and not the object, which does the work. There is a modicum of truth in this. Faith, by its very power to organize man's faculties and give them definite set and drive, is itself a master force, and if a man has no interest beyond the achievement of some immediate end, like conquering nervous qualms or getting strength for a special task, he may achieve that end by believing in almost anything, provided he believes hard enough. *But to believe in some things may debauch the intelligence and lower the moral standards, even while it achieves a practical end.* To win power for a business task by believing in a palm-reader's predictions is entirely possible, but it is a poor bargain; a man sells out his intelligence for cash. The object in which a man believes does make an immense difference in the effect of his faith on his *mind* and *character*. An African savage may gain courage for an ordeal by believing in his fetish—but how immeasurable is the abyss between the meaning of that faith for the whole of life and the meaning of a Christian's faith in God! We have no business, for the sake of immediate gain, to allow our faith to rest in anything lower than the highest.

Blessed be the God and Father of our Lord Jesus Christ, who according to his great mercy begat us again unto a living hope by the resurrection of Jesus Christ from the dead, unto an inheritance incorruptible, and undefiled, and that fadeth now away, reserved in heaven for you, who by the power of God are guarded through faith unto a salvation ready to be revealed in the last time. Wherein ye greatly rejoice, though now for a little while, if need be, ye have been put to grief in manifold trials, that the proof of your faith, being more precious than gold that perisheth though it is proved by fire, may be found unto praise and glory and honor at the revelation of Jesus Christ: whom not having seen ye love; on whom, though now ye see him not, yet believing, ye rejoice greatly with joy unspeakable and full of glory: receiving the end of your faith, even the salvation of your souls.—I Pet. 1:3-9.

Gracious Father of our spirits, in the stillness of this worship may we grow more sure of Thee, who art often closest to us when we feel Thou hast forsaken us. The toil and thought of daily life leave us little time to think of Thee; but may the silence of this holy place make us aware that though we may forget Thee, Thou dost never forget us. Perhaps we have grown careless in contact with common things, duty has lost its high solemnities, the altar fires have gone untended, Thy light within our minds has been distrusted or ignored. As we withdraw awhile from all without, may we find Thee anew within, until thought grows reverent again, all work is hallowed, and faith reconsecrates all common things as sacraments of love.

If pride of thought and careless speculation have made us

doubtful of Thee, recover for us the simplicity that understands Thou art never surer than when we doubt Thee, that through all failures of faith Thou becomest clearer, and so makest the light that once we walked by seem but darkness. Help us then to rest our faith on the knowledge of our imperfection, our consciousness of ignorance, our sense of sin, and see in them shadows cast by the light of Thy drawing near.

If Thy purposes have crossed our own and Thy will has broken ours, enable us to trust the wisdom of Thy perfect love and find Thy will to be our peace.

So lead us back to meet Thee where we may have missed Thee. Amen.—W. E. Orchard.

COMMENT FOR THE WEEK

I

The forgiveness which the Gospel offers—reinstating a man in the personal relationships against which he sinned, and giving him another chance—opens opportunity, but by itself it does not furnish power. The saviorhood of Christ, however, so far from failing at this crucial point, makes here its chief claim to preeminence. However one may explain it, the normal quality of a genuine Christian life is moral energy. The Gospel not alone to Paul, but to all generations of Christ's disciples, had been "God's saving power for everyone who has faith" (Rom. 1:16, Moffatt).

Faith always supplies moral dynamic. Emerson's challenge "They can conquer who believe they can," is easily verified in daily life. In practical business, in social reform, in personal character, no more common or fatal barrier to success exists than disbelief in possibilities. While some who think they can when they cannot, prove the rule by its exception, we are sure in advance that one who believes he cannot, has lost his battle before it has begun. Granted a task worth doing, sufficient strength for its accomplishment, and motives in plenty to make success desirable, and one insinuating enemy can spoil the enterprise. Let the subtle fear that the task is impossible obsess the thought, paralyze the nerve, and no hope is left. Like chlorine gas, such fear defeats us before we have begun to fight and fills our trenches with asphyxiated powers.

Anyone who is to be a savior to mankind, therefore, must be able to make men say, "I can." That Christ has had that influence on men is the commonplace of Christian biography from the beginning until now. "In him who strengthens me I am able for anything" (Phil. 4:13, Moffatt's Translation) is a word of Paul's which the best Christian experience confirms. It does not mean that men can do what they will, overriding all obstacles to chosen goals; it means that they are aware of resources in reserve, of power around them and in them, so that they are not afraid of anything which they may face. If a duty ought to be done, they are confident that they can do it; if a trouble must be borne, they are assured that they can bear it.

This buoyant faith is more than a grace of temperament. In Paul's case, for example, it was not due to rugged health, for that he lacked; it was not the easy optimism of some happiness cult, for he was a persecuted man, bearing in his body "the marks of the Lord Jesus"; and such a note of assured resource as we just have quoted did not come from the hopefulness of fortunate circumstance, but from a prison where he wore a chain. Paul himself is certain that his sense of power springs from discipleship to Jesus. And when one turns to the gospels, he sees that whenever the Master had opportunity to exert to the full his influence on men, some such result as here appears in Paul is evident. A contagious personality always enlarges the sense of possibilities and powers in other men. A man, leaving Trinity Church, where he had heard Phillips Brooks, exclaimed, "He always makes me feel so strong." It was said that one could not stand for a moment with Edmund Burke under an archway, to let a shower pass by, without emerging a greater man. Each one of us knows folk who so impress him. We go into their presence, weak, self-pitiful; when we come out, the horizons are broader, the possibilities have enlarged, there is more in us than we had suspected, we are convinced that we *can*.

To a degree that escapes our estimation Jesus exerted that influence on men. Napoleon said that he made his generals out of mud. Out of what, then, did the Master make his apostles? At the beginning, Peter, for example, is protesting, "Depart from me, for I am a sinful man, O Lord," and Jesus is bending over him, saying: "Come after me, and I will make you a fisher of men; if you will, you can." After months of influence, Peter, still shamed and weak, is pleading his love against his deed, and Jesus is saying: "Feed my sheep; feed my lambs; if you will, you can." In Jesus' relationship with his disciple, a great personality stands over a lesser one, by life and word insistently saying, *You can,* until power is vitally transmitted, and in the vacillating, vehement Simon there emerges rock-like, stable Peter.

Throughout the Christian centuries nothing has been more typical than this of the Master's influence on men. He has come to innumerable sodden lives, held slaves to tyrannous sin, saying in the hopelessness of bondage, "I cannot," and he has touched them with his contagious confidence, until they rose into freedom, saying, "By the help of God, I can!" He has come into social situations where ancient evils, long entrenched and seemingly invincible, withstood the assault of reformation, and he has put inexhaustible resource into his people, until they said with an old reformer, "Impossible? If that is all that is the matter, let us go ahead!" He has come to his Church, reluctant to undertake a world-wide mission, staggered by the task's magnitude, and he has made men pray with *life* and not alone with lip, "Thy Kingdom come, Thy will be done on earth as it is in heaven." Wherever the influence of Christ vitally has come, the horizons of possibility have widened and the sense of power grown inexhaustible.

Such influence is of the very essence of saviorhood and the attitude that appropriates it is saving faith. When John B. Gough, desperately enmeshed in habit, faces the Christian Gospel of release one easily may trace his changing response. Dubious at first, he wants to believe it but he does not dare. He wishes it were true, but the whole logic of his situation, his long habit, his spoiled reputation, his weakened will, argue against the possibility. As Augustine said about his lust, "The worse that I knew so well had more power over me than the better that I knew not." Still, a note of authority in the Gospel, as though spoken by one whose power to perform is equal to the thing he promises, arrests Gough's mind, captures his imagination, awakens his spirit's deep desire, until at last the Master's call, "You can," is answered by the human cry, "I will," and the man moves out into new possibilities, new powers, and increasing liberty. That *is* salvation. It is no formal status decreed by legal enactment, as though a judge technically acquitted a prisoner. It is new life, inward liberation from old habits, apprehensions, anxieties, and fears. It lifts horizons, consumes impossibilities, and at the center of life sets the stirring conviction that what ought to be done can be done.

Christians who are accustomed lightly to assert that they are saved need specially to take this truth to heart. Some speak as though salvation were a technicality and they sing about it,

> "'Tis done, the great transaction's done."

To many such, were candor courteous, one would wish to say: Saved? Saved from what? You are habitually anxious. Your life is continually vexed with little fears and apprehensions. When trouble comes, you are sure that you cannot stand it; when tasks present themselves, you are certain that you cannot perform them. You have pet self-indulgences, from major sins to little meannesses; you know that they are wrong; but when suggestion comes that you surrender them, you are sure that you have not the strength. When causes, plainly Christian, on whose successful issue man's weal depends, appeal to you for help, you weaken every enterprise by your disheartenment. Saved from *what?* Not from fear, timidity, selfishness, and stagnation! And if you say, "Saved from Hell"—what is Hell but the final subjugation of the soul to such sins as you now are cherishing? The words of Jesus are promises of saviorhood from real and present evils: "Be not *anxious*" (Matt. 6:34); "Go, *sin* no more" (John 8:11); "*Fear* not, little flock" (Luke 12:32). When one, by faith, turns his face homeward from such destroyers of life, he begins to be saved; but only as he lives by faith in fellowship with the Divine and so achieves progressive victory, does he keep on being saved. *The heart of salvation is victorious power.*

Not all men feel the need of the power which comes from discipleship to Christ. They live content without such increment of strength as Christians find in faith. Their power is equal to their tasks because their tasks are levelled to their power. One cannot understand, therefore, what the saviorhood of Christ has meant to men, unless he sees how Christ has created the need of the very power he furnishes. He has done this, in part, *by awakening the desire for an ascending life*. Men do not naturally want to believe in possibilities too great and taxing; it always is easier to leave undisturbed the *status quo*. Even changing one's residence is difficult. Though one may move to a better house, yet to decide to move, to break old relationships, to tear up and refit the furnishings, and to adjust oneself to new associations mean stress and strain. So men come to be at home with habits; they are comfortably accustomed to timidity and self-indulgence. Release into a new life does not lure as privilege; it repels as hardship. Some sins, indeed, are followed by remorse, but others, grown habitual, bring a sense of well-being and content. We like ourselves; we do not want a better life; we are unwilling to pay its cost. Our sins are no bed of nettles, but a lotus land of decent ease. Were we candidly to speak to them, we should say, "O Sin, you are a comfortable friend!" When most we want forbidden fruit you suggest excuses. You side happily with our inclinations and save us from the struggle that high duty costs and the sacrifice of striving for the best. Among the blessings of our lives, we count you not the least, O decent, comfortable, self-indulgent Sin!

Idlers thus drift listlessly and refuse a voyage with a purpose and a goal; youths living by low standards, look on Christlike character as beyond their interest and possibility; undedicated men find excuse for holding back devotion to great causes in the world—we shelter ourselves from aspiration and enterprise behind our faithlessness. Into such a situation Christ repeatedly has come, bringing a vision of what life ought to be, too imperative to be neglected, too challenging to be denied. Men have been shaken out of their content; the true color of their lives has been revealed against his white background, the meanness of their plans against the wide ranges of his purpose. From seeing Him they have gone back to be content in their old habits, but in vain. Can one who has seen a home be happy in a hovel? Ranke, the historian, says, "More guiltless and more powerful, more exalted and more holy, has naught ever been on earth than his conduct, his life, and his death. The human race knows nothing that could be brought even afar off into comparison with it." So he has been the disturber of man's ignoble self-content, and to say that we believe in him means that, no longer able to endure the thing we are, we go on pilgrimage toward the thing he is. Faith means that we decide to *move*. This first essential work of saviorhood Christ has wrought, and when men start to follow him, they feel the need of power.

For another thing, Christ has created a thirst for the power he furnishes by *revealing the quality of character in the possession of which salvation ultimately consists.* At the beginning of the ethical development whether of the individual or of the race, goodness is defined in terms of prohibitions. There are many things which men ought *not* to do; they walk embarrassed in the presence of their duty like courtiers before an exacting prince. How negative and repelling such goodness is! As another exclaims: "They do not break the Sabbath themselves, but no one who has to spend it with them likes to see the dreadful day come round. They do not swear themselves, but they make all who know them want to. They are just as good as trying not to be bad can make them."

Discerning spirits, therefore, turn to goodness positively conceived. "Thou shalt not" becomes "Thou shalt"; duty consists of rules to be kept, precepts to be observed, principles to be applied, and we go out to do good deeds to men. But whoever seriously tried to do deeds really good, faces a need of moral elevation, as much beyond the outward act of good as that surpasses the observance of prohibitions. *Good deeds are not a matter of will alone, but of spiritual quality*. Let the wind blow to fan the faces of the sick, but if it discover that it is laden with disease, what shall it do? To blow this way or that may be within volition's power, but not to *cleanse* oneself. The task of character reaches inward, beyond the things we do or refrain from doing to the man we are. Goodness is something more than girding up the loins, blowing upon the hands, and setting to the work of being dutiful. It springs from the spirit's depths; it is tinctured with the spirit's quality; and deeds are never really better than the soul whose utterances they are. From "Thou shalt not do" to "Thou shalt do" and from "Thou shalt do" to "Thou shalt be," man's flying goal of goodness moves. And this ideal in Christ has been incarnate, visible, imperative. He *was* right in the inner quality and flavor of his life; and to be like him involves a pure and powerful personality. Whoever sets that task ahead knows that he cannot strut proudly into it. Like Alice entering Wonderland he must grow very small before he can grow large. The Christ who has power to give has revealed the need of it.

Not only by the intensifying of the ideal, but by its extension, has Christ created thirst for divine help. In youth the problem of character concerns personal habits. Our untamed strength must be broken to the harness, and the snaffle bit be used upon our wayward powers. We justly fear our sins and in their triumph we see the wreck of individual prospects and the ruin of our families' hopes. Our concern centers about ourselves, and its crux is self-mastery. But when in maturity, somewhat "at leisure from ourselves" in settled habits, we no longer fear our own ruin or think it probable, goodness extends its meaning. To play our part in man's advancement, to live, work, sacrifice, and, if need be, die for causes on which our children's hopes depend, becomes our ideal. As boys in springtime when the ice is melting see from a hilltop the swirling flood that overflows the plain, and know that somewhere underneath the unfamiliar and tumultuous rapids the main channel runs, from which the floods have broken, to which in time they must return, so in a generation when man's life has broken its banks in fury we still believe that the main course of the divine purpose is not forever lost. To believe that, and in the strength of it to toil for the ends God seeks, becomes to awakened spirits the essential soul of goodness.

When such meanings enter into his ideal, a man runs straight upon the need of God. For we may make our contribution to the cause of man's good upon the earth and our children may make theirs, but if this world is a spiritual Sahara, never meant for character and social weal, and against the dead set of the desert's power we are building oases here with our unaided fingers, then the issue of our work stands in no doubt. The Sahara will pile its burning sands about us and hurl its blistering winds across us, and we and our works together come to naught. By as much, then, as a man really cares about democracy and liberty and social equity, about human brotherhood and Christian civilization, by so much he needs God, who gathers up the scattered contributions of his children and builds them into victory. A man alone may keep the decalogue, but alone he cannot save the world. Who dreams of that wants power. And Christ has made men dream of that, believe in that with passionate certainty, until "Thy Kingdom come" is the daily prayer of multitudes. To no human strength can such prayer be offered; we are not adequate to an eternal, universal task. Again Christ has brought us to the need of power, and his people call him Savior, because the need which he creates he also satisfies.

In one of the tidal rivers near New York, the building of a bridge was interrupted by a derelict sunk in the river's bottom. Divers put chains about the obstacle and all day long the engineer directed the maneuvering of tugs as they puffed and pulled in vain endeavor to dislodge the hulk. Then a young student, fresh from the technical school, asked for the privilege of trying, and from the vexed, impatient chief obtained his wish. "What will *you* do it with?" the engineer inquired. "The flatboats in which we brought the granite from Vermont," the young man answered. So when the tide was out, the flat boats were fastened to the derelict. The Atlantic began to come in; its ynghty shoulders underneath the boats lifted—lifted until the derelict had to come. The youth had harnessed infinite energy to his task. To the consciousness of such resource in the spiritual world Christ has introduced his people. They have meant not formula but fact, not technicality but experience, when they have called him Savior.

III

This consciousness of power has come in part from Christ's revelation of God the Father. Whoever has sinned against his friend or unkindly wronged a child knows what sin does to personal relationships. How swift a change comes over a son's thought of his father when the son has sinned! The wrong may have been done secretly so that his sire does not know, and the boy alone on earth is conscious of it. But for all that the filial relationship has lost its glory. Before the sin, the son was happy with his father near; they were companions, confidants, and to the boy fatherhood was very beautiful. Now, he is most unhappy with his father near; the father's eyes like a detective's pierce him through, the face like a judge's waits sternly to condemn. He is looking at his father through the dark glasses of his sin, and they distort his vision. When one considers the gods whom men have worshiped, approaching them by bloody altar-stairs, offering their first-born to assuage wrath or win from apathy to favor, he sees, extended to a racial scale, our boyhood's tragedy. *Mankind has been looking at the Father through its ignorance and sin and it has seen him beclouded and awry.* Christ changed all that. By what he taught, by what he was, by what he suffered he has said to man, so that man increasingly has believed it—You are wrong about God. He does not stand aloof—careless or vindictive; he is not as he looks to you through the twisted lenses of your evil. He loves you. He *cares* beyond your power to understand, and all my compassion but reveals in time what is eternally in him. He is pledged to the victory of goodness in you and in the world, and you have not used all your power until you have used his, for that, too, is yours.

From that day the fight against sin has been a new thing, and men have gone into it with battle cries they never used before—"*God* was in Christ, reconciling the world unto himself" (II Cor. 5:19); "*God* commendeth his own love toward us, in that, while we were yet sinners, Christ died for us" (Rom. 5:8); "If *God* is for us, who is against us?" (Rom. 8:31).

This access of power has come in part from Christ's revelation of *man*. When a jewel is taken from darkness into sunlight, there is a two fold revealing. The sunlight is disclosed in new glory, for it never seemed so beautiful before as it appears breaking in splendor through the jewel's heart. And there is a revelation of the jewel. Dull and unillumined in the dark, it is lustrous when the sun enlightens it. So Christ brought us an unveiling of the

Father; the Divine never had seemed so wonderful as when it poured in glory through his purity and love. And he brought as well a new revelation of man. Our human nature, bedimmed by sin and lusterless, he in his own person took up into the light, and lifting it where all mankind could see he cried—This *is* human nature—man as God intended him to be—no slave of fate and dupe of sin, but a free man and a victor. And from that day the war on sin has had new spirit in it, and battle cries that presage triumph have grown familiar on the fighters' lips: "Now are we children of God, and it is not yet made manifest what we shall be" (I John 3:2); "Till we all attain unto the unity of the faith, and of the knowledge of the Son of God, unto a full-grown man, unto the measure of the stature of the fulness of Christ" (Eph. 4:13); "His precious and exceeding great promises; that through these ye may become partakers of the divine nature" (II Pet. 1:4).

IV

Christ's double revelation of God and man, however, has had its vital impact of power on life in what Christians have always called *the experience of the Spirit.* When the New Testament speaks its characteristic word about the Spirit, it means the conscious presence of the living God in the hearts of men, and that is the very essence of religion. The first Christians did not know God in one way only; they knew him in three ways. So one man might know Beethoven the composer and be an authority upon his works; another might know Beethoven the performer and delight in his playing; and another might know Beethoven the man and rejoice in his friendship—but no one could know the whole of Beethoven until he knew him all three ways. The New Testament Christians came thus to God. He was the Father, Creator of all; he was the Character, revealed in Jesus; but as well he was the Spiritual Presence in their lives, their sustenance and power. "The grace of the Lord Jesus Christ, and the love of God, and the communion of the Holy Spirit" (II Cor. 13:14)—such was their experience of the Divine. It was not dogma; it was *life.* God was Creator, Character, and Comforter.

Christian experience is in continual danger of drifting from this vital center. In our age especially, we are prone to find God at the end of an argument and to leave him there. We have been compelled by militant agnosticism to put our apologetic armies on the defensive. Finding it impossible to hold the respect of men's intelligence without reasonable arguments in the faith's behalf, we have had to draw such inferences from the nature of the material universe, from the necessities of human thought, the demands of human conscience, and the progress of moral evolution in history, that materialism should be made, what indeed it is, a discredited affair. But God so arrived at, by way of reason, is an external matter. He is an hypothesis to explain the universe. "He sitteth upon the circle of the earth and the inhabitants thereof are as grasshoppers before him." Granted the incalculable value in such faith, putting unity into history and purpose into life—it is not religion and it never can be. *Religion begins when the God outwardly argued is inwardly experienced.* Religion begins when we cease using the tricky and unstable airplane of speculation to seek Him among the clouds, and retreat into the fertile places of our own spirits where the living water rises, as Jesus said. God outside of us is a theory; God inside of us becomes a fact. God outside of us is an hypothesis; God inside of us is an experience. God the Father is the possibility of salvation; God the Spirit is actuality of life, joy, peace, and saving power. God the transcendent may do for philosophy, but he is not enough for religion.

Without this completion of the Gospel, Christ's savior-hood does not reach inward to our need. For lacking it, we stand before the Master with the same admiration that a man who is no painter feels when he sees a Raphael. He knows the work is sublime, but he is not proposing to reproduce it. He is conquered by its beauty, but he knows no possibility of its imitation. If, however, there were a spirit of Raphael that could lay hold upon a man's life and transform him to the master's skill and power, then his admiration would become inwardly effective. *It takes the spirit of Raphael to do Raphael's work.* If this gospel of an indwelling dynamic is not coupled with our admiration for Jesus, we are like a student practicing the fingering of the "Hallelujah Chorus" on an organ from which the power has been shut off. With what accuracy his fingers travel the keys, who can tell? Once Handel's soul, on fire with the passion of harmony, burned itself into that composition. He wrote it upon his knees. But with whatever agility the student's fingers follow the notes, no "Hallelujah Chorus" comes from his organ to praise God and move men. So the record of this matchless character handed to us in the Gospels, like notes of music meant to be played again, is but our despair, if we must attempt its reproduction on a powerless organ. Our admiration for it is external and ineffectual. We fall thereby into a static religion of creed; we have no dynamic religion of progress and hope. This then is the glorious message, where the Christian Gospel reaches its climax, and which alone puts fullest meaning into Jesus' perfect life: *the Spirit of God in Jesus made his quality; that same Spirit is underground in our lives, striving to well up in characters like his, until we live, yet not we, but Christ lives in us.*

Any spring day may serve to illustrate this faith. Where does the restlessness in nature have its source? Every tree, in discontent, hastens to make buds into leaves, and every blade of grass is tremulous with impatient life. No tree, however, is a sufficient explanation of its own haste and dissatisfaction; no flower has in itself the secrets of its eager growth. The spirit of life is abroad, and crowding itself everywhere on old, dead forms, is making them bloom again. Explain then, the moral restlessness of our hearts in other wise! We do ill, and are distraught with remorse until we repent and make reparation. We attain money or talents, and are chased day and night by the urgent call to their spiritual dedication. We conform ourselves to decency and still hear a call for goodness beyond all earthly need. We succeed as the world calls it, and we know that it is failure; we fail as the world sees it, and our hearts sing for joy because we know that we have succeeded. Everywhere we are confronted with a pulsing life that longs to get itself expressed in us. We cannot get away from God. He is not far, he is here. This Spirit, for whom there is no better name than the Spirit of Jesus, is our continual companion. We are locked in an enforced fellowship with him. There is no friend with whom we deal more directly and continually than with him. Every time we open an inspiring book and devoutly study it, this Spirit is pleading for entrance. Every time we pray he stands at the door and knocks. Every time some child in need, or some great cause demanding sacrifice, lays claim on us, this Spirit is crying to be let in. Men's hunger for food, their love for family and friends, are not more direct, concrete, immediate experiences than our dealings with this Spirit of the Lord. He is not only God the Father; he is God the Spirit, striving to dwell in us and work through us.

Into a vital use of this relationship with the Divine, Christ opened the way and multitudes have followed. He has taught men to find that same resourcefulness in the spiritual world which science finds in the physical. Every successful invention of a man like Edison involves a twofold faith: that there is inexhaustible power in the universe and that, with persistent patience and cooperation, there is no telling what marvels yet may come from the employment of it. Faith is science's flying column. It runs out into engineering, agriculture, medicine, and refuses to limit the possibilities. Science is a tremendous believer; it lives by faith that almost anything may yet be done. Such a relationship Paul sustained with the Spirit. He was confident of resources there, "exceeding abundantly above all that we ask or think" (Eph. 3:20). He was a spiritual Edison, a believer in the divine reality and power and their availability by faith in human life.

Only such a Gospel is adequate to man's deepest need. Sin, whether its forms be decent or obscene, cripples men's wills with the appalling certainty that they are slaves. As a hypnotist draws imaginary circles around his victims, across which they cannot step, so sin, that Svengali of the soul, whether in personal or social life, paralyzes its dupes with disbelief in possibilities. To innumerable folk, imprisoned by their fears and sins, Christ has been the Savior. He has awakened that faith which, as he said, is the greatest mountain-mover known to men. They have been "strengthened with power through his Spirit in the inward man" (Eph. 3:16).

V

When one considers, as we have in these two chapters, what Christ has meant in the experience of his people, little wonder can remain that they have called him by such high names as have aroused man's incredulity. For this Gospel of power has never been separable from him, as though he were its historic fountain and could easily be forgotten by those who far down stream enjoyed the water. His personality itself has been the inspiration of his people. At Marston Moor, when the Puritans and Cavaliers were aligned for battle and all was in readiness for conflict to begin, Oliver Cromwell came riding across the plain. And the chronicler says that at the sight of him the Puritans sent up a great victorious shout, as though their battle already had been won. Some such effect our Lord has had on his disciples. To explain that effect one would have to speak not so much of his teaching as of himself—his character and purpose; nor so much of them as of the Cross where all he taught and was came to a point of flame that has set the world on fire. Christ was the

> "nerve o'er which do creep
> The else unfelt oppressions of the earth."

He suffered with man and for man. He uniquely embodied in his own experience the universal law that the consequences of sin fall in part on the one who loves the sinner and tries to save him; and in that sacrifice his work for man was consummated, and his influence over man confirmed. When his people have bowed before him in unutterable devotion they have been thinking not only of what he has done for them, but of what it cost him to do it.

Why, therefore, should we wonder that his disciples at their best have called Jesus divine? His first followers began with no abstract ideas of deity; they began with "the man, Christ Jesus" (I Tim. 2:5). They had no idea at the first that he was more. His bodily and mental life had obeyed the laws of normal human development, advancing "in wisdom and stature, and in favor with God and man" (Luke 2:52). He hungered after his temptation, thirsted on the Cross, slept from weariness while the boat tossed in a storm, and exhausted, sat beside the well. Like other men he had elevated hours of great rejoicing; times when compassion moved him to tears, as when he saw a multitude unshepherded or, swinging round the brow of Olivet, beheld Jerusalem; and hours of hot indignation, too, as when he found his Father's house a den of thieves or spoke out his heart against the Pharisees. He asked questions, and was astonished, now at the people's lack of faith, again at the centurion's excess of it. His fellowship with God was nourished by secret prayer, his power replenished by retreat to quiet places for communion, and all his life was lived, his temptations faced, his troubles borne, and his work done in a spirit of humble, filial dependence on his Father.

Thus real and human, a sharer in their limitations, their sorrows, and their moral trials, the first disciples saw the Master. But ever as they lived with him, whether in physical presence or in spiritual fellowship, he wrought in them a Savior's work. He became to them manhood indeed, but manhood plus. He grew in their apprehension, as though a boy had thought an ocean's inlet were a lake enclosed, and now discovers that it is the sea itself, and all its tides the pulse of the great deep. How should they name this greatness in their Lord? They were not utterly without a clue, for he himself had introduced them to the life divine. They had learned through him to say about themselves that they were temples in which God dwelt (II Cor. 6:16), that God abode in them (I John 4:12), that he stood ever waiting to come in (Rev. 3:20), and that the possession of the divine nature was the Gospel's promise (II Pet. 1:4). By what other element in their experience could they interpret the greatness of their Lord? It might be inadequate, but it was the best they had. They rose to understand the divine life in him from the experience of the divine life in themselves. "God was in Christ," they said. They never dreamed of claiming equality with him. Like pools beside the sea, they understood the ocean's quality from their own. There are not two kinds of sea water; nor, with one God, can there be two kinds of divine life. But so understanding the sea, shall the pool claim equality with it? Rather, the sea has deeps, tides, currents, and relationships with the world's life that no pool can ever know. So Christ was at once their brother and their Lord. He was real, because they interpreted his life divine from the foregleams of God's presence in themselves. He was adorable, because he was an ocean to their landlocked pools, and they waited for his tides.

Only by some such road as these first disciples trod can men come to a vital understanding of the Lord. Nothing but *experience* can give us a living estimate of anything; without that theory is vain. Let a man live with the Master's manhood until it grows luminous and through it he sees the character of God; let a man avail himself of the Master's saviorhood until forgiven and empowered he finds the "life that is life indeed"; let a man grow in the experience of God's presence until he knows not only the God without but the God within; and then if he rises to estimate his Lord, he will not hesitate to see in Jesus the incarnate presence of the living God. After that, theology may help or hinder him, according as it is wise and vital or cold and formal; but with theology or not, he knows the heart of the New Testament's attitude toward Jesus. He understands why the first Christians summed up their faith as "believing in the Lord Jesus Christ."

CHAPTER XII

The Fellowship of Faith

DAILY READINGS

Our thought turns, in our closing week of study, from believers taken one by one, to believers gathered in fellowship. This community of faith has wider boundaries than the organized churches; in a real sense it includes all servants of man's ideal aims; yet in the Church we naturally seek the chief meanings of fellowship for faith. Why men do not go to church, is often asked. But why men do go, so that in spite of countless failures in the churches, attendance on public worship and loyalty to organized religion are among mankind's most usual habits, is an inquiry far more important. To that inquiry let us in the daily readings turn our thought.

Twelfth Week, First Day

But woe unto you, scribes and Pharisees, hypocrites! because ye shut the kingdom of heaven against men: for ye enter not in yourselves, neither suffer ye them that are entering in to enter.

Woe unto you, scribes and Pharisees, hypocrites! for ye compass sea and land to make one proselyte; and when he is become so, ye make him twofold more a son of hell than yourself. . . .

Woe unto you, scribes and Pharisees, hypocrites! for ye tithe mint and anise and cummin, and have left undone the weightier matters of the law, justice, and mercy, and faith: but these ye ought to have done, and not to have left the other

undone. Ye blind guides, that strain out the gnat, and swallow the camel!—Matt. 23:13-15, 23-24.

Jesus' indictment of the Jewish Church is terrific, and yet no one who knows the story of the Christian churches can doubt that they often have deserved the same condemnation. They have at times committed all the sins that can be laid at any institution's door; they have been selfish, formal, worldly, cruel. A wonder-story from the Arctic says that once the candle flames froze and the explorers broke them off and wore them for watch charms; the flames of the great fire congealed and were wound like golden ornaments around men's necks. So repeatedly the burning words of Scripture, the blazing affirmations of old creeds, on fire at first with the passion of souls possessed by God, have been frozen in the churches' Arctic climate, and handed to men like talismans and amulets, with no saving warmth or light. Creeds, rituals, organizations—how often these frozen forms of life have taken the place of inward spiritual power! Dr. Washington Gladden would not be alone in saying: "While therefore I had as large an experience of church-going in my boyhood as most boys can recall, I cannot lay my hand on my heart and say that the church-going helped me to solve my religious problems. In fact, it made those problems more and more tangled and troublesome." And yet the Church goes on. Voltaire prophesied its collapse in fifty years, and in fifty years the house where he made the prophecy was a depot for the circulation of the Scriptures. The Church's persistence, continual adaptation to new conditions, and apparently endless power of revival must have some deep reason. It may be because prayer like this which follows has never utterly died out in the sanctuary.

O Thou that dwellest not in temples made with hands! We ever stand within the courts of Thy glorious presence only we open now the gates of our poor praise. Thou hast enriched this day of rest, O Lord, with Thy choicest gifts of peace; and lo! Thou unforgetting God, its record is before Thee, for ages past, moistened with penitential tears, and illumined with glad hopes, and hallowed by the innumerable prayers of faithful and saintly men. In this our day may the churches of

Thy Holy One seek Thee still in spirit and truth; may we also enter in and find our rest, being of one heart and mind, and serving Thee with a wakeful and humble joy. Teach us now how we may converse with Thee, for we cannot order our speech by reason of darkness. We are naked and without disguise before Thee; oh! hide not Thyself from us behind our ignorance and sin. May we at least in this Thine hour shake off the sluggish clouds of sense and self that cling around our souls; and strenuously open our whole nature to the breath of Thy free spirit, and the healthful sunshine of Thy grace. Let the divine image of the Son of God visit us with power; driving out, with the chastisement of penitence, all obtruding passions that profane the temple of our hearts, and turn into a place of traffic that native house of prayer. O God of glory, God of grace! let not the things which are spiritually discerned by foolishness unto us through the blindness of our conscience: Thou knowest the thoughts of our wisdom that they are vain; take them from us, and bid them vanish away, lost in that wisdom from above which is revealed only to the pure in heart. Not unto us, O Lord, not unto us, but unto Thee be every thought of praise! Amen.—James Martineau.

Twelfth Week, Second Day

Some men doubtless go to church from traditional habit only, but such a motive obviously is not adequate to explain why the recurrent tides of humanity, even after an ebb in interest, sweep back to the Church again. In the eighteenth century, for example, Butler reports the common opinion that all that remained for Christianity was decent obsequies. But in a few years the Wesleys began a movement that changed the spiritual complexion of the English-speaking world, and swept multitudes into Christian fellowship. One reason for this repeated fact is clear. Mankind cannot and will not consent to live without faith in God, and faith in God in its genesis and its sustenance is largely a matter of contagion. We are not so much taught it; we catch it. It is vitally imparted in the family circle, and wherever kindred and believing spirits gather. No man is so independent as to escape the vital fact that his noblest emotions, attitudes, ideals, and faiths are socially engendered and socially sustained; he never would have had them in a solitary life and a solitary life would soon spoil those which he has now. A man may believe in his country and love her; but let him join in a patriotic movement or even attend a high-spirited patriotic meeting, and he will believe in her and love her more ardently. Man's religious life is not lawless; it is regulated by the same necessities of fellowship. The Church has made many mistakes, but on her altar the fire has never utterly gone out, and in her fellowship the faith of multitudes has been kindled.

Let us hold fast the confession of our hope that it waver not; for he is faithful that promised: and let us consider one another to provoke unto love and good works; not forsaking our own assembling together, as the custom of some is, but exhorting one another; and so much the more, as ye see the day drawing nigh.—Heb. 10:23-25.

Great is Thy name, O God, and greatly to be praised. In Thee all our discordant notes rise into perfect harmony. It is good for us to think of the wonder of Thy being. Thou art silent, yet most strong; unchangeable, yet ever changing; ever working, yet ever at rest, supporting, nourishing, maturing all things. O Thou Eternal Spirit, who hast set our noisy years in the heart of Thy eternity, lift us above the power and evils of the passing time, that under the shadow of Thy wings we may take courage and be glad. So great art Thou, beyond our utmost imagining, that we could not speak to Thee didst Thou not first draw near to us and say, "Seek ye my face." Unto Thee our hearts would make reply, "Thy face, Lord, will we seek." . . . We thank Thee for our birth into a Christian community, for the Church and the Sacraments of Thy grace, for the healing day of rest, when we enter with Thy people into Thy House and there make holyday; for the refreshment of soul, the joys of communion, the spiritual discipline, the inspiration of prayer and hymn and sermon. . . . We praise Thee for the myriad influences of good, conscious and unconscious, that have been about us, deeply penetrating our inner life, shaping and fitting us for Thy Kingdom. Thou has indeed forgiven all our iniquities, and healed all our diseases, and redeemed our life from destruction, and crowned us with lovingkindness. Therefore would we call upon our souls, and all that is within us, to bless Thy holy Name. Amen.—Samuel McComb.

Twelfth Week, Third Day

For ye, brethren, were called for freedom; only use not your freedom for an occasion to the flesh, but through love be servants one to another. For the whole law is fulfilled in one word, even in this: Thou shalt love thy neighbor as thyself. But if ye bite and devour one another, take heed that ye be not consumed one of another.—Gal. 5:13-15.

One fundamental reason for the endless revival of the Church is that faith never is satisfied until it issues in work. It insists on our being "servants one to another." We have spoken of God's merciful acceptance of a man when out of sin he turns his life by faith toward Christ; but to interpret this as meaning the adequacy of faith without effective service is to misread Scripture and to demoralize life. Faith that does not lead to service is no real faith at all. But whenever men endeavor to express in work any faith which they may hold they must come together. Service involves cooperation. A hermit may have faith, but his faith does not concern any ideal hopes on earth; it has no outlooks save upon his own soul's condition in the world to come; it is a narrow, selfish, inoperative thing. As soon as men are grasped by some moving faith about what ought to be done for God's service and man's welfare here and now, a hermit's solitude or any sort of unaffiliated life becomes impossible. They must combine in a fellowship of faith and of labor to seek common ends. They begin to say with Edward Rowland Sill, "For my part I long to 'fall in' with somebody. This picket duty is monotonous. I hanker after a shoulder on this side and the other." And to fall in with others to serve Christian ends means some kind of church. Let us pray today for a church more fit to express this passion to serve.

God, we pray for Thy Church, which is set today amid the perplexities of a changing order, and face to face with a great

*new task. We remember with love the nurture she gave to our
spiritual life in its infancy, the tasks she set for our growing
strength, the influence of the devoted hearts she gathers, the
steadfast power for good she has exerted. When we compare
her with all other human institutions, we rejoice, for there is
none like her. But when we judge her by the mind of her
Master, we bow in pity and contrition. Oh, baptize her afresh
in the life-giving spirit of Jesus! Grant her a new birth,
though it be with the travail of repentance and humiliation.
Bestow upon her a more imperious responsiveness to duty, a
swifter compassion with suffering, and an utter loyalty to the
will of God. Put upon her lips the ancient Gospel of her
Lord. Help her to proclaim boldly the coming of the
Kingdom of God and the doom of all that resist it. Fill her
with the prophet's scorn of tyranny, and with a Christ-like
tenderness for the heavy-laden and down-trodden. Give her
faith to espouse the cause of the people, and in their hands
that grope after freedom and light to recognize the bleeding
hands of the Christ. Bid her cease from seeking her own life,
lest she lose it. Make her valiant to give up her life to
humanity, that like her crucified Lord she may mount by the
path of the cross to a higher glory. Amen.*—Walter
Rauschenbusch.

Twelfth Week, Fourth Day

For the scripture saith, Whosoever believeth on him shall
not be put to shame. For there is no distinction between Jew
and Greek: for the same Lord is Lord of all, and is rich unto
all that call upon him: for, Whosoever shall call upon the
name of the Lord shall be saved. How then shall they call on
him in whom they have not believed? and how shall they
believe in him whom they have not heard? and how shall they
hear without a preacher? and how shall they preach, except
they be sent? even as it is written, How beautiful are the feet
of them that bring glad tidings of good things!—Rom.
10:11-15.

The necessity of affiliation for effective faith is clear when
one considers the missionary enterprise. One of the noblest
qualities in human life is our natural desire to share our

blessings. Every normal child is happier when some other child is joining in the play; every lover of music is gladdened by sharing with a friend enjoyment of a favorite symphony; save in singularly churlish folk the love of having others partake our joys is spontaneous and hearty. To those whom Christian faith has blessed with hope and power, the undeniable impulse comes to share these finest benedictions with all other men. The missionary enterprise does not rest upon a text; it wells up from one of the worthiest impulses in man's life. One may be fairly sure, that save as some perverted theology inhibits a spirit of love, a man's missionary interest will be proportionate to the reality and value of his own experience. If he himself has something well worth sharing, he will want to share it. But the missionary enterprise is more than any individual can compass; it demands organization, cooperation, and massed resources; it cannot be prosecuted without a church. The further our thought proceeds the more clear it becomes that the question is not, shall we have churches? but rather, since churches are inevitable, of what sort shall they be?

O Thou who has made all nations of men to seek Thee and to find thee: bless, we beseech Thee, Thy sons and daughters who have gone forth, into distant lands, bearing in their hands Thy Word of Life. We rejoice that, touched with the enthusiasm of Christ, so many have consecrated their lives to proclaiming the message of Thy love to those other sheep of Thine who are not of our fold, that they may be united with us and that there may be one flock and one Shepherd. Help Thy ministering servants to recognize the fragments of truth and goodness that are ever found where men are sincere and to claim these glimpses of Thyself as the prophecies of a fuller revelation. When discouraged by the hardness of their task, and the meager fruit of all their labor, give them faith to see the far-off whitening harvest. Inspire them with Thy gracious promise that though the sower may go forth weeping, bearing precious seed, he will come again with joy, bringing his sheaves with him. Comfort them in their exile and loneliness with a sense of Thy companionship and with the prayers and sympathy of their brethren at home. Through them let Thy Word have free course and be glorified. And so let Thy Kingdom come, and Thy Will be done on earth as in Heaven, for Jesus Christ's sake. Amen.—Samuel McComb.

Twelfth Week, Fifth Day

After this manner therefore pray ye: Our Father who art in heaven, Hallowed be thy name. Thy kingdom come. Thy will be done, as in heaven, so on earth. Give us this day our daily bread. And forgive us our debts, as we also have forgiven our debtors. And bring us not into temptation, but deliver us from the evil one. For if ye forgive men their trespasses, your heavenly Father will also forgive you. But if ye forgive not men their trespasses, neither will your Father forgive your trespasses.—Matt. 6:9-15.

The central ideal of Christian effort is set for us in the first petition of the Master's prayer. But a Kingdom on earth, with God's will done here in heavenly fashion, is a social idea. It means not only right personal quality; it means right family life, and economic, political, and international relationships Christianized. No amount of fine individual character, necessary as it is, will of itself rectify the social maladjustments and inequities. Were everyone as good as possible, we still should need organized action. All parts of an engine may be correct, and yet they may be wrongly fitted together. As it is, social relations obviously demand concerted action; we must join together to combat immoral industrial conditions, to throttle the liquor traffic, to make human fraternity a fact and not a dream. The opposition to all such reforms is organized, and no haphazard attack will succeed. Now, many organizations may arise to serve special ends and may do excellent service to the cause, but what has proved true in the conflict with the liquor traffic, is true also of enterprises for industrial justice and international cooperation—*only when the churches see the moral issue and put their power in, is there any hope of victory.* A Christian whose faith involves the Kingdom sees plainly that he cannot go on without the Church.

O Lord, we praise Thy holy name, for Thou hast made bare Thine arm in the sight of all nations and done wonders.

But still we cry to Thee in the weary struggle of our people against the power of drink. Remember, Lord, the strong men who were led astray and blighted in the flower of their youth. Remember the aged who have brought their gray hairs to a dishonored grave. Remember the homes that have been made desolate of joy, the wifely love that has been outraged in its sanctuary, the little children who have learned to despise where once they loved. Remember, O Thou great avenger of sin, and make this nation to remember.

May those who now entrap the feet of the weak and make their living by the degradation of men, thrust away their shameful gains and stand clear. But if their conscience is silenced by profit, do Thou grant Thy people the indomitable strength of faith to make an end of it. May all the great churches of our land shake off those who seek the shelter of religion for that which damns, and stand with level front against their common foe. May all who still soothe their souls with half-truths, saying "Peace, peace," where there can be no peace, learn to see through Thy stern eyes and come to the help of Jehovah against the mighty. Help us to cast down the men in high places who use the people's powers to beat back the people's hands from the wrong they fain would crush.

O God, bring nigh the day when all our men shall face their daily task with minds undrugged and with tempered passions; when the unseemly mirth of drink shall seem a shame to all who hear and see; when the trade that debauches men shall be loathed like the trade that debauches women; and when all this black remnant of savagery shall haunt the memory of a new generation but as an evil dream of the night. For this accept our vows, O Lord, and grant Thine aid. Amen.—Walter Rauschenbusch.

Twelfth Week, Sixth Day

Neither for these only do I pray, but for them also that believe on me through their word; that they may all be one; even as thou, Father, art in me, and I in thee, that they also may be in us: that the world may believe that thou didst send me. And the glory which thou hast given me I have given unto them; that they may be one, even as we are one; I in them, and thou in me, that they may be perfected into one;

that the world may know that thou didst send me, and lovedst them, even as thou lovedst me.—John 17:20-23.

To the Christian the Church is a problem, just because she is a necessity. He caught his faith from the contagion of her fellowship and he sees that if he is to serve effectively the ideals of Christ and the coming of the Kingdom he must work through some church. But because the Church is necessary, he is not thereby made content with her. She is at once helping and hindering the spread of the faith; she is the source of immeasurable good and yet she is not "one, that the world may believe." A traveler across the American plains in springtime sees fences, tiresomely prominent, staring at him from the landscape; but in summer when he returns the fences are invisible. The wheat and corn are growing, the earth is bearing fruit, and while the old divisions may be there, they all are hidden. One suspects that if Christians everywhere set themselves with hearty zeal to bear the fruit of service for the common weal, if they gave themselves to achieve the aims of Christ for men with ardor and thoroughness, the sectarian divisions would grow unimperative and disappear. We may not be able to think the disagreements through, but we may be able to work them out; even where we cannot recite a common creed, we can share a common purpose. The War, where Jewish rabbis have held crucifixes before the eyes of dying soldiers, and where Catholic priests have met death, as one did at Gallipoli, following a Wesleyan chaplain—"my Protestant comrade"—into danger, has revealed how deeply underneath our sharp divisions our spiritual loyalties seek unity when crisis comes. For all the unity that can come without compromise to conscience, surely the Christian people are bound to pray and work.

O God, the Father of our Lord Jesus Christ, our only Saviour, the Prince of Peace; give us grace seriously to lay to heart the great dangers we are in by our unhappy divisions. Take away all hatred and prejudice, and whatsoever else may hinder us from godly union and concord; that as there is but one body and one Spirit, and one hope of our calling, one Lord, one faith, one baptism, one God and Father of us all, so we may be all of one heart and of one soul, united in one

*holy bond of truth and peace, of faith and charity, and may
with one mind and one mouth glorify Thee, through Jesus
Christ our Lord. Amen.*—"The Book of Common Prayer."

Twelfth Week, Seventh Day

**For I am already being offered, and the time of my
departure is come. I have fought the good fight, I have
finished the course, I have kept the faith: henceforth there is
laid up for me the crown of righteousness, which the Lord,
the righteous judge, shall give to me at that day; and not to
me only, but also to all them that have loved his
appearing.—II Tim. 4:6-8.**

The fellowship of faith is not bounded by the earth. Paul's
expectation took into its account a communion that far
overreached the confines of temporal experience. The New
Testament believers not only held but vividly apprehended
that the "whole family" to which they belonged in Christian
communion was "in heaven and on earth." Their outlook
Wordsworth has expressed in modern words:

> "There is
> One great society alone on earth:
> The noble Living and the noble Dead."

To that society of the world's prophets and martyrs, seers
and servants, it may well be a man's ambition to belong.
And that ideal is not impossible to anyone, for the mark and
seal of their fellowship is that they have "kept the faith."
When others despaired, lost heart, and deserted causes on
which man's welfare hung, they kept the faith. When
mysteries perplexed their minds and discouragement, to
human vision, was more rational than hope, they turned
from sight to insight and they kept the faith. When new
knowledge, half-understood, disturbed old forms of
thought and multitudes were confused in uncertainty and
disbelief, they kept the faith. And they often came to their
end, like Paul, having "suffered the loss of all things"—yet
not *all,* for they had kept the faith.

"For all the saints, who from their labors rest,
Who Thee by faith before the world confessed,
Thy name, O Jesus, be forever blest,
Alleluia!

O may Thy soldiers, faithful, true, and bold,
Fight as the saints who nobly fought of old,
And win with them the victor's crown of gold,
Alleluia!

O blest communion, fellowship Divine!
We feebly struggle; they in glory shine;
Yet all are one in Thee, for all are Thine.
Alleluia!"

O God, Thou only Refuge of Thy children! who remainest true though all else should fail, and livest though all things die; cover us now when we fly to Thee. Thy shelter was around our fathers. Thy voice called them away, and bids us seek Thee here till we depart to be with them. In Thy memory are the lives of all men from of old. Before Thy sight are the secret hearts of all the living. We stand in awe of Thy justice which, since the ages began, hath never changed: and we cling to Thy mercy that passeth not away.

Almighty Father, Thou art a God afar off as well as nigh at hand. Thou who in times past didst pity the prayers of our forerunners, and especially of that suffering servant of Thine whom Thou hast made our Leader unto Thee! be pleased to strengthen us now, O Lord, to bear our lighter cross and surrender ourselves for duty and for trial unto Thee. Show us something of the blessed peace with which they now look back on their days of strong crying and tears, and teach us that it is far better to die in Thy service than to live for our own. Rebuke within us all immoderate desires, all unquiet temper, all presumptuous expectations, all ignoble self-indulgence, and feeling on us the embrace of Thy Fatherly hand, may we meekly and with courage go into the darkest ways of our pilgrimage, anxious not to change Thy perfect will, but only to do and bear it worthily. May we spend all our days in Thy presence, and meet our death in the strength of Thy grace, and pass thence into the nearer light of Thy knowledge and love. Amen.—John Hunter.

COMMENT FOR THE WEEK

I

So far in our studies we have been dealing with the individual believer in his search for a reasonable faith. But we must face at last what from the beginning has been true, that there is no such thing as an individual believer. *All faiths are social.* However little we may be aware of each other's influence, however intangible the social forces which shape the convictions by which we live, no man builds or keeps his faiths alone. We may pride ourselves on our independent thought, but the fact remains as Prof. William James has stated it: "Our faith is faith in some one else's faith, and in the greatest matters this is most the case."

The realm of religious conviction is not the only place where we hold with a strong sense of personal possession what has been given us by others, and often forget to acknowledge our indebtedness. We believe in democracy and popular education, not because by some gift of individual genius we are wiser than our unbelieving sires, but because, in the advance of the race, that faith has been wrought out by many minds, and, with minute addition of our own thought, we share the general conviction. As a man considers how rich and varied are the faiths he holds, how few of them he ever has thought through or ever can, and how helpless he would be, if he were set from the beginning to create any one of them, he gains new insight into Paul's words, "What hast thou that thou didst not receive? but if thou didst receive it, why dost thou glory as if thou hadst not received it?" (I Cor. 4:7).

Indeed, this same truth holds in every relationship. Nothing is more impossible than a "self-made man." In no realm can that common phrase be intelligently applied to anyone. If in business one has risen from poverty to wealth, he has used railroads that he did not invent and telephones that he does not even understand; he has built his business on a credit system for which he did not labor and whose moral basis has been laid in the ethical struggles of unnumbered generations. For the clothes he wears, the food he eats, the education he receives, he is debtor to a social life that taps the ends of the earth and that has cost blood not his and money which he never can repay. If granting this, a man still says, "My power and the might of my hand hath gotten me this wealth" (Deut. 8:17), he may well consider whence his power has come. His distant ancestors stalked through primeval forests, their brows sloped back, their hairy hides barren of clothes, and in their hands stone hatchets, by the aid of which they sought their food. What has this twentieth century boaster done to change the habits of the Stone Age to the civilization on which his wealth is based or to elevate man's intellect to the grasp and foresight of the modern business world? All the power by which he wins his way is clearly a social gift, and any contribution which he may add is infinitesimal compared with his receipts.

By this truth all declarations of individual independence need to be chastened and controlled and all boasting cancelled utterly. Normal minds have their times of self-assertion in religion, when they grow impatient of believing anything simply because they have been told. As a college junior put it: "I must clear the universe of God, and then start in at the beginning to see what I can find." But to assert a reasonable independence ought not to mean that one cut himself off from the support of history, the accumulated experience of the race, the insight of the seers, and in unassisted isolation walk, like Kipling's cat, "by his wild lone." No man can do that anywhere and still succeed. Imagine a man, in politics, dubious of his old affiliations and disturbed by the conflicting opinions of his day. If, so perplexed, he should throw over all that ever had been thought or done in civic life, and in an unaided individual adventure attempt out of his own mind to constitute a state, in what utter confusion would he land! No mind can begin work as though it were the first mind that ever acted, or were the only mind in action now. All effective thinking is social; contributions from innumerable heads pour in to make a wise man's knowledge. And to suppose that any man can climb the steep ascent of heaven all alone and lay his hands comprehensively on the Eternal is preposterous. No one ever apprehended a science so, much less God! Even Jesus fed his soul on the prophets of his race.

II

Indeed, Jesus' attitude toward the fellowship of faith is most revealing, seen against the background of his nation's history. In the beginning, there was in Israel no such thing as individual religion. In the earliest strata of the Bible's revelation, we find no indication of a faith that brought God and each of his people into intimate relationships. Jehovah was the God of the nation as a whole and not of the people one by one. When he spoke, he spoke to the community through a leader; "Speak thou with us and we will hear," the people cried to Moses, "but let not God speak with us lest we die" (Exod. 20:19). It was at the time of the Exile, when the nation fell in ruins, and the hearts of faithful Jews were thrown back one by one on God that individual trust, peace, joy, and confidence found utterance. It was Jeremiah (Chap. 31) and Ezekiel (Chap. 18) who saw men individually responsible to God, and who opened the way for loyal Jews to be his people even when the nation was no more. And what they began Jesus completed. He lifted up the individual and made each man the object of the Father's care. "It is not the will of your Father . . . that *one* of these little ones should perish" (Matt. 18:14). "What man of you, having a hundred sheep, and having lost *one* of them . . ." (Luke 15:4). "The very hairs of your head are all numbered" (Matt. 10:30). As for religion's inner meaning, it became in Jesus' Gospel not a national ritual but a private faith: "But thou, when thou prayest, enter into thine inner chamber, and having shut thy door, pray to thy Father who is in secret" (Matt. 6:6).

While Jesus, however, so emphasized the inward, individual aspects of religion, he did not leave it there, as though persons could ever be like jugs in the rain, separate receptacles that share neither their emptiness nor their abundance. He bound his disciples into a fellowship. He joined their channels until, like interflowing streams, one contributed to all and the spirit of all was expressed in each. He braided them into friendship with himself and with each other, so close that the community did what no isolated believer ever could have done—it survived the shock of the crucifixion, the agony of sustained persecution, the frailties of its members, and the discouragements of its campaign.

On the *group* the Master counted for his work: "The gates of Hades shall not prevail against it" (Matt. 16:18). And when the New Testament Church emerged, the fellowship which Christ himself had breathed into it was clear and strong. Men who became Christians, in the New Testament, came into a new relationship with God indeed, but into a new human fraternity as well. They were "builded together for a habitation of God through the Spirit" (Eph. 2:22), and even when death came that fellowship was not destroyed. They were still "the whole family in heaven and on earth" (Eph. 3:15). John Wesley was right: "The Bible knows nothing of a solitary religion." In the Old Testament religion was predominantly national; in the New Testament, individuals rejoicing in the "Beloved Community" could not describe their life without the reiteration of "one another." They were to "pray one for another" and "confess sins one to another" (James 5:16); they were to "love one another" (I Pet. 1:22), "exhort one another" (Heb. 3:13), "comfort one another" (I Thess. 4:18); they were to "bear one another's burdens" (Gal. 6:2) and in communal worship "admonish one another with psalms and hymns and spiritual songs" (Col. 3:16).

So when they thought of their faith, they never held it in solitary confidence; they were "strong to apprehend *with all the saints* what is the breadth and length and height and depth, and to know the love of Christ which passeth knowledge" (Eph. 3:18).

III

When a modern believer endeavors to interpret this spirit in the New Testament in terms of his own wants, he sees at once that he needs fellowship for the *enriching* of his faith. Cooperation for achievement is a modern commonplace, but when Paul prayed, as we have quoted him, that the Ephesians might be "strong to *apprehend* with all the saints," he was stating the more uncommon proposition that men must cooperate for knowledge. He saw the divine love in its length, breadth, depth, and height on one side, and on the other a solitary man endeavoring to understand it. Impossible! said Paul; the divine love in its fullness cannot be known in solitude, it must be apprehended in fellowship.

At first nothing seems more strictly individual than knowledge. To know is an intimate, personal affair; it cannot be carried on by proxy. But even casual thought at once makes clear that in solitude we cannot know even the physical universe. No man can go apart and through the narrow aperture of his own mind see the full round of truth. For astronomers study the stars, geologists the rocks, chemists know their special field and physicists know theirs; each scientist understands in part, and if one is to know the breadth and length and height and depth of the physical world he must be strong to apprehend with all the scientists.

In religion this necessity of cooperation in knowing God may not at first seem evident. In the secret session behind closed doors, as Jesus said, one finds his clearest thought of God, and in the individual heart the divine illumination comes. So some insist; and the answer does not deny, but surpasses the truth in the insistence. *Is yours the only heart where God is to be found? Does the sea of his grace exhaust itself in what it can reveal in your bay?* Rather, in how many different ways men come to God, how various their experiences of him, and how much each needs the rest for breadth and catholicity of view!

One man comes to God by way of intellectual perplexity and he knows chiefly faith's illumination of life's puzzling problems; another comes through the experience of sin and he responds to such a phrase as "God our Saviour" (I Tim. 1:1); another comes to God through trouble and has found in faith "eternal comfort and good hope through grace" (II Thess. 2:16); and another by way of a happy life has found in God the object of devoted gratitude. One, a mystic, finds God in solitary prayer; another, a worker, knows him chiefly as the Divine Ally. Some are very young and have a child's religion; some are at the summit of their years and have a strong man's achieving faith; and some are old and are familiar with the face of death and the thought of the eternal. How multiform is man's experience of God! Some compositions cannot be interpreted by a solo. Let the first violinist play with what skill he can, he alone is not adequate to the endeavor. There must be an orchestra; the oboes and viols, the drums and trumpets, the violins and cellos must all be there. So faith in God is too rich and manifold to be interpreted by individuals alone; a fellowship is necessary. Even Paul, in one of his most gloriously mixed-up and yet revealing sentences, prays for fellowship that his faith may be enriched: "I long to see you, that I may impart unto you some spiritual gift, to the end ye may be established; that is, that I with you may be comforted in you, each of us by the other's faith, both yours and mine" (Rom. 1:11-12).

Poverty of faith, therefore, is not due only to individual lapses of character and perplexities of mind; *it is due to neglect of Christian fellowship*. One who with difficulty has clung to his slender experience of God, goes up to the church on Sunday. Even though it be a humble place of prayer, if the worship is genuine, the hymns, the prayers, the Scriptures gather up the testimony of centuries to the reality of God. Here David speaks again and Isaiah answers; here Paul reaffirms his faith and John is confident that God is love. Here the saints before Christ cry, "Jehovah is my rock, and my fortress, and my deliverer" (Ps. 18:2), and the sixteenth century answers, "A mighty fortress is our God"; and the nineteenth century replies, "How firm a foundation, ye saints of the Lord!" We go up to the church finding it hard to sing, "*My* Jesus, *I* love thee, *I* know thou art *mine*"; we go down with a *Te Deum* in our hearts:

"The glorious company of the apostles praise thee;
The goodly fellowship of the prophets praise thee;
The noble army of martyrs praise thee;
The holy Church throughout all the world doth acknowledge thee."

In the rich and varied faiths of the Church we find a far more fruitful relationship with God than by ourselves we ever could have gained. Without such an enriching experience men can only with difficulty keep faith alive. Twigs that snap out of the camp fire lose their flame and fall, charred sticks; but put them back and they will burn again, for fire springs from fellowship. Amiel, after an evening of solitude with a favorite book on philosophy, wrote what is many a Christian's prayer: "Still I miss something—common worship, a positive religion, shared with other people.

Ah! when will the church to which I belong in heart rise into being? I cannot, like Scherer, content myself with being in the right all alone. I must have a less solitary Christianity."

IV

Men need fellowship, not only for the enrichment of their faith, but for its *stability.* No man can successfully believe anything all alone. Let an opinion in any realm be denied, despised, neglected by common consent of men, and not easily do we hold an unshaken conviction of its truth. But let it be agreed with, supported and endorsed by many, especially by men of insight, and with each additional testimony to its truth our faith grows confident. A fundamental experience of man is that his faiths are socially confirmed.

Authority of some sort, therefore, never is outgrown in any province of knowledge, and strugglers after faith have solid right to the sustenance which it can give. For one thing the authority of the *expert* is acknowledged everywhere. When a great astronomer speaks about the stars, most of us put our hands upon our mouths and humble ourselves to listen. If in science, expert knowledge has this authority— not artificial, infallible, and externally enforced, but vital, serviceable, and real—how much more in realms were insight and spiritual quality are indispensable! Such authority comes in the spirit of Paul: "Not that we have lordship over your faith, but are helpers of your joy" (II Cor. 1:24).

An amateur stands before a picture like Turner's "The Building of Carthage" and either does not notice the details, or noticing sees no special meaning there. But when Ruskin, Turner's seer, begins to speak—how wonderful the children in the foreground sailing toy boats in a pool, prophecy of Carthage's future greatness on the sea!—one by one the details take fire and glow with meaning as our eyes are opened. Such is the service of a real authority. It does not, as Weigel says, put out a person's eye and then try to persuade him to see with some one else's. It rather cures our blindness and enables us to see what by ourselves we were incapable of seeing. Christ supremely, when allowed to be himself, has helped men thus. He has not oppressed the mind with burdensome authority, denying us our right to think. He has come appealing to our little insight with his own clear vision, "Why even of yourselves judge ye not what is right?" (Luke 12:57). Things which we see dimly he has clarified; things which we did not see at all, he has made manifest. He has been what he called himself, the Light, and his people have said of him what the man in John's ninth chapter said, "He opened mine eyes" (John 9:30). A struggler after faith may well count among his assets the insights of the seers and of the Seer. As another states it: "Our weak faith may at time be permitted to look through the eyes of some strong soul, and may thereby gain a sense of the certainty of spiritual things which before we had not."

Beside the authority of the seers, there is *the authority of racial experience,* to which indeed no mind ought slavishly to subject itself, but from which all minds ought to gain insight and confidence. Tradition has done us much disservice. Oppressions that might long before have been outgrown have been counted holy because they were hoary. There must be something to commend an opinion or a custom beside its age, and all progress depends upon recognizing that

"Times makes ancient good uncouth."

But if out of the past have come evils to be overthrown, out of the past also have come the best possessions of the race. "Traditional" has grown to be an adjective of ill repute; it signifies in common parlance the inheritance of oppressive ideals and institutions that hold the "dead hand" over hopes of progress. But our best music also, our poetry, and our art are traditional; the discoveries of our scientists on the long road from alchemy to chemistry, from magic to physics are traditional; all that each new generation begins with, fitted out like the well-favored child of a provident father is traditional. No one can describe the utter barrenness of life, if we could not build on the accumulations of our sires, using the result of their toil as the basis of our work, their hardly won wisdom as our guide. To discount anything because it is traditional is to discount everything, except that comparatively minute addition which each new generation makes to the slowly accumulating wisdom and wealth of the race. As Mr. Chesterton has put it: "Tradition may be defined as the extension of the franchise. Tradition means giving votes to the most obscure of all classes, our ancestors. It is the democracy of the dead. Tradition refuses to submit to the small and arrogant oligarchy of those who merely happen to be walking about. All democrats object to men being disqualified by the accident of birth; tradition objects to their being disqualified by the accident of death. Democracy tells us not to neglect a good man's opinion, even if he is our groom; tradition asks us not to neglect a good man's opinion, even if he is our father."

Now racial experience is dubious at many points and at very few does it approach finality. But on one matter it speaks with a unanimity that is nothing short of absolute. *Man cannot live without religion*—like the earth beneath the mountain peaks this universal experience of the race underlies the special insights of the seers. When during the mid-Victorian discomfiture of faith at the first disclosures of the new science, Tennyson's "In Memoriam" appeared, Prof. Sidgwick wrote of it, "What 'In Memoriam' did for us, for me at least in this struggle, was to impress on us the ineffable and irradicable conviction that *humanity* will not and cannot acquiesce in a godless world." That conviction is confirmed by the whole experience of the race. To be sure religion, like love, exists in all degrees. From degraded lust to the relationship of Robert Browning and Elizabeth Barrettt, love is infinite in variety; it takes its quality from the character of those whom it affects; yet through all its changes it is itself so built into the structure of mankind, that though there be loveless individuals, life as a whole is unimaginable without it. So religion runs the gamut of human quality. In a Hindu idolater it performs disgusting rites to placate an angry god, and in Rabindranath Tagore it cries: "If thou speakest not I will fill my heart with thy silence and endure it. I will keep still and wait like the night with starry vigil and its head bent low with patience. The morning will surely come, the darkness will vanish, and thy voice pour down in golden streams, breaking through the sky." In Torquemada it is cruel; in Father Damien it becomes a passion for saviorhood. Religion helped Sennacherib to his campaigns and Isaiah to his prophecies; it preached the Sermon on the Mount and it dragged Jesus before Pilate. Can the same spring send forth sweet water and bitter? But religion does it, for religion is life motived by visions of God; it is tremendous in strength, but with man's unequal power to understand the Divine, it is ambiguous in quality. Like electricity, it is magnificent in blessing or terrible in curse. Yet through all its degrees man's relationship with the Invisible is so essentially a part of his humanity that lacking it he has never yet been discovered, and without it he cannot be conceived. It was this impressive witness of racial experience that made John Fiske, of Harvard, say, "Of all the implications of the doctrine of evolution with regard to man, I believe the very deepest and strongest to be that which asserts the Everlasting Reality of Religion."

This testimony of the spiritual seers and this cumulative experience of the race have a right to play a weighty part in any consideration of religious faith. Even a rebellious youth might pause before he scoffs at a mature and thoughtful mind, letting his Church, his Scripture, and his Christ speak impressively to him about the reality of God. What we all do in every other realm, when we are wise, this mind is doing in religion. His individual grasp on truth he sets in the perspective of history. He does not feel himself upon a lonely quest when he seeks God; rather he feels behind him and around him the race of which he is a part and which never yet has ceased to believe in the Divine, and he sees his own insights illumined by those supreme spirits who have talked with God "as a man talketh with his friend." He knows as well as any youth that authority has been stereotyped in theories of artificial infallibility, to which no mature mind for a moment can weakly surrender its right to think, but he refuses to give up a real authority because some have held a false one. The authority of the dictionary is one thing—literal and external. But the authority of a good mother moves on a different plane. It is not artificial and oppressive. It is vital and inspiring. She has lived longer, experienced more than her children; she is wiser, better, more discerning than they. A man who has had experience of great motherhood comes to feel that if his mother thinks something very strongly and very persistently, he would better consider that thing well, for the chances are overwhelming that there is truth in it. How much more shall he feel so about the age-long experience of the saints with God! In this respect at last there still is truth in Cyprian's words, "He that hath God for his Father hath the Church for his Mother."

V

Faith needs fellowship not alone for enrichment and stability, but for *expression.* For faith, as from the beginning we have maintained, is not an effortless acceptance of ideas or personal relationships; it is an active appropriation of convictions that drive life, and Christian faith especially has always involved a campaign whose object is the saving of the world. Such an expression of religious life involves cooperation; men cannot effectively support the "work of faith" (I Thess. 1:3) apart from fellowship.

The necessity for this cooperative expression of religion is clear when we consider the *one in whom we believe.* How anyone can expect in solitude to believe in Christ is a mystery. For Christ, with overflowing love to those who shared his filial fellowship with God, said, "No longer do I call you servants . . . I have called you friends" (John 15:15); his care encompassed folk who never heard of him and whom he never saw, "Other sheep I have, which are not of this fold: them also I must bring . . . and they shall become one flock, one shepherd" (John 10:16); and beyond his generation's life his love reached out to followers yet unborn, "Them also that believe on me through their word" (John 17:20). Whatever other quality a movement sprung from such a source may possess, it must be social. Moreover, Jesus' faith was active; the meaning of it he himself disclosed, "All things are possible to him that believeth" (Mark 9:23). In such a spirit, both by himself and through his followers, he sought the lost, healed the sick, preached the Gospel, and expectantly proclaimed an earth transformed to heaven. Such a character cannot be known in contemplation under the trees in June or through the pages of an interesting book. If Garibaldi, leading his men to the liberation of Italy, had found a devotee who said, I believe in you; I love to read your deeds, and often in my solitary, meditative hours I am cheered by the thought of you—one can easily imagine the swift and penetrating answer! That you believe in me is false; no one believes in me who does not share my purpose; the army is afoot, great business is ahead, the cause is calling, he who believes follows. Such a spirit was Christ's. The hermits, whether of old time in their cells, or of modern time with their unaffiliated lives, are wrong. *The final test of faith in Christ is fellowship in work.*

The Church itself has been to blame for much undedicated faith. Correctness of opinion has been substituted, as a test, for fidelity of life. "Believe in the Lord Jesus Christ and thou shalt be saved," has been interpreted to mean: accept a theory about Christ's person and all is well. But one need only go back in imagination to the time when first that formula was used to see how vital was its import. To believe in Christ then meant to accept a despised religion, to break ties that men value more than life, to face the certainty of contempt and the risk of violence. To believe in Christ then meant coming out from old relationships and going to a sect where one was pilloried with derision, that one might work for the things which Christ represents. No one did that as a theory; it required a tremendous thrust of the will, a decision that reached to the roots of life. All this was involved in believing on Christ and our decent holding of a theory about him, in a time when all lips praise him, is a poor substitute for such vital faith. John tells us that once a multitude of Jews professed belief in Jesus, but the Master, hearing their affirmations, saw the superficial meaning there. "Many believed on his name," says John—"but Jesus did not trust himself unto them" (John 2:23-24). How many believe in Christ in such a way that he cannot believe in them! They forget that while the test of a man is his faith, the test of faith is faithfulness. An apostolic injunction needs modern enforcement, "that they who have believed God may be careful to maintain good works" (Titus 3:8).

The necessity for a cooperative expression of religion is evident again in the *truth which we believe.* Take in its simplest form the Gospel which Christianity presents, that God is in earnest about personality, and what urgency is there for associated work! For personality is being ruined in this world. False ideas of life, idolatry whether to fetishes in Africa or to money here, irreligion in all its manifold and blighting forms, are destroying personality from within, and from without sweatshops, tenements, war, the liquor traffic, industrial inequity, are engaged in the same task of ruin. The common contrast between individual and social Christianity is superficial. The one thing for which the Christian cares is personal life, and in its culture and salvation he sees the aim of God and Godlike men. Whatever, therefore, affects *that* is his concern, and what is there that does not affect it? What men believe about life's meaning and its destiny strikes to the core of personal life, and the houses in which men live, the conditions under which they work, the wages that they are paid, and the environments which surround their plastic childhood— these, too, mould for good or ill the fortunes of personality.

The Christian, therefore, who intelligently holds the faith that he professes cannot be negligent either of evangelism, education, and missionary enterprise upon the one side, or of social reformation on the other. These are two ends of the tunnel by which the Gospel seeks to open out a way for personality to find its freedom. A man who says that he believes in Jesus Christ, and yet is complacent about child labor and commercialized vice, poor housing conditions and unjust wages, the trade in liquor and the butchery of men in war, stands in peril of hearing the twenty-third chapter of Matthew's gospel brought up to date for his especial benefit by the same lips that spoke it first. The indignation of the Master falls on priests and Levites who, speeding to the temple service, "pass by on the other side" the victims of social injury.

Isolated Christians, however, cannot further this campaign for personality redeemed from inward ills and outward handicaps. *Evil is organized, and goodness must be, too.* As wisely would a single patriot shoulder a rifle and set out for France as would an unaffiliated Christian set his solitary strength against the massed evil of the world. Men increase effectiveness by a large percent through fellowship, as ancient Hebrews saw: "Five of you shall chase a hundred, and a hundred of you shall chase ten thousand" (Lev. 26:8).

VI

Many secondary fellowships offer to a Christian opportunity for associated service; no cooperative endeavor to make this a better world for God to rear his children in should lack Christian sympathy and support. But the primary fellowship of Christians is the Church. Some indeed would have no church; they would have man's spiritual life a disembodied wraith, without "a local habitation and a name." But no other one of all man's finer interests has survived without organized expression. Justice is a great ideal; any endeavor to incarnate it in human institutions sullies its purity. One who dwelt only on the lofty nature of justice, who thought of it uncontaminated and ideal, might protest against its embodiment in the tawdry ritual and demeaning squabbles of a law court. Between the poetry of justice and the recriminations of lawyers, the perjury of witnesses, the fumbling uncertainty of evidence, the miscarriages of equity, how bitterly a scornful mind could point the contrast! But a reverent mind, sorry as it may be at the misrepresentation of the ideal in the human institution, is ill content with scorn. He who with insight reads the history of jurisprudence, perceives how the courts of law, with all their faults, have conserved the gains in social equity, have propagated the ideal for which they stand, have made progress sometimes slowly, sometimes with a rush like soldiers storming a redoubt, and in times of stress have been a bulwark against the invasion of the people's rights. The poetry of justice would have been an ideal dream without equity's laborious embodiment in codes and courts.

Some minds dwell with joy upon the spiritual Church. Its names are written on no earthly roster, but in the Book of Life; its worship is offered in no earthly temple, but in the trysting places where soul meets Over-soul in trustful fellowship; its baptism is not with water but with spirit, its eucharist not with bread but with the shared life of the

Lord. Or, ranging out to think of the Church as an ideal human brotherhood, men dream as Manson did in "The Servant in the House":

"If you have eyes, you will presently see the church itself—a looming mystery of many shapes and shadows, leaping sheer from floor to dome. The work of no ordinary builder! . . . The pillars of it go up like the brawny trunks of heroes: the sweet human flesh of men and women is moulded about its bulwarks, strong, impregnable: the face of little children laugh out from every corner-stone: the terrible spans and arches of it are the joined hands of comrades; and up in the heights and spaces there are inscribed the numberless musings of all the dreamers of the world. It is yet building—building and built upon. Sometimes the work goes forward in deep darkness: sometimes in blinding light: now beneath the burden of unutterable anguish: now to the tune of a great laughter and heroic shoutings like the cry of thunder. Sometimes, in the silence of the night-time, one may hear the tiny hammerings of the comrades at work up in the dome—the comrades that have climbed ahead."

All such ideals, like pillars of fire and cloud, lead the march toward a promised land. They are to the actual Church what the poetry of justice is to the actual courts. But in one case as in the other, such ideals are dreams if, with labor and struggle, through many mistakes, against the disheartenment of man's frailty and sin, we do not work out an institution that shall embody and express man's spiritual life. Even now a discerning spirit whose own faith has been nourished at the altar regards the Church with boundless gratitude. She has indeed been to the Gospel what courts are to justice, indispensable and yet burdensome, an institution that the ideal cannot live without and yet often cannot easily live with. No one feels her faults so acutely as one who devotedly values the Gospel and longs for its adequate expression on the earth. Yet the Church conserves the race's spiritual gains, fits out our youth with the treasure of man's accumulated faith, is a power house of endless moral energy for good causes in the world, exalts the ideal aims of life amid the crushing pressure of material pursuits, holds out a gospel of hope to men whom all others have forsaken, and to the ends of the earth proclaims the good news of God and the Kingdom. No other fellowship offers to men of faith so great an opportunity to make distinctive contribution to the race's spiritual life. In the presence of the Church's service and the Church's need an unaffiliated believer in Jesus Christ is an anomaly. For enrichment, stability, and expression, faith must have fellowship.

"O magnify Jehovah with me, and let us exalt His name together" (Ps. 34:3).

SCRIPTURE PASSAGES
USED IN THE DAILY READINGS

EXODUS 3:1-5 (VI-5); 4:24-26 (II-4).

DEUTERONOMY 28:65-67 (VIII-2).

II KINGS 21:3-6 (IV-5).

JOB 30:20-21, 25-27 (X-4); 37:23 (V-3); 38:31-38 (VII-1).

PSALMS 16:5-11 (III-5); 23:1-4 (X-3); 27:1-6 (VIII-5); 27:7-14 (V-7); 51:1-4 (III-3); 55:1-7 (VIII-1); 56:1-3 (VIII-3); 73:2-3, 16-17, 24-26 (II-6); 103:1-5 (III-2); 118:1-6 (VIII-7); 145:1-10 (III-7); 146:1-5 (IV-1).

PROVERBS 2:1-5 (II-3); 4:1-9 (II-2).

ECCLESIASTES 3:11 (V-3).

ISAIAH 1:10-17 (VI-2); 40:26-31 (V-4); 51:9-16 (VI-6); 55:1-3 (II-7).

AMOS 5:21-24 (IX-4).

MICAH 6:1-8 (IX-3).

MATTHEW 6:6-14 (III-1); 6:9-15 (XII-5); 6:24-33 (VI-6); 7:15-20 (V-6); 7:24-27 (VI-7); 13:54-58 (XI-3); 17:19-20 (XI-4); 18:12-14 (II-4); 21:28-31 (X-1); 23:13-15, 23-24 (XII-1); 25:34-40 (IX-7).

MARK 12:28-30 (V-1).

LUKE 6:12-16 (IX-2); 7:48-50 (XI-2); 18:9-14 (IV-3); 22:31-32 (XI-6).

JOHN 3:21 (IX-5); 4:23-24, (IV-5); 6:16-17 (IX-5); 6:27-29 (XI-1); 7:16-17 (IX-5); 14:25-27 (VII-2); 17:20-23 (XII-6).

ACTS 17:22-28 (IV-6).

ROMANS 8:1-6 (X-7); 8:14-16 (V-5); 8:24-25 (III-4); 10:11-15 (XII-4); 11:33-34 (V-3); 11:33–12:2 (IX-6); 15:13 (III-4); 16:1-8 (IX-1).

I CORINTHIANS 2:10-14 (VII-4); 3:4-9 (III-6); 3:18-23 (VII-6); 4:11-13 (VI-2).
II CORINTHIANS 5:5 (V-2).
GALATIANS 2:20 (XI-5); 5:13-15 (XII-3); 5:16-23 (IV-7).
EPHESIANS 1:15-19 (VII-5); 4:13-15 (X-5).
PHILIPPIANS 3:12-16 (X-6).
I THESSALONIANS 3:1-2, 10 (XI-6); 5:21 (V-1).
II THESSALONIANS 1:3 (XI-6).
I TIMOTHY 6:20-21 (II-5).
II TIMOTHY 1:3-5 (II-1); 4:6-8 (XII-7).
HEBREWS 1:1-2 (VII-7); 2:8-10 (VI-3); 4:1-2, (I-6); 10:23-25 (XII-2); 10:32-36 (I-4); 11:1 (I-1); 11:3, 6 (I-5); 11:8-10 (I-2); 11:13-16 (I-1); 11:24-27 (I-2); 11:32-40 (I-3); 12:1-3 (VI-4); 13:7 (I-7).
JAMES 1:2-8 (X-2); 2:14-21 (VI-4); 5:13-16 (VIII-4).
I PETER 1:3-9 (XI-7); 4:12-16, 19 (VI-1).
II PETER 1:5 (V-1).
JUDE 20-25 (VII-3).

SOURCES OF PRAYER
USED IN THE DAILY READINGS

ALFRED, KING—IX-3. "A Chain of Prayer Across the Ages," by S. F. Fox.

ANSELM, ST.—XI-6. "A Chain of Prayer Across the Ages," by S. F. Fox.

ARNDT, JOHANN—IX-1; X-1. "A Chain of Prayer Across the Ages," by S. F. Fox.

ARNOLD, THOMAS—VII-5. "A Chain of Prayer Across the Ages," by S. F. Fox.

BACON, FRANCIS—VII-2. "A Chain of Prayer Across the Ages," by S. F. Fox.

BEECHER, HENRY WARD—I-4; I-7; II-7; III-5; III-7; IV-7; V-7; VI-6; X-5. "A Book of Public Prayer."

BOOK OF COMMON PRAYER—XII-6.

DAWSON, GEORGE—X-4. "A Chain of Prayer Across the Ages," by S. F. Fox.

HALE, SIR MATTHEW—VII-4. "A Chain of Prayer Across the Ages," by S. F. Fox.

HUNTER, JOHN—I-1; IV-5; XI-2; XI-3; XII-7. "Devotional Services for Public Worship."

JENKS, BENJAMIN—X-2. "A Chain of Prayer Across the Ages," by S. F. Fox.

McCOMB, SAMUEL—I-6; II-1; III-1; VI-3; VIII-1; VIII-2;; VIII-3; VIII-5; VIII-6; VIII-7; IX-2; XI-1; XII-2; XII-4. "A Book of Prayers for Public and Personal Use."

MARTINEAU, JAMES—III-4; IV-4; V-2; VI-2; XII-1. "Prayers in the Congregation and in College."

NEWMAN, FRANCIS W.—VI-1; VI-7. "A Chain of Prayer Across the Ages," by S. F. Fox.

ORCHARD, W. E.—I-2; I-3; II-2; II-3; II-4; II-5; II-6; III-2; IV-3; IV-6; V-1; V-3; V-6; VI-5; VII-1; VII-3; VII-7; VIII-4; IX-5; X-7; XI-5; XI-7. "The Temple."

PARKER, THEODORE—I-5; V-4; V-5; VI-4; VII-6; X-6. "Prayers."

RAUSCENBUSCH, WALTER—III-6; IV-1; IV-2; IX-4; IX-6; XII-3; XII-5. "Prayers of the Social Awakening."

ROBINSON, HELEN RING—XI-4. "Thy Kingdom Come," by Ralph E. Diffendorfer.

SHAFTESBURY, EARL OF—IX-7. "A Chain of Prayer Across the Ages," by S. F. Fox.

STEVENSON, ROBERT LOUIS—III-3. "Prayers Written at Vailima."

VAN DYKE, HENRY—IV-6. "Thy Kingdom Come," by Ralph E. Diffendorfer.

WEISS, S.—X-3. "A Chain of Prayer Across the Ages," by S. F. Fox.